PRAISE FOR *YOUR BLUE IS NOT MY BLUE*

"Aspen Matis is a hero and inspiration. *Your Blue Is Not My Blue* will open the door to empathy, compassion, and healing for you and all those affected by you."

—Deepak Chopra, author of *Metahuman: Unleashing Your Infinite Potential*

"*Your Blue Is Not My Blue* is a sudden classic. Matis's poetic language renders such a shocking story relatable and tear-jerking. She is a champion with a tender heart and fierce courage. This book isn't for reading, but rather for transforming the filter and frame through which we view life and each other. A masterpiece!"

—Kelly Sullivan Walden, author of *I Had the Strangest Dream*

PRAISE FOR *GIRL IN THE WOODS*

"Beautiful and so wildly engaging."

—Lena Dunham, author of *Not That Kind of Girl*

"Mercy. I love this story."

—Cheryl Strayed, the #1 *New York Times* bestselling author of *Wild*

"A lovely tribute to the healing power of wilderness."

—Nicholas Kristof, winner of the Pulitzer Prize for Commentary

Your Blue Is Not My Blue

ALSO BY ASPEN MATIS

Girl in the Woods: A Memoir

Your Blue Is Not My Blue

A
MISSING PERSON
MEMOIR

Aspen Matis

Published by Little A, New York

www.apub.com

Amazon, the Amazon logo, and Little A are trademarks of Amazon.com, Inc., or its
affiliates.

Lyrics to "Come Back Here" used with permission from David Lockwood.

ISBN-13: 9781542007894 (hardcover)
ISBN-10: 1542007895 (hardcover)
ISBN-13: 9781542007917 (paperback)
ISBN-10: 1542007917 (paperback)

Cover design and illustration by Liz Casal

Printed in the United States of America

First edition

For my extraordinary parents

Contents

AUTHOR'S NOTE

Chronology has been altered for literary cohesion, and some names and identifying characteristics have been changed.

PART I

ASHES

*Our chief want is someone who will inspire us to be what we
know we could be.*

—Ralph Waldo Emerson

1

MAN IN THE WOODS

I'd first met Justin by stunning coincidence in the summer of 2009 when we were hiking—separately—in shaded pinewood forests, backpacking from Mexico to Canada. We'd given up indoor plumbing, beds, and friends, both hiding shameful reasons for abandoning our lives. Nineteen years old, I had dropped out of my college, disappearing. He was nearly thirty, lean and tall with pale sapphire eyes; and I was drawn to him, curious what had taken him into these dark woods. As he smiled, his puffy lips became slightly asymmetrical, the bottom one pinker, and a shadow of scruff darkened his hollowed cheeks—so handsome I couldn't look away.

Held in his piercing powder-blue vision, I froze. A butterfly awakened in my chest.

For almost four months I'd been walking alone, trekking northward, unaware that this man had been trailing me, tracking my line of footsteps, ever-nearing. On the August day he caught me, wind moaning as we spoke, two souls alone in the trees, we discovered that he had *also* started off at the Mexican border in April—just two days after I had. For two thousand miles we'd been walking in nearly perfect sync. Having long endured identical terrain, our union seemed fated.

We stepped together for one hundred miles; then, two hundred. Under gold clouds, he pushed the limits of my body, setting a faster pace—some days surpassing forty rugged miles, unstopping through morning's thick peach haze; noon's warmth; red evening sun. I surrendered into his intensity with growing affection for the challenge. And each night by silver starlight, I set up my little tent, which fast-became our home.

One day in mid-September in the remote Indian Heaven Wilderness, walking together in quiet wonder, we traversed a lake-jeweled land carpeted with low bushes of ripe berries; in a murky fern-green valley, we arrived at the weather-worn trunk and dead branches of a fallen tree, deep roots eroded—their strong hold gone, cut out of black earth by the steady grating of the river. Balancing like an acrobat, wanting desperately to drop to my knees and crawl, I faked confidence as I tightroped over freezing pulsing waters, their current violent and storm-cloud steel. On land again, the other side, I stood in awe of Justin's apparent fearlessness. I felt powerful, bolder in his presence.

That night in cool milk moonlight, he brought out the little stove he'd been carrying. Over the bloom of a blue-gold flame, he cooked pasta elbows in butter. "For us," he said. Everything I had eaten on the trail in the long months pre-Justin had been cold. With my first big bite, the warm fat of creamy starch dissolved in my watering mouth.

Talking into the small hours of bitter winds, an arctic gust stinging our exposed cheeks, he told me about the aggressive fire that had burned down his childhood house. His baseball card collection, everything that had meant anything to him, was gone forever. He was eleven. "My family never discussed it."

"I'm sorry," I whispered, squeezing his palm for the first time.

∼

Four hundred fifty miles into our shared hike, a whiteout hailstorm high on a ridge trapped us at dusk. In blinding snow-fog I became colder and colder, unable to close my hands. Shaking, I felt strange burning, fumbling to remove my iced shirt from my torso.

Immediately Justin stripped off all his clothes—shockingly risking his own safety to give me all his warmth, my faint body at the verge of actual freezing. Behaving like a medic, Justin told me to sip his water as he set up our tent, his naked skin pink with biting hail and wind. Inside our cloth shelter, my hands heated up against his stomach, my cheeks thawed against his neck.

Cuddling in our sleeping bags wrapped in night's indifferent air, he asked me distracting questions, trying to take my mind off the dead cold. My favorite flavor of ice cream? And what was it I wanted to do with the rest of my life?

"Salted Caramel Core," I mumbled. "You have any?" I smiled slightly, my upper lip so stiff that it split from the pressure of just this small movement. He brushed my mouth with his thumb, wiping away a crack of blood. My thoughts broad strokes in the mind-mist of near-hypothermia, I confided that I wanted to someday be a writer.

He kissed my mitten. "Then we'll get you to New York," he said. He described Manhattan as an epicenter of creativity, a midnight tar-paved island where the young artists of the world go to pursue themselves. Listening, growing warmer, I peered up through the tent's mesh roof at faraway stars, faint glitter, giddy.

Justin told me that he'd lived in the famous city just two years ago, wearing a suit to work in finance. More resourceful now that he'd survived out of a backpack for half a year, he insisted the "expensive" metropolis wasn't as unaffordable as people claimed. "I've got some tricks," he promised. He pressed a quick peck on my cheekbone, his lips soft—I moved toward him, mouths locking in blue velvet space, smiling.

That night he nearly froze keeping me alive.

I woke from shivering sleep to find I'd suddenly fallen—I loved him.

Feeling better on the footpath the next morning, we picked plump huckleberries, frosted silver with bloom-wax like summer plums. Lingering in a bush, we invented names for our make-believe children: our boy Winter and little girl Marin. I was exhilarated—still a teenager, I had never discussed parenthood with a man or even had a real boyfriend yet; and my hands, grasping at fruits, became unsteady. The berries stained my fingers and mouth unearthly purple; Justin snapped a photo, smirking. But I didn't care. Walking together, I imagined he was leading me into a secret future.

Where the Pacific Crest Trail faded at a clearing in the pines—mile 2,663, the Canadian border—we held each other and swayed. A violet-green swallow was warbling its mating call, a rhythmic whistle. This gap in the forest seemed an arbitrary end.

I stood in that woodland spot, shifting my weight amid the evergreens, feeling accomplished. Wanting to stay with Justin forever on the quiet footpath, staring at his face, I heard a car's tinny engine and could see an old Jeep passing through the trees.

"I guess we're done," I said softly, unsure if this proudest landmark was our goodbye.

He squeezed my shoulder, his hold firmer. "Now's the scary part."

As we strode along the silent moss-edged path to the highway, empty of words, I realized I had to tell him what I'd withheld. "I move into an apartment in Colorado in ten days," I said, not looking up from the stony soil and ferns. Because I craved experiencing myself in his presence, I hadn't wanted to voice this inevitable farewell.

"I thought you were out of school," he said. His stride had stopped.

When I'd first begun my big walk, leaving school five weeks before the academic year ended, I was certain I was never going back to Colorado College. Yet I had promised my concerned parents that this excursion was "just a leave of absence." Backpackers themselves, they profoundly grasped my desire to undertake this wilderness challenge—they supported me through the hike with the understanding, the *agreement*, that I would return to college in winter. And as my summer of wonder unfolded, they'd helped me secure an October apartment just off the edge of campus.

My mom and dad had just endured nearly half a year of worry in their wary hearts—their daughter's remote recklessness in hostile climates. Nervous for my safety, my mother had told me when I called her from somewhere in Washington that she hadn't slept well "since Mexico"—I couldn't subject her to the pain of breaking my word, now. I told Justin I would be a student again. My decision was already made.

Listening, he had resumed our path; and I stepped quicker, staying at his side. "So we have ten days," he said. He seemed unfazed.

His simple words of implied tomorrows made me feel secure, adored—we had reached a solid ground, paved road. For so long, I'd been following a singular footpath, a mindless liberating task. The thing to do was ever-clear, the immediate world marked on my map in shades of blue, a bold red-dotted line showing me the way. Now, there were choices; other routes to go. Infinite options, a little disorienting, exciting my imagination.

Impulsive, we boarded a bus to Vancouver, where we found a youth hostel.

After sharing a warm shower, my trail-friend gazed at me, grinning—I was struggling to break through a tight knot of curls. "You look so . . . normal," he spoke. I sensed I no longer appeared as a dirt-cheeked wild child. He plucked my miniature brush out of my fingers and brushed my hair, as if I were a doll. Finished detangling me, he touched his nose to mine.

On that first post-trail night, I made us dinner in the little kitchenette, playing house.

For five days we explored the garden-parks and café-bars of this other country, the softer sister of our own. Until we rode a ferry to the mainland coast of northern Washington, reentering America. Justin rented a car and drove us south, tracing the glinting Pacific Ocean, boundless. The pace of life on the highway was so fast, the ancient redwoods and petals of California poppies only dreamed-up smears of half-thoughts in my passenger-side window.

We coasted into Berkeley—to Justin's hometown, where his parents still lived. Rolling to a stop, we parked out front of an elegant house perched high in wooded hills. The structure crouched like a great stone tiger on a slope of the East Bay, resting on the cliffside with calm grace.

In the driveway, Justin took my hand; and I was uneasy, nervous to meet the parents of this man I loved but hardly knew. He whispered in my ear, "I haven't been here in a while." Releasing my clammy grip, he pressed the doorbell, which made a playful digital ding, and we waited in the tulip-gold new-autumn sun.

The towering wood door swung, smelling of fresh cedar—a woman appearing. Gray-haired with frost-pale eyes and Irish features, she shared her son's same delicate nose and plummy lips. "Who's this?" she asked, her growing smile genuine.

I looked to Justin to respond. But he was quiet, his face relaxed, expressing nothing. I felt a painful pinch of panic in my stomach— Justin had met me as Wild Child, my trail name. His was Dash. We had both used thru-hiking as an opportunity to capture the aspects of ourselves we wanted to magnify, escaping our associations of the past— using the culture of the woods to rename ourselves, redefine ourselves. Had I even told him my real name? "It's so nice to meet you," I said to his mom. "I'm Debby."

She said that she was Lucy, and we hugged.

Almost immediately, Justin left for "the laboratory" to pick up his father, who I learned was an astrophysicist. "He bikes down the hill to work, but needs a ride back up," Lucy explained.

Inside, wide windows free of glare soared five times my height— creating the illusion that the lemon trees, too, were a part of this house.

The glossy concrete floors were heated from beneath, as if the foundation were a perpetually sunlit ground.

Justin's mother led me into the kitchen, the foyer sweeping, and I felt clumsy and tense, alone with her in this great home's foreign beauty. Putting on a pot of Pure Gold Irish breakfast tea, she said, "Let me ask you something. Are you Justin's girlfriend?"

I felt my face flush hotter. I didn't honestly know. I told her, trying to joke, "You're going to have to ask Justin that, I think."

~

After our precious week-and-a-half in civilization together, culminating in two connective nights with Justin's parents, he drove me to the San Francisco airport. I would fly to Colorado Springs—returning to my life's pre-laid plans, without him.

In the overcrowded terminal, Justin put his arm around my waist. "Maybe we'll go skiing this winter," he told me as my tears broke, silently falling to the gray-flecked linoleum floor.

Then we kissed in the center of a swarm of travelers, my eyelashes wet. "Come sooner," I mumbled, a little embarrassed that I appeared so devastated—I had only known him for six weeks.

But landing alone on the runway's dark tarmac, I couldn't grip the kite string of my heart. Already, I missed him. Rolling up to the gate, I texted Justin that I had "landed safe," as if he were my boyfriend.

Back in the mountain-edged city, unpacking in heavy silence, I checked my little flip-phone, craving some response. But day faded to darkness; no word came.

Heart erratic as a wind-picked leaf, I smelled him on my jacket, that baby-powder sunscreen scent still kissing my imagination. Later, I lay awake, reliving summer. Smiling at an echo of his voice on my mind's stage, I felt the void of all I hadn't said. My expression froze as

I remembered how, not wanting to seem overzealous, I had been too scared to tell him how I loved him.

A fear emerged in me, blooming like a black-blue thread of ink in disturbed water: maybe he had only seen us as a fling.

Over the next week, as I wandered the beige otherworld of Colorado Springs, a vast and continuous strip mall, this artless red-white-and-blue town became my home, again. My heart felt tight—

Meeting Justin was an amazing serendipitous happening, certainly, but I had been perfectly joyful for two thousand solitary miles, before him. Yet something had changed. Swallowed up in the belly of the whale of infatuation, I now needed to distract myself in order to stay happy. Because our unknowable future shadowed the countenance of my soul.

Passing a Taco Bell and the gray-gold plastic crown of a Burger King, pacing repetitive boulevards, I sensed the mountains were out there, somewhere beyond the concrete plains; I missed their quiet aliveness, beauty. At dusk Monument Creek shimmered through the black trees, long and winding, a blue vein of water.

Nights alone in my yellow kitchen, I made myself hot chocolate. I missed my mother. In my window, maple leaves rusted, young fall blooming.

The only comfort I found was in planning to disappear. I considered the appeal of thru-hiking: the experience of technicolor concentration, the way the woods intensified all life. I cherished the way that, in deprivation—a hundred miles with only peanuts and stale crackers—a watermelon became more than itself, the juicy pink fruit's sweetness explosive on my parched tongue. In bed between dreams, I imagined running away to the remote Great Divide Trail through Canada, a path Justin had mentioned he might be walking next, chasing his ghost.

Two weeks from the afternoon we'd kissed goodbye, I drifted up the block to the Conoco convenience store and bought a one-pound bag of Jolly Ranchers, the pink watermelon kind, and chain-popped them as I walked to the river. I pictured not stopping, just stepping north indefinitely, sleeping in silent bushes whenever I got tired—the insanity and liberation in that. In leaving civilization again—forgetting school, abandoning my promise.

Reversing direction, I stepped back toward my dark apartment, white aspens and the bone-beige dirt earth falling into blueness: swallowed up by night.

And melancholy in my room, too warm at home, I sensed I shouldn't be here. I packed a backpack full of trail mix, and a tent, hopeful my mom and dad would understand.

2

TRAIL MAGIC

While searching for my forest-green wool socks, I heard the doorbell. It was ten o'clock at night, and I was almost ready to leave. When I opened up my screen, Justin was there, standing in worn-soft blue jeans, smiling huge. "Can I come in?" he asked.

"You're here," I said, dumbfounded.

He told me he had driven here from Berkeley—twenty-five hours straight, stopping only to pee. "I was going to move to Colorado anyway," he said, half-smirking.

Stunned, I invited him into my unheated room, "the ice chamber," where we made love.

On a gray morning in mid-October six days later, Justin rented his own apartment—not twenty yards from mine, across the street. Sitting cross-legged on the hardwood of his unfurnished living room, we toasted his new home with black coffee, backs against the plaster wall.

Joined in the world of electricity and rooftops, we slept on a mattress on the floor of my apartment, and then in his bed. We lived in my college town's rediscovered beauty, walking under golden aspens as the green leaves changed.

One midnight we took a trip to the ghostly dunes of southern Colorado, our little car threading the velvet night like a bright needle. Parking in a vacant lot of stones eleven miles beyond the hills of sand, we dipped in glassy blue hot springs at sunrise.

For our inaugural Halloween, he was a cave man and I was a wild woman. At a costume party in the student center, little freshmen twirling around us, masked and childlike, Justin joked, "I picked you under-ripe." This mysterious man from Cascade woods had become my first orgasm, first love—first everything.

The next morning, I awakened with a skin of sweat. I was caught in thick dizzy copper haze as Justin took my temperature: 103.

Melting into him in a fogged half-dream, I felt Justin lift me up. He carried me in his arms for a quarter mile to the medical center across campus.

I called him "my boyfriend" to the nurse, claiming the word for the first time. When he didn't protest, I felt giddy. To cool my body, the nurse gave me fever-reducing pills and an orange popsicle—I was now a few tenths of a degree shy of 105, unsafe. Just three months of knowing this man, I was envisioning becoming his wife, *his*.

~

On my twentieth birthday, late January, I woke to the *ding-dong* of the doorbell.

I opened the front door to a stout man's outreached arms. "Delivery for Deborah Parker."

Blossoms—snow-white and powdery Egyptian-blue hydrangea blooms, petite spray roses the deep red color of blood, elegant and tiny, glossy snake-green sprigs of friendly leaves. The sweet arrangement was gathered in a gleaming jade glass vase, weighty and solid. Tearing the tiny envelope, I found a small note of affection from my mom and dad, the sky-colored card expressing their vast love.

I called and thanked my parents for the colorful bouquet. I couldn't stop smiling, the whole apartment smelling of fresh petals. They knew how I treasured flowers, sweet buds both wild and mine. As I told them about my spring classes, excited, I detailed each subject, describing my professors' distinct teaching styles. In the fluidity of their voices, I could hear a vivid happiness, their overwhelming *relief*. Because their beloved child was back in college; safe. Both hardworking lawyers, they deeply valued education. We didn't speak for long, but we shared a tender kind of love; newly rebuilt. A little fragile.

In the kitchen, Justin was frying us eggs. Offering a warm mug of milky coffee, he whispered in my ear that he would be throwing me a birthday party tonight, his place.

Later, he draped tiny twinkling Christmas tree lights along his walls and doorframes; swept and mopped; placed a gigantic circular cake the sunny color of rich buttercream on a folding table he'd picked up at a downtown thrift shop. A smile in his eyes all day, Justin hooked up big speakers and laid out Solo cups and a few dozen cans of beer. Standing on a chair, I placed the aromatic bouquet from my parents atop the high cupboard above the stove, proactively protecting it from the danger of dancing bodies.

When the stated start time came, no one had arrived yet. An hour later, still it was just us. Justin turned on the music, and it blasted from the speakers to create the sense of a party, in case people were not finding the off-campus apartment, somehow missing our celebration.

By the end of the night, only two people had come; and after just fifteen minutes, they left.

But swaying in my boyfriend's arms as quiet midnight passed, I didn't feel upset—in truth, the two of us alone was my first choice.

In bed, his little spoon, I speculated that his age—a decade older than my peers—might have kept people away. But despite reason, I smiled in the dark; that night under our covers, we were a beautiful and thriving island.

As the semester progressed, snow blooming on the quad in shimmering mounds, the flake-thick air sparkling, I was often up all night completing class assignments. Justin didn't mind that I would work in bed, lights on until daybreak, typing on the pillow beside him.

For Valentine's Day, a cold weekend, we flew down mountains from morning until dusk, skiing. Justin had competed in Alpine on his college team at Cornell, I had Nordic ski raced back in high school—and on that first adventure to snowy peaks together, he pushed my limits further, my turns faster. Sunday, we ice-climbed a frozen waterfall in the "Switzerland of America," the rugged mountain town of Ouray, Colorado. Spending the night in a cozy cottage along a thermal pool, we swam as snow danced in the steely air, wildly alive.

On the last day of February, we walked together through the Garden of the Gods, a beautiful red-rock park and national landmark. Erect pinnacles of stone shot into pristine sky, silhouetted dots of people clinging to them, climbing. Strolling hand-in-hand, I could smell the clay-earth and Justin's shampooed hair. Without planning to, I asked him, "Do you think we'll ever get married?"

"Yes," he answered quickly. Then he squeezed my hand twice, lightly. "Do you *want* to get married?" he asked me, seeming surprised and very happy.

I responded, heart fluttering, "I do."

Hours later, we parked his car outside the dorm where I had lived my freshman year. We were about to go in, to sing karaoke in the commons. But I needed confirmation, touching his shoulder. He leaned back in the driver's seat, turning the car off.

I asked him what I wondered. "So are we engaged now?"

"What?" he said. It was as if he had forgotten. But then he seemed to remember. He put his palm on my cheek, cradling my face. "Yes!"

Overjoyed, I kissed him on the lips, then on the neck, and we ran into the dormitory, where we sang horribly, so happy and foolish that people must have assumed we were high. Because my mind remained in the Garden of the Gods, walking that gorgeous red Eden, clasping each other's hands.

The next sunrise, I slipped into the white tile bathroom while Justin lay asleep. I called home, beaming and excited to share my future with my parents. "Hi Mom," I said, voice cracking with my first words of young morning.

"Sweetheart!" she said and called to my dad, "Steve, pick up!"

Without flowery introduction, I announced to my mother and father that I was getting married! "Justin proposed yesterday," I told them. "So, I am officially engaged."

They congratulated me, and we all sat in energetic silence. In the lull that followed, my mother filled the void. "So what does Justin do?" she asked. "Is he looking for a job in Colorado?"

"Actually, no," I answered, my words too fast. "He says he needs to do 'something that matters' or nothing at all—" I stopped myself. In reacting to her direct question, my tone had become defensive. Seeing that she was only being protective, I softened. "He saved up a lot while working in finance," I explained. "I really admire his commitment to making a positive impact."

"What does Justin do all day?" my dad asked. My father seemed intrigued.

I thought for a moment, and the extent of this mystery occurred to me. "Actually, I have no idea," I said. I didn't really *know* what Justin was up to while I was attending class. "But we spend most of our time together, and he's really sweet to me."

I heard the bed creaking in the other room, Justin waking. "Aren't you a little young to get married?" my dad asked me. He spoke softly, his low tone causing me to pay acute attention. Our line was free of static, crisp, and I sensed that he was closer than Massachusetts, almost whispering in my ear.

"Dad, you were twenty when you married Mom," I reminded him, voice firm. Cracking the door, I could see Justin putting on his socks.

"We were still in college," my mom added. She had been twenty-two when they had wed.

My father spoke, "That's true." I sensed his smile—concession. Their shared life the fruit of young connection, my parents understood that good love is not age-bound.

Like new sun breaking over a horizon, gold warmth blooming, their joy rose as we discussed a wedding. They said they would do everything they could to help with the big day.

~

As the green blessing of spring kissed the plant life of Colorado, an atmospheric shift, Justin delayed telling his parents our news. When I'd ask him why, he'd say "I will—it's not the time." I grew uncertain if my fiancé's hesitation was a product of his dissociation with his parents, or if his reluctance was the result of second thoughts.

Not realizing it was a mistake, I booked a photographer online for August 28, an arbitrary date—*before* we had a chosen location. But then venues I called were unavailable on that late-summer Saturday. I had never even planned a dinner party, overwhelmed. Noticing how I was struggling, my lack of prowess surprising to him, Justin began assisting—and as we compiled our lists of friends and family, I saw that he was only inviting about a dozen people, his circle much smaller than I'd assumed.

Conceiving the day together, we both sensed how little we knew each other.

When school ended for summer break, Justin and I returned to the wild. We spent June and July in the Rockies, growing stronger, feeling feral in the untamed range of mountains. By days we trudged across fields of lacy wildflowers and behind the glass walls of waterfalls in summer's friendly sun; and nights in our tent, awake in the cool white light of our headlamps, we designed blue invitations.

The subject of last names came up as we were stopped for a dinner of almonds and beef jerky on a granite boulder. Chewing our lackluster nourishment, we agreed that the convention of the woman automatically adopting her husband's surname, forfeiting her history by default, seemed antiquated and a little strange. Justin felt that it was sexist. But at the same time, we definitely wanted to share one family name, a singular entity. So we came up with our own solution:

We decided to flip a nickel—the loser would adopt the winner's name. If I were to win, Justin would be a Parker, like my mother and father. This idea excited me—as if we were pioneers.

The moonlight turned rosy, clouds coalescing into indigo fog; and calling tails, I lost.

But speaking "Deborah Matis" aloud, it sounded wrong. I touched Justin's hand, swallowing in the faint light. Sheepish, I asked to keep my last name, after all. I hoped he wouldn't mind my sharp reversal.

He smiled. "Sure."

$\sim$

I badly wanted to wear contact lenses for our wedding day. Though I'd thought about getting them for thirteen years, I'd always been too squeamish to touch my finger to my pupils. But I didn't want to be staring through thick glass as I said "I do." So a week before our ceremony, Justin scheduled me a contact-putting-in lesson with an optometrist.

In the small overlit office, I rinsed my hands and poked and poked and poked the limp lens at my eye and blinked and blinked and knocked it out with my eyelashes. The doctor tried, a frightening thrust of her red fingernail toward my retina; I squirmed and tensed my cheeks. After her third jab I stood up and ran out blind into the hall.

Justin joined me under the fluorescent lobby light. He kissed my cheek and asked if he could try.

His first attempt was close—the lens touched and lingered for a quick instant, sticking until my lashes batted it out. It fell to the carpet; and before I could think to dodge, he found it, squirted it with solution, and placed it directly onto my cornea. I froze, stunned.

And then, with care, Justin put the second lens in, giving me my eyes. Turning to the mirror on the wall, I saw myself, unblocked by glass and wire. I felt beautiful, changed—freed from the identity of the "girl who wears glasses."

On the eve of our vows, oblivious to the tradition of sleeping separately, we stayed together. Limbs intertwined under white covers, Justin expressed that he didn't want a separation of the bride's side and the groom's side of the aisle, tomorrow. I found this sweet, our families one.

Then he became serious. He told me that dependency on my parents was keeping me tied to childhood neediness. He urged me to cut up the credit card that my parents paid on my behalf. Blindly complying, I snipped the shiny plastic into two perfect red halves, which fell to the nightstand, now useless. They *click-clicked* against the blue-glass table, a subtle double-*ping*.

Justin held me tighter. "You won't ask permission anymore," my fiancé told me, confident as a prince. "Do what you want now."

Emboldened by his tone, I tossed the crimson shards into the trash can. His condemning observations made exciting sense—I'd never really felt that my parents held me back, but doing precisely what felt right to me sounded pretty nice. "I want to drop out of college," I announced, resting my head on his chest. "This time for good."

∼

A backlit mist bathed the Cascade foothills in silver as Justin and I pledged our love before a justice of the peace. Standing in the same lush mountains where we'd first met, we exchanged rings, grinning on a stone stage in a fog-flowered forest clearing.

At our reception in a leafy emerald garden, my new mother-in-law motioned me over to a head-high patch of sunflowers that seemed to be smiling. "I am so happy you're marrying Justin," she told me, a slow rain falling in swollen droplets, gentle and huge. In the chilling platinum sun-shower, she placed her hand on the small of my back. "I've always wanted a daughter." I felt relieved that she approved of our swift union, just a year and a week from the day I'd met her son.

In the new pearl dawn, Justin drove us into sun-glinted Seattle, its buildings high and June-sky blue. He led me to a crowded area of concrete and glass skyscrapers, people in suits striding. We entered a bright-green and silver storefront called Fidelity, a huge television with fiscal news analysis blaring. "We'd like to open some accounts," he told a lanky woman in a chic salmon dress-suit, her blonde hair pulled back in an elegant topknot. He took my hand. "This is my wife."

I followed the lady and my new husband into a small glass room, answering basic questions—date and place of birth; social security number.

When we left just fifteen minutes later, I asked Justin, a little awkward, "What did we just do?" I was embarrassed to reveal I was uncertain.

"We opened you an investment account," he answered. He smiled. "Different from a bank account," he said, anticipating my next question.

"I have investments?"

"Now you do." He explained that he already had a Fidelity account of his own. "I also opened us a joint account and invested all our wedding-gift money."

Sensing his extensive financial competence, I was impressed. Rising to tippy-toes, I kissed his cheek and whispered, "Thank you."

~

For our honeymoon, Justin and I drove up through a slim gap between black-ink peaks, and then downhill along the ribbon-road, a mute car threading through dusk's blue and carrot air—toward the Pacific Crest Trail. Our backpacks leaned against each other on the backseat, all our belongings filling so little space. We'd met carrying our individual lives on our backs, and sped west now with my socks in the same duffel bag as his. To celebrate our union, we wanted to perform "trail magic," random acts of kindness for thru-hikers.

Nearing the expansive footpath, Justin sprung at me, pecked me quick behind the ear. We bumped and swayed our way down an uneven dirt road to a grassy glade in the cool shadow of frost-studded peaks— my jaw hurt from grinning, from the huge shock of his soft kisses on my tensed cheeks and the concept of "forever."

Parking in the deep pine forest, we set up a foldable table and loaded it high with six dozen eggs; thirty pounds of potatoes; a pyramid of onions and tomatoes; stacks of frozen pizza to heat over the camp-stove flame; and a five-pound block of orange cheddar cheese. We hauled a cooler the size of a treasure chest filled with all the wine, beer, and soda left over from our wedding onto the untamed needle grass.

That sundown in our tent, the new night's luminescent indigo darkening, decaying to fierce black, I lay still as my lover's full lips parted slightly, and he slept. I kissed him in his dreams a dozen times, cradled his limp wrist in my hand and felt my pulse drum against his lilac vein.

We camped, resting in dark evenings hip-to-hip—feeding passing hikers in the drizzle of days, exchanging fragments of diverse and odd life stories.

Learning the common threads that had led backpackers to our table in deep woods, I saw how some people were hiking because they were looking for their place in the world; others because they didn't believe a place for them in this world *existed*.

I listened, enraptured as Justin shared a story with a group of young men about how, while working in an office high in the Chrysler

Building in Manhattan, he suddenly lost all hearing in one ear. "For the first time I understood that my body wasn't permanent," he told the bearded boys. "It could fail me." He explained to them how, shortly after, he'd left his job—choosing to use his temporary life for something more meaningful than making "disgustingly rich" people even richer.

We stayed at that glade beside our beloved trail until, after four nights and three days of trail magic, every last beer and potato was gone.

3

BASECAMP BERKELEY

Newly married, Justin and I evacuated the woods where we had once lived as nomads. We would no longer pass sweet breezy days in our sleek tent, in mossy hills and sun, showering in waterfalls. That era was now our memory, a shared dream. We fused universes—

Two weeks after our vows we moved in with his parents in the high hills of the outer Bay, a spectacular view, now ours.

Our new life existed in a crack between two worlds, built directly on the borderline of Oakland and Berkeley. The house was massive, "adobe modern," a style inspired by his dad's time at a laboratory in New Mexico when Justin and his older brother were little kids. Unpacking in a bone-white room in golden sunshine, Justin told me to compliment the construction to his father—to remark that the stairs and corners were all rounded, a home with no sharp edges—his dad would like that.

It was as if I had inherited a palace by virtue of simply being in love. I'd walked through a portal—out of my leafy New England childhood, into novel architecture of tremendous beauty. And this new world felt untethered, fresh as a foreign tongue—

I loved living amid the rosy perfume of strange trees, unlike the pines and maples of my Massachusetts upbringing. I drank the clean Bay air. Hidden away within the soft charm of green knolls, we didn't have a plan yet. We had no future in the works. We now slept in an extra bedroom, both unemployed and unseen; we lived in a sunlit castle in the land of dreams, in my mind.

I enjoyed our impulsive drives up and down the grassy inclines or along the glistening waterfront, winding. In brilliant September, dreaming in tandem, we hiked footpaths through the redwoods, along those gorgeous coasts of longing: the Lands End Trail out to Point Reyes, back again. Walking remained ritual.

Yet as our North Bay strolls grew longer, sometimes wandering felt like pacing, adrift. I had no direction, only a romantic wish: to become a professional writer.

But whatever terrain existed between my body and a body of work I might create seemed mysterious and vast, unknown. Most days, the sky was satin, markless blue. But below, fog hung like a suspended field of snow that never melted, the boundless dampness muting San Francisco's lights. And the path to that summit of composing even one novel was invisible.

~

Crossing a hill in mid-autumn, striding, Justin suggested that I return to college, "this time in New York." He told me: this was my next step.

"Slow down," I called ahead to him, trying to keep up. I felt blindsided—he sounded like a parent. "I don't want to think about that right now," I mumbled, recouping my breath.

For stiff minutes, we walked without talking, not connecting. I tried to see his face, but it was obscured by his baseball cap, a shadow. I couldn't catch the blueness of an eye.

Something was wrong—"What's the matter?" I asked him. Finally, he looked at me, expression empty. "Love you," I whispered. "I'm sorry."

The trail had grown wider, broad enough for the two of us to share its width, and he took my hand in his. Passing a miniature train that snaked through the undergrowth, whistling and pouring a blue river of smoke, he led me deeper into waxy bushes, farther off the traveled way. Walking through forested slopes, Justin showed me Tilden Park, a wooded playland. He told me that somewhere in these trees, he'd built something when he was seventeen.

We arrived at the base of a stone stairway that connected two trails. Climbing up from the bottom, Justin explained that constructing these hundred steps had been his "aimless Eagle Scout project." I was impressed that it still stood, intact through thirteen years, a mossy fixture. His posture seemed straighter and very proud.

At the top, the bay leaves shimmered in the sun, their canopies like quivering manes, alive. And I became fixated by the life above my head, an unfamiliar species in the sky—flowering trees with pallid leaves and petite rosy blooms, so tall that the tops intermingled, becoming one crown. They populated the forests, exhaling perfume. I'd never seen such beautiful giants on my coast. The floral scent overwhelmed the stony smell of dried earth, the fumes as intoxicating as my first-ever sip of wine, which crossed my lips at fourteen. All mystery and the possibility of the world existed in that taste.

"If you don't want to be in school," Justin said, "you should at least be writing daily." The conviction in his voice changed my stare's direction. "You are gifted, and cream rises," he declared.

My heart revved at his words. I blushed hotter. Through my childhood, I was happiest when I was creating artwork—painting watercolors, throwing pottery, or making up new stories, more present to my imagination and ambition. The soil beneath our swift running shoes smelled of iron and fresh milk, wonderfully sweet; and I stepped closer to him.

We rested at a redwood tree older than America's nationhood, wide as the house I was raised in, its hairy bark the bright hue of old steel rust; and I was leaning. Tilting into something spectacular and simple, we came up with the playful little idea that would alter our future: a blog that would attract a following.

"It could be called Basecamp Berkeley," I announced. "I'll tell stories from our dreams and from the hills."

"And who are you?" he asked.

I pressed my cheek into the rough red bark. "A pen name?"

"Your name. The author."

I considered. "Something Hemingway," I said as he started walking away. I'd spoken *Hemingway* for the wishful, aspirational reason; a ghostly blue butterfly passed us. "Aspen."

I'd learned from my father on a long-ago backpacking trip in Wyoming how aspen trees are linked below the earth, their roots a vast interconnected network that spans miles and unifies existences.

"Aspen Hemingway," my husband called back to me.

~

In the beginning, I felt lucky, inexplicably chosen by this family.

Evenings, I asked my new dad-in-law, Walter, my questions about astrophysics and his research. A tall and weighty figure, he was a natural teacher; both curious, we shared in the pursuit of glimpsing how scientific textbooks "knew" what they asserted about the wordless history of our ephemeral world. Related, we became friends.

One fall night, talking in his home office, I asked Walter about the flowering tree I'd been noticing that didn't exist where I'd grown up, excited to learn its name. But the sun had set, and so outside the window there was nothing I could point to. I conjured the leaves from memory: "A thousand pale green fingers. They form soft tufts like bushes in the sky, and the bark's like army camo," I described, recalling tan and mint pastels in the precise pattern of the woodland uniform.

Walter nodded—told me in a low voice, "*Eucalyptus.*"

I told him that I loved them. "They're beautiful."

"They're invasive." In the unrest in Walter's eyes, I felt as if I'd cussed. "Many houses burn down because they're taking over." He spoke with stiffness, as if of a secret war, explaining the culpability of this striking species of tree—their terrible role in exacerbating deadly flames. He told me that eucalyptus sap is flammable, and their bark, like tinder, flies off when it's singed, igniting new fires up to a hundred yards away. Then, appearing sullen, Walter revealed something. "This house," he said, "was built on top of where our last home stood"—shelter remade after the great Oakland Hills fire of 1991, a shocking disaster that devastated the community.

I imagined the smoky scene nineteen years back, eleven-year-old Justin escaping this scorched ground littered with coal and ash.

The next day, my husband and I investigated the regenerated grounds of his childhood neighborhood. The clear-eyed light of noon was on our cheeks. Sunny bodies, we mounted a high crest between twin streets. "What was it like after the fire?" I asked him at the top.

Justin narrowed his eyes at the sun. "Different," he said. He told me how his family was displaced and, in the chaos, he got separated from his mother and older brother for twenty hours. "We were reunited in a gymnasium set up as a shelter by the Red Cross," he told me. "We lived in temporary housing for a year." He grasped my curls, tugging my hair teasingly to reverse our direction—we backtracked, descending toward a familiar cluster of newer buildings. "My pet rat, Lizzy, burned to death, and we lost all our toys," Justin said, eyes smiling. "But the good news is we got a new Nintendo."

I laughed. We walked back to his revived house in tender silence, the dry gold land freckled with young pines and red flowers.

Back inside the kitchen, my mother-in-law was juicing fresh lemons and pouring a stream of white sugar-dust, a saccharine puff. Adding ice cubes, she served us the most spectacular lemonade.

The world smelled sweet as cream, and Lucy and I took a drive to town together. The breeze spilled over us, steady from the eucalyptus groves atop the hill. At a hectic market filled with California produce, I was mesmerized by the rows of citrus species in every size and color, captivated by an entire wall of distinct mushrooms, more than a hundred forms, velvety and whitish and richest button-black. My mother-in-law told me to choose freely.

That evening we gathered in the dining room, a forty-foot-high-ceiling atrium with indoor plants and outdoor blooms separated by tall windows—the impression of great openness, even while sheltered. I'd selected asparagus in hues of purple and springtime green, cooking a colorful supper, which Lucy savored. Chewing sweet roasted eggplant, the thin clouds spark-red flares, soft sunlight caramel gold, Lucy joked, "I usually just microwave potatoes." Smiling back, I daydreamed of Justin and me in twenty years, visiting this home, our kids playing in the backyard blossoms.

After the meal, inspired by the forceful splendor of sky's fire, I began writing. Bright yellow lemons twinkled in the twilight sun on a terrace tree, and far beyond my window, San Francisco lay, flat like a pastel toy. As dishes clinked in the kitchen, I was typing a new story, my screen like a faint nightlight, glowing.

When tomorrow broke, our hillside home filled up with honeyed light, a fish tank. Fierce orange at the eastern edge, dawn kissed my face; and I finished the last sentence. This new tale was brief as a spark, only five hundred words.

With that first sleepless night, I started a practice of composing a story each morning—the beginning of a new creative diligence. The birth of *Basecamp Berkeley*, dispatches from a nonexistent person. The "blog" was fiction, episodes from the life of a character I'd invented. And each day I lost myself in her emergent world; joyfully, I infused reveries with the foggy spirit of the California coast.

As I wrote one morning, obsessing over an ending, I overheard Justin helping his mother with the crossword. Lucy loved the sunrise ritual of completing the tidy boxed puzzle, her mind lit up with connections, solutions. Both quick thinkers, they were well-matched, swiftly finding the answers in a smooth dance of suggestion and epiphany. I liked eavesdropping on Justin's quiet kindness, his family's apparent harmony.

On that foggy afternoon, hazy with sunlit mist, he programmed the old plastic cat feeder—automating it, so his parents would no longer need to remember to feed the two cats, Elton and Giuseppe. He used his intelligence creatively, rewiring and upgrading technologies around the house, loving to fix things.

Justin talked about finding a volunteer job—he claimed he was very interested in helping homeless families find affordable housing. But weeks passed, and he never acted.

Instead, he loved showing me the hidden beauty of the Bay, secret fire roads and old footpaths through spiny overgrowth. On Sundays, he would map out hikes for the four of us to take together, as a family. Driving to whatever dirt trailhead he'd discovered through careful research, we unloaded in the woods, walking in line, a little pack.

One gem-blue day in November, sky boundless, my husband asked me if I'd like to take a bike ride to Lake Merritt.

I blinked at him, embarrassed. "I never learned to ride one," I confessed. Mischievous, he took my arm and led me to the garage—he clipped a neon helmet on my head.

At the bottom of the hill, steadying my hips with his firm palms, he taught me how to balance—guiding me to a vacant playground lot behind his middle school as I tentatively pedaled. Wobbling, I was riding! Justin released me as I churned my feet violently, captaining his mom's old bicycle. I made a wide, shaky turn along the lot's edge, stopped with both feet.

Justin jogged up to me, slowly clapping. "That was nice," he said. He pointed to the rusted monkey bars. "This was my favorite place to hang out when we were between houses." I wiped sweat from my face, smiling. I loved sneaking peeks of this world where he had grown. And over the next hours, patient as a coach, he taught me how to ride a bike—

Coasting down a gentle hill, Justin jogging alongside me, we made it all the way to College Avenue. Exhausted, I took a seat at a white marble countertop in the Elmwood Café, an old-timey soda fountain converted into a coffee shop; and Justin ordered us a fudge brownie sifted with powdered sugar. Before handing it to me, he took a big bite, grinning, the tip of his nose white with the soft dust.

That evening after dinner, I picked lemons from the tree in the backyard, the fruits golden bulbs under the rising moon. Lucy found me in the blooming darkness. "It's good to see Justin this happy," she told me. As if an afterthought, she added that his distance while "figuring things out" had been a little hard for her and Walter.

Trying to understand better, I asked, "You weren't in touch?"

"Just off and on," she said, raising her lean broad shoulders, her clumsy movement girlish. "But that was what he needed. No harm done."

I wanted to ask her what had happened, why he'd been absent. "Justin seems so at home here," I said, my cheeks stiffer, cold in the night's sharp air as I spoke.

Then she told me, "You have changed my son." Her candid tone was blunt, and I loved her directness, unapologetic as the weather.

~

On a lavender morning in December, Justin woke me with a small kiss on the mouth at dawn and spoke into my chest, "I have something to show you."

Rising, I followed—climbing stairs to a smaller bedroom; ascending a narrow ladder to a lofted childhood space, a sanctuary of his past. I settled beside him, cross-legged on a twin mattress; and the world through the high window was pink with mist.

Tapping his laptop awake, the black screen brightening, he showed me the surprise—

By my husband's mastery, an email had gone out to every sophomore, junior, and senior at Colorado College, stating that Ernest Hemingway's granddaughter—current undergraduate Aspen Hemingway—had started a popular literary blog, *Basecamp Berkeley*. Justin had hacked my former school's student Listserv—creating a little trick, trying to help me. He said more eyes would find my writing this way.

The message appeared to be personalized to each student, slightly fewer than two thousand altogether. And included was a link to the blog-of-imagination that I now wrote daily.

The thrill of our con pounded like knocks in my heart—and in the first hour alone, my website had six hundred visits. In celebration, we took a long stroll in open fields, the fading sky glowing amethyst and copper. Justin's kaleidoscope attention touched every aspect of my mind, every cell and dream, his presence in my evolving nature as subterranean as a deep well whose source I could not fathom.

My chest drummed, and at the top of a sweetgrass hill speckled with orange-gold California poppies, I danced like a little kid, adrenaline rushing. A sense of great possibility charmed me. A wicked white jolt, wonderful and wrong.

4

First Movement

I woke at ten o'clock to no husband in my bed and an email from my mother. Proud, she wrote that my oldest brother had "started Northeastern law school," and I imagined her green eyes beaming. I missed hearing her familiar voice. Since the wedding, I'd been bad about calling home, and we had spoken on the phone just a few times. Her message ended with a question: "How do you like San Francisco?"

Late morning's sun buried in opaque gold haze, my laptop was hot in my damp hands. I clicked Reply, ready to tell her how I really liked the city—but we hadn't actually been to San Francisco since we'd moved here.

Flopping my legs off the edge of the bed, I pulled on Justin's sky-blue shirt, abandoning the message. In Berkeley, eleven or even noon had become regular rising times, and considering this now as I stood, a little lazy, I thought how we never had any concrete reason to wake.

Living with Justin in his childhood home, my love and I had formed an island—a nation-state of two, sleepy and safe. We had only planned to stay with his family for a few weeks after the wedding—three months had passed. Days in our private culture were peaceful, smooth as a frozen lake, our souls stilled. This life with my in-laws was a comfortable hibernation, easy.

Searching the house, I called out for Justin. But I couldn't find him in any room, all quiet. Collapsing into a woven couch, fine threads of white and yellow, I felt an inexplicable melancholy—even the excitement of last night had dissipated like seeds strewn through a field, invisible now.

Dizzy, I finally found Justin. He was in the driveway, washing his mother's car with a garden hose; and noticing me, he switched off the loud spray.

Restless, I took his nozzle. "Want to go to San Francisco?"

He smiled and gazed downward, his eyes shining blue slits. "Today?" I couldn't tell what he was thinking. The sky was clearing, an open pool emerging from a field of silver clouds.

I handed back the hose. "We still haven't crossed the bridge."

~

That afternoon, we slipped under a thousand shades of green-blue water. We rode the Transbay Tube, a four-mile underwater rail tunnel that leads large modern trains beneath the San Francisco Bay. Rocketing at eighty miles per hour through a submerged portal 135 feet below sea level, I leaned into my husband's balancing body, swaying in sync, his forearms pressing my hips.

Emerging in a windowless station of concrete flooring, we found a stairway of smiling mosaic faces and climbed upward. Stepping out above ground into a realm of honking cars and chirping birds gathered high in a bush of yellow blossoms, we wandered up a steep rainbow-painted sidewalk lined with narrow pastel houses—down another, even steeper, to the sea. The air smelled fresh, of floral trees and salt.

We walked for peaceful hours, sliding in and out of quirky districts: the waterfront world of the Embarcadero, past the Ferry Building's fresh citrus stands and seaside cafés, into a community constructed along a three-mile engineered seawall from which wide clusters of floating wooden rafts housing plump sunbathing sea lions extended into the Bay, the creatures' rhythmic barks like feral songs; North Beach with its Italian coffee bars and red and beige tablecloth homemade pasta shops, and the notorious storefront of City Lights bookstore like a sacred beat-nik temple, its black and white checkered floor and arched wood door-ways to corridors of books in every color, a high wide rainbow of brave stories; coastal Fort Mason, that hamlet with periwinkle hills beyond vibrant turquoise water and grass pure shamrock green, smelling of sunbaked rocks, the distant great orange-rose Golden Gate Bridge like a dollhouse model of itself, a wonder; the willow groves and red maples of the Presidio, leafy and profoundly lush.

Intoxicated by the eclectic charm of San Francisco, I felt swell-ing aliveness—*happiness.* We followed a dirt trail through cypress trees along a narrow beach, and pausing on a cliff above the seaweed-scented spray of crashing waves, I rose to my tiptoes and kissed Justin square on the lips.

To my surprise, he grabbed both my arms, pulled me into him—and spun me like a rag doll. Exploring the beauty of this city, he seemed spirited, more openly affectionate outside the walls of his parents' home. As if we'd escaped the tamer force-field of his childhood, back in the independence of our bubble, freer. Spontaneous as the white birds cir-cling above the sea, uninhibited, occasionally diving.

~

A white-domed Roman palace grew from the horizon like a figment vision. We approached a wide shaded passageway lined with towering rock pillars that traced a small cobalt lagoon, the pool's expanse creating a mirror to the grand columns and the flawless sky, most beautiful at a distance, the vista of a dream. Up close, the great white-capped central structure levitated, visible from every angle, like a moon.

I took thirty pictures from a single perspective, the many resulting images near-identical—too pretty to abandon. Photography a secret oasis, the discerning act of focusing my lens also heightened my awareness.

Inside, woody vines wove through a crisscrossed open lattice above our heads, the plant's strange snowy blossoms elegant. Australian eucalyptus trees fringed the eastern shore, that dangerous invasive species. Swans drifted in the inlet like ornaments, and a turtle peeked its little frowning prehistoric head.

"Follow me," Justin said, tugging my outstretched arm. He told me we were at the Palace of Fine Arts—"a phoenix." This marvel had risen from the rubble of the 1906 earthquake and consequent fires that leveled miles of San Francisco's infrastructure.

Wandering the grounds, we wordlessly linked fingers, passing beneath an engraved band of three allegorical figures carved from speckled stone, representing *Contemplation*, *Wonderment*, and *Meditation*. Staring into this creation, at once at home and invigorated, I felt a connection between my resilient husband and this city.

That night, starving from five hours of sustained walking, we climbed a gentle hill—rising to Chinatown as sunset blossomed its gold petals across the thin wisp-clouds. Matte lilac mist rimmed with radiant apricot light floated in fierce blue air above, casting us in an impressionistic painting; and giddy with bliss and great appetite we kept ascending, passing under the courtyard of sturdy concrete apartments threaded with red and yellow fabric triangles. Within these festive flags, we noticed a hole-in-the-wall restaurant tucked behind a tree of pale pink flowers.

At that basement café, nearly empty, dim sum dissolved in our mouths. Unable to contain the fire of my excitement, I said, "Today is my favorite day of our whole marriage."

Taking a sip of water, Justin narrowed his light eyes, blue playful pools. "We should move here," he told me, "for the Asian food."

I smiled, twisting my cloth napkin into a thick band. "Really?" I asked. "We could?"

"Why not." He took a big bite of pork bao.

My parents had lived in California, long ago, when they were twenty and twenty-two, also newly married. This distant knowledge romanced me like a whiff of honey, the sweet and mythic prehistory of my existence.

Spirit dancing, I envisioned a place inside this energetic city, ours: a classic townhouse on a steep street with expansive views of the Pacific, the magenta siding sun-faded—a third-story perch, thick platinum haze embracing our new home. My eyes shut in strange joy.

The next day, we crossed the vast blue bay to San Francisco, again. We craved new independence, greater adventure and terrain unknown to us. Back in the cloudy hills, cold wind excited my imagination, my dreams awake—and we hunted for the first address from Craigslist. Inside, the studio was tiny as a walk-in closet, and when I turned on the faucet, the sink smelled of leaking cooking gas, unnerving. The burnt-orange rug was unraveled at one end, a pallid softness underneath my shoes. We left without explanation, disappointed.

The next apartment we stepped into was the antithesis of the first: the entire second story of a buttercream townhouse with a shimmering view of the silver-blue Marina, roof kissed by fog.

Outside, the surrounding neighborhood was peppered with young families, and pretending we were permanently settling here, home-hunting for our "whole family," we again whispered of children. Our strapping Winter; sweet, beautiful Marin—kidding, I became more and more excited for the new world we were building.

We signed a two-month lease, not knowing what would come after. But this was our proud first movement—at last leaving his parents' sun-spilled castle.

~

Living together in a brick-and-mortar apartment felt surreal, our Victorian on a translucent hill of mist. The only place we'd shared alone, before, had been a little tent. Our old hiking gear and climbing rope now fit nicely underneath a plush queen bed.

And I was joyous in this urban base camp. In our Pacific Heights hideaway, I wrote with new vigor, working on stories for an amorphous "book."

Justin would also be on his laptop as I typed, his body facing mine across our kitchen table. I assumed he was looking for jobs or volunteer opportunities, though whenever I would try to peek over, he'd shield his screen. And if I asked what he was up to, he would say, "Just researching."

Despite his taciturn responses, we were harmonious—and he was supporting us, so I didn't think it fair to interrogate him. I was content to see my love upbeat and stimulated.

But my work soon felt too tangled. The themes and the plot of my novel were ever-evolving, changing with me. Routinely, I'd write a thousand new words in a frenzied afternoon, only to delete them the next morning, starting over. And while my *Basecamp Berkeley* blog was cool and reached a few hundred strangers, its creation didn't challenge or ignite me. I wished to find some definitive track—a bridge to true and formal publication.

Searching online in bed, I discovered Shut Up & Write!, San Francisco get-togethers at which dozens of strangers gathered at the same local bar or coffee shop—commuting simply to produce their pens or laptops and write in silence, together. The idea was accountability, and community. I was intrigued, wishing to find a guide, the elusive "mentor" of my hopes.

I attended my first gathering at the Amsterdam Café, a maroon-walled bar in the Tenderloin, an infamously gritty district of downtown. For ninety minutes, I wrote rapidly—yet aimlessly. As the sun sunk, my words felt gravely undirected, documenting the shooting-star whims of my thoughts.

After the session was over, a few writers were socializing, ordering house wine, and as ruby lights flicked on, I hoped I wouldn't be carded—I was still just a hair underage.

Satin-striped scarlet curtains ballooned like velvet flags in the crisp breeze from an open window, and—glass bottle of Diet Coke in hand—I wandered the dive, an awkward outsider. Feeling too young, not from here. Nervous, I stepped up to a small cluster of eccentric adults, predominantly men, standing in a loose circle. And though they seemed perfectly nice, I shifted my weight from one foot back onto the other, soundlessly tilting, visibly uncomfortable—and I realized I wasn't even sure what I wanted to know, what questions to ask.

So after fifteen minutes, I disappeared onto the train toward new home, safer. I'd never spoken a word, not even hello.

~

I turned twenty-one. We filled our water glasses with wine. January raindrops glittering on the window, Justin and I touched cups, blessing our freedom and our love; he blessed my breasts. I blessed his oversized lower lip, which I'd learned had been hit by a baseball when he was a child, and had never recovered. Now it was thicker on the right side than the left, strangely exciting.

We opened a second bottle of Merlot on the soft leather of our pretty mint-green couch. I'd been intoxicated only a handful of instances in my life. Bittersweet truth blooming, a dandelion in my heart, I confessed to him that I was feeling rootless. I whispered in the small cave of my love's ear, "I am a lost ship."

Justin laughed. I had been serious as ice, intense and true, but he seemed only amused. He wrapped me firmly in his large hands and began to rock me.

Swaying back and forward, I became drunker. I was soft butter in my husband's arms, at ease, when he asked, "What about college in Manhattan?" We were curled into a pretzel on the sofa, a baby-blue comforter like a smooth cloud over us.

My first instinct was *no*. College had always felt more like an anchor than a kite, a tedious and time-eating entrapment. Studying for pointless tests stole away nights, rote memorization disappearing the freedom of creation. Yet my fundamental lack of direction—floating through days like a leaf in twirling springtime breeze—prevented my flat objection. Deflecting, I asked him, "Why New York?"

"It's the literary hub of the universe," he spoke. "You're a born writer. And going to school there is a way to become a professional." He assured me that greater structure would benefit my energetic soul.

I sat up a little straighter, pulling away. "*Thank you*," I said, overenunciating both syllables. "But in creative fields, a degree is a prerequisite for nothing." Annoyed, I took another sip of wine.

Justin gripped the back of my neck, bizarrely soothing. "It's not about the piece of paper," he told me. "It's the people you'll meet, professors and connections. Even just from a statistical perspective, ignoring all the positive intangibles, you'll be maximizing the chance of greater opportunity." He spoke as if the plan had already been written. "You have to trust me."

Shaking my head, I grinned in my defiance, and the room and the whole world became soft and buzzing, lights dangerously unfocused. Our shadows intermingled, a Chagall on the pale wood floor. My thoughts sudden and intriguing, like a rainbow you see for only a second—

Touching my nose with his thumb, Justin called me his "investment," declaring that my writing would someday support us both—a mad sureness. This confidence in me seemed unfounded, simply wishful.

A single black ant sped across the floor beyond our naked toes, and I wondered why I felt so oppositional. His expression of unflappable faith had touched a profound place, the deep wellspring of my purpose—my future dream I cradled like a soft and formative pearl.

I could not deny that in this attractive city, without compelling assignments or any deadlines to reach for, all painful catalysts for growth had been eliminated, erased from my existence like the rogue lines in a sketch—the unexpected marks that make the picture's expression passionate and real, gone now. Living here, I was growing complacent again, seduced by a stagnant state of mind I hated to indulge—

Seamless like a fall leaf changing color, my will switched powerfully. "You make sense," I told him. "I want to go back."

I trusted my husband so purely, as raindrops trust the ocean as they're falling.

Not pausing, Justin grabbed my laptop and opened applications for me to return to college, the moon framed in our kitchen, winking in the window from behind a slate storm-cloud. He asked me questions from the forms aloud, marking my responses—applying me to schools in New York City.

One college I learned of, The New School, possessed a quiet history of revolution, the institution bravely offering asylum to the world's exiled artists and scholars, great minds in hiding. Reading about the rebellious institution, I saw that Marlon Brando, a former student of the university, praised the school as "a sanctuary for hundreds of extraordinary European Jews who had fled Germany . . . enriching the city's intellectual life with an intensity."

Over the next week, drunk on young drive, I typed impulsive college essays, personal arguments defending creative freedom, inspired. I wrote these rants myself—but everything else was Justin. He was excellent at doing things for me.

In the small hours of a cold February dawn, Justin and I walked to the Pacific, high cliffs eroding over the ocean, crashed and crashed by lapping salty waves. Their spray misted us in day's young purple air, exhilarating. Walking the Golden Gate Bridge, our world receding, pale gold sunrise lit thin fog, morning coloring us like a faded fairy tale.

Day vivified the city, and we found a rogue path through the dunes down to the beach, the foam edge of teal sea. The whole sky celestial sapphire. We were celebrating my admission to The New School in New York City.

We joked about our new Manhattan residence, "maybe slightly bigger than a tent."

$\sim$

Before settling in our new city, we craved one last great adventure. Our idea had formed through a mutual friend's bright lure: While backpacking the Pacific Crest Trail, we'd met a man named Mystic; we had walked with him, devouring his manic stories. He saw beauty in pure blue lakes, in girls, food, birds, common things. In just walking.

Mystic spoke of a woodland footpath indicated by blazes—smears of white paint on trees and rocks that mark the Appalachian Trail. The hiking route extends from Georgia to central Maine, expansive—an estimated 2,200 miles, though the exact length changes over time as sections of the path are modified or rerouted, a moving maze.

Justin and I drove across America, from San Francisco to the East Coast—to the beginning of another pilgrimage. In Georgia, we entered the cold forest, together.

On our first afternoon on the trail, the branches bare, two fireflies appeared in the same instant. The lightning bugs twirled sparks and squiggles of pure yellow gold, sometimes taking turns and sometimes harmonizing, their air-flecking fine as precious metal—blinking close, and then diverging, as if they were gently dotting the path of a conversation. They danced in reality; we followed the movement of one spark.

I felt connected to the luminescent creatures, my mind airborne with them. Trails enabled me to better see the world, to notice fine aspects invisible from an airplane, the most basic things we miss. Seeing life at a pace at which you can actually observe nuance, the speed of stepping, the beautiful inspiring texture of "plain" reality becomes visible—God smiling in the detail.

That night in our tent, Justin told me how, ten thousand years ago, human beings were migrant—we were like the birds. The average human would see only about a hundred people in her lifetime and would know each one profoundly, deeply bonded. Today, humans in cities will see a hundred beings in just minutes, naming them *strangers*, a dehumanizing designation.

The next morning, I woke to wet rocks glittering in the slanted light, the day's warmth shining in bars through the sparse canopy of maples. Happy here, I began to fear our next destination, hectic Manhattan—a surreal flip to witnessing ten thousand people a day. In these deep thickets, we walked a path that was streamlined, simple and clear.

We were in the woods, and not a parent or a friend on earth knew where. At this moment, we were untraceable, this notion an odd pleasure. A patch of fallen leaves glowed in a pool of golden sun, and the dim forest air smelled sweet, of young lilac, invisible sage.

Ferns blanketing the entire forest floor like the grounds of another era, Justin and I hiked the southern half of the Appalachian Trail— eighty days and 1,020 miles through the green tunnel of creaking trees.

～

We emerged from Bear Mountain's leafy woods and appeared just two hours later in the long shadow of skyscrapers, the sun caught high on a tall glass building, a reflection. Exiting a bus, déjà vu overwhelmed me, that ephemeral phenomena of alignment so perfect it is eerie.

Thus we joined spirit with Joan Didion and Patti Smith and about a million other dreamers who, against all odds, had landed here, moving on fumes of reveries, to New York City.

The bus left us on dark pavement outside of Port Authority, yellow cabs dotting this new world—a wave of bodies crossing the jammed-up Midtown street; we followed.

5

TURQUOISE WALLS, NEW YORK

The New York sidewalk led us along a little corner park rimmed with yellow-orange and violet pansies that seemed to be smiling, their faces upturned, and past a bagel shop that smelled of sesame and salt, delicious warm air. We passed an empty wine bar with a pink chandelier, whimsical and dim inside, and a neighborhood diner with its blue neon sign huge and lit up, little white line-cook hats—the city seemed in my vision like a multifaceted gem, spectacular. I wished I could keep everything I witnessed like a photograph, to forever hold this electric aliveness. The colors of the flowers and the clothing were crisp and rosy, hyper-bright against the subdued sun-drenched pigments of the streets and the brick buildings, all seeming faded, softer than real. Pops of coral and red—a scarf, a lady's lips—were pops of life.

Between us, we had only our hiking backpacks. Exhausted, we rented a room at the Latham Hotel, the cheapest we could find in Midtown Manhattan.

Justin had to show his ID to enter—the establishment, which doubled as a home for battered women, had a problem with abusive partners showing up unwanted, looking for their sheltered wives and girlfriends. Stuffed into the tiny half-lit elevator with a girl about my age and her crying infant, I was grateful. I thought, *I am with a good man.*

In our tiny room, the walls were shiny medical white with no artwork or any humanizing adornment. The space had no blankets, either; we pushed our two low cots together on the floor, touching except the small gap of metal edges—approximating a bed.

We had good reason to be anxious, beginning anew without a clue or map, but on our backs in that unnatural whiteness, we lay peaceful as waterfront sunbathers. Our plan was loose and as undefined as the path across a beach—any route seemed possible, all effective in crossing. And a calm energy lit my heart, perceptible in my movements, which seemed slower.

Justin switched off the light; momentarily spooked, I wanted to hear his voice. I spoke into dim space: "I bet *you'll* do big things here too—"

"I never want to work again," he cut me off, his unexpected decree like stardust in the darkness. For a moment, the blankness of New York's canvas took on an energetic tone of backstage butterflies.

"I know, Charlie," I whispered. I called him Charlie when I was being tender. "You're going to do something meaningful."

"Long-term, I want to be a stay-at-home dad." Our one-year wedding anniversary would come next week, and this was the first time he'd brought up his role with our children. "While you're writing books, I'll take care of the kids. I'll make blueberry pancakes."

I laughed, worried and excited. "I just hope I can support us, writing," I joked. I didn't know exactly how much money he had saved. "And if I don't, I'm sure you'll find a job you love."

My husband adjusted his body, turning away from me to face the wall. He cradled his bent arm firmly in the other, the deadweight limb apparently asleep.

~

When I woke, our white room glaring in the new sun, Justin was watching me, lying in his cot but already dressed for the day.

Seeing my opened eyes, he took my face up in his palms, my cheeks damp with August heat. "In this bright light you look more beautiful," he spoke, as if perplexed.

I blushed hotter, flattered. "You're handsome," I said back, "same as always."

He opened his laptop and showed me a picture of a "cozy" Greenwich Village apartment he'd found online. My dad, a born New Yorker, had told me stories of the Village, a lively network of cobblestone streets and jazz dives, coffee houses and folk clubs with no cover fee—and I felt a surge of light-headed ambition. "Though it's kind of strange," Justin continued, "there is no bathroom inside. Our toilet would be down a public hallway."

We walked two bustling miles, arriving at a slender six-story structure of mushroom brick—one of the converted tenements of MacDougal Street, a famed haven for artists. Bob Dylan had gotten his first stage-time downstairs, right in this building, at a little club called Kettle of Fish; Jack Kerouac penned *The Dharma Bums* in a manic spill across the street, in rickety Caffe Reggio.

Inside, hand-painted tiles were faded and lovely, creating a sand-blond and orange floral patterning in the narrow lobby. Cast-iron stairs, ebony and ornate, spiraled upward. The old construction now housed twenty units, and the hallways came not to a flat end but instead to a sharp point, like the acute tip of a geometric diamond, a design out of *Alice in Wonderland*. The walls were indistinct pale and the doors were heavy and black, lanterns mounted up above our heads glowing rich buttery gold. The apartment we were viewing was perched on the fifth story, a walk-up with turquoise walls like an oasis pool.

The place would cost $1,775 a month—hand-in-hand, we huddled in the sharp-tipped hall, our quiet voices echoing against our wills. Justin told me that they required six months' rent, up front. "But trust me, it's a special find. It's a good deal."

Staring at the cast-iron swirls and black hearts of the guardrail's spiral downward, I pictured our life here. We would live in this nexus of magic, our sky-top nest. We would love it—

Three days later, we moved in.

~

Sitting with a hundred transfer students at folding tables in a small auditorium, I fantasized about becoming a novelist, the architect of worlds, making a living dreaming wild dreams. Considering possible courses, my top choice was Intermediate Fiction.

Yet when I got to the front of the "approval" line, a trim lady informed me, "You'll need to take the prerequisite, first. It's Beginning Fiction Workshop, but it's full." Her glasses were thick horizontal eggs, the rims smooth milk-white shells, and for a moment I imagined I could trick her, just slip my enrollment card past her. But she didn't once look away. She asked me, "What do you want to take instead?"

I didn't want to go all the way to the back of the line to reselect my fourth class—quickly, I flipped through the catalogue and noticed Writing for New York City Newspapers and Magazines: Instant Gratification Takes Too Long. The description explained that the objective in this class would be "to write and publish a beautiful piece by the end of the course." I liked the sound of this vocational approach.

The lady wouldn't let me into Intermediate Fiction, I didn't want to wait—so I signed up for Instant Gratification Takes Too Long.

The following Monday, I entered a room where a big fan spun, combating humid heat. Though it was 8:00 p.m., the sun blinked, silver in the western window, as if this fourth-story classroom were a magic safeguard against the fall of night.

Three long taupe plastic tables were arranged into a U, and as we settled into our modern slate bucket chairs, Professor Nicole Solomon told us a story, her fawn eyes glinting bright with expectant energy. A twenty-year-old graduate student fleeing "the repression of the Midwest," she had cast herself as a chain-smoking confessional poet, an outcast. She always wore all black, midnight her fashion—my new teacher spoke rapidly, without resting. "Arriving in Manhattan for graduate school," she recalled, "I noticed every girl in sight was dressed head-to-toe in black identical to mine. I'd found that while in Michigan I was radical and edgy, in New York City I was merely mainstream."

The classroom bubbled with laughter, faces basking, a half-moon of thin smiles, enraptured.

Then she told us how she'd graduated with all the prestige of her lauded New York University master's degree in poetry—utterly lost. "I didn't even know how to craft a cover letter to submit the precious pages I'd spent two years perfecting," she explained, rising to her feet to pass around our thick course packets. "I've invented the course *I* needed to take back then."

I felt lit up, as if someone had reached into my heart and flipped an inner switch, turning me on, brighter.

Until I saw our first assignment: "Write three pages on your most humiliating secret."

~

Opening my apartment's heavy black door, I came home to a small miracle—on a new wooden table, a delicate wheel of soft cheese, triple crème. Medjool dates and Turkish golden apricots sat on the white linoleum of our kitchen countertop.

Justin was lying on his back on our new faux-leather futon, his head resting on his emptied thru-hiking backpack. Examining these exquisite treats, I asked him, "Where'd you get all this?"

"They were free," he said. A puckish, faraway smile cracked his stare. "I found them. Handpicked in SoHo." He told me how he'd scavenged these treasures—collecting them from the sidewalks of upscale areas, the fine foods discovered outside fancy grocery stores, discarded. With these scraps, we had the makings of a feast.

I was excited by his resourcefulness—his municipal foraging reminded me of his scrappy industriousness, back on the trail. In the mountains, he would find us delicious edible berries and gather up flourishing wild green patches of miner's lettuce.

"Wow," I murmured. This sudden sweet loot appearing, I felt like we were tricking the world—living in urban loopholes.

Handing me a vibrant golden peach, Justin said softly, "This is the way it's gonna be." He had saved up enough to pay our rent and bills for a decade, he told me, *if* we were careful. "So we're not going to waste our money taking taxis," he went on. "We'll be smart."

Processing this decree, I saw the logic in his vision. "You're smart," I echoed. I loved walking, anyway, and the subway was a fun adventure, available whenever we wanted to explore farther.

Using sourdough bread he'd found, some dried black cherries, and the brie, I designed a little cheese plate, the dark fruits arranged on the porcelain into a cockeyed smiley face.

Justin stood and opened a bottle of wine—one spoil not found but purchased.

Like old best friends on a first date, we stayed up through the night, half-charmed by wonder. Tipsy, I considered how people might view Justin's rummaging as wrong and grungy. *But why should this food go wasted?* Too curious, I took a risk and asked him, "Were you embarrassed that someone might see?"

He swigged a gulp of wine and placed the bottle on the ground. "Why would I be?" Reclining deeper into our non-bed, just a flat foam mattress on the floorboards, he slipped his naked arm around my back.

"Sorry," I whispered, wishing I hadn't pressed him. "I just wondered."

He stared at me. "Every person exists in their own shallow bowl, and they can't see over the rim," he explained. "But they think that their world *is* the world—the truth. When in reality, no two bowls are identical, and all people are stuck trapped in their own."

Listening to my love, I felt as if we were transported back to the trail, staring at the inky field of ghostly stars. My hair dangling off our bed and onto the hardwood floor, almost upside down, I challenged him, intoxicated. "No that's silly. We see the color of the walls, the same."

"There is no way to prove that your blue is my blue," he said.

I placed my palm softly on his face, as if thwarting the momentum of this challenging line of thinking. "We all want love and human connection," I said, perky, "the same things."

The block of sky in our twin high windows became a nectarine, amber and rose pink, and we lay in silence as white sunlight broke. We'd flipped places—he was now on his side, and I flat on my back. And sobering, I began seeing how my love's allegory was a hard truth, very dark—how our shallow bowls, differences of perspective, account for all declarations of others' "wrongness" (one's own rightness), and the sense of being wronged.

"You were right, by the way," I told him, rolling over onto my stomach, closer to him. "I love New York."

As my husband drifted off, smiling with lips parted like a child's in the brilliant day's intensifying blueness, I decided what my first essay would be about: our great hike, *us*.

~

At a coffee shop with a vibrant yellow awning, I ordered a latte, which came in a white ceramic bowl with pale foam in the smooth shape of a heart. At a communal granite table, I wordlessly began to write the story of first walking alone, typing rapidly and with pure awareness—revisiting the footpath on my shining screen. How—before Justin—I had yelled out simply to hear my echo, Oregon's volcanic rock like a husk of dead earth beneath my running shoes.

Composing my first assignment, hours passed, noon became dusk, the city sky rose and golden; and I imagined I was merging with The New School's radical movement, a student of creativity and free expression.

Stepping outside, all finished, gold porchlight kissed my forehead. The animated nighttime island was a concrete jungle wild with promise, and around any cobblestone corner my big break might exist, disguised as a simple café, waiting for me to open the door.

Arriving home at nine, I found the apartment empty. I made a cup of mint tea and texted Justin, "Home!" A half-burned stick of sandalwood incense was still lit, its long tip glowing orange, unnerving. Settling onto the futon with my warm mug, I wondered where he might be.

An hour elapsed with no response, but I didn't worry—ever since I'd first landed in Colorado Springs, I had learned to interpret his silences as meaningless: Justin being Justin.

I exhaled when he finally walked through the doorway. He sat down beside me, his eyes ignited. "I have some news," he said. "I'm going to be a math and science tutor."

I was relieved. "Where?" I asked him, embracing his ribs.

"All around New York," he said. "Just three to four days a week, teaching kids the fun of applied logic." He explained that the job was not for pay, and I admired his generosity and altruism. "I'll need my car," he added. Before we'd hiked the Appalachian Trail, he'd left it in a long-term lot in Georgia. As if an afterthought, he told me, "Next two days, I'll be gone."

6

A Thousand Miles to Tell the Truth

One night in late September, Professor Solomon emailed me, asking if I could take a walk with her. "Want to discuss your essay?" her message said. "Does midnight work?"

I'd heard from a few of my classmates about these energetic sessions, which took place at the witching hour and always traced the periphery of Washington Square Park—her unique interpretation of "office hours." Unconventional, these power-walks were famous. I was honored, even a tad nervous.

I showed Justin the invitation and then twirled, skipping around our apartment. He laughed at me, happy—excited too.

When I arrived five minutes before midnight, Nic was changing out of elegant black pumps. Her apartment was beautiful, a great open atrium, the walls lined with tall bookshelves, completely filled. A bouquet sat on her kitchen counter, red and golden blossoms. Glancing at the card, I saw it was from a former student who had just gotten a book deal, sent in gratitude.

Nic insisted I take my heels off, too, telling me, "You'll wreck your feet and back," handing me loaner sneakers. Her concern seemed warm and motherly, not critical but caring.

We stepped into the city night. The unnatural brightness was composed of a million spotlights, storefront lanterns and neon words. Bypassing hollow small talk, she told me she liked my essay's language, calling my descriptions of the woods and cold blue lakes "pretty and atmospheric."

From the author of ten books, this praise felt meaningful. Trying to conceal my glee, I just said, "Thank you!"

"But truthfully, it's too cryptic," she told me. "It's well written, but there's no blood there." She encouraged me to bare my heart in my sentences. "Your essay is just pretty air."

I bit my lip. I had the piercing urge to walk away, but doing so would have been ridiculous. "There wasn't so much blood on the trail, unfortunately," I protested. *Pretty air is far more valuable than ugly blood,* I thought—the music of the sentences is what *creates* the nuance of emotion, not the drama. "The hike was wonderful, and then I fell in love."

"What made you think of this story as a humiliation?" she asked. Nic's pace was brisk, and I felt flushed, warm with exertion. "I was left wondering why you decided to take such a long walk by yourself."

The true answer held my chest like an unwanted hand's sudden touch, uncomfortable and unfeeling. "You can't tell anyone," I told her without stopping to think, "and I would never want to write about this. But freshman year . . ." I paused to breathe. "I was raped."

Nic turned to find my eyes, which glanced away, cautious. "And then you left school to backpack for half a year, alone?"

My face and my whole body felt clammy. Other than Justin and my family, and the administration of Colorado College, almost no one knew. "I did," I finally said.

"That's your beginning." Nic encouraged me to write about the violation, even if the pages were only for myself.

Barely believing my own words, I promised her I'd try.

~

Walking downtown in a cool October drizzle, Justin and I were offered an umbrella by a middle-aged stranger in an olive bowler hat. "It's extra," he said, bowing down slightly. "I brought it because I knew someone would need it." A palpable force seemed to be unifying the people of the city, the sudden camaraderie of solidarity.

Arriving in the Financial District, we saw a tent city in Manhattan's heart. A thousand people were gathered on the grass of Zuccotti Park, wielding cardboard signs with powerful reminders: "None are more hopelessly enslaved than those who falsely believe they are free" and "We are the 99%." Chatting with the campers, individuals who strongly reminded us of thru-hikers from the trail, we learned that this patch-work rally was a coordinated response to our country's growing wealth gap.

This protest spoke to me—the humanist principles felt connected to the minimalist essence of long-distance hiking, the desire to transcend the smoke and mirrors of our country's established society, revealing what remains in all its splendor: the magnificent, resilient human soul.

Walking back home that afternoon, I felt more aware of the poverty and opulence on every sidewalk—we brushed past a raven-haired lady with a thousand-dollar handbag and a skinny child with toeless shoes begging for change.

Over the next weeks, neglecting Professor Solomon's assignment, I began a new project: a photo-essay about the Occupy Wall Street movement that was overtaking Manhattan.

Inspired, I snapped hundreds of photographs, wanting to document this singular moment in New York's pulsing body, watching people flooding the sidewalks like human rivers, converging at the green park as one ocean. I took shots of the sharpest signs and strangest masks; the angry bankers in their crisp blue button-downs; the lines of bored-faced cops, slouching with thick arms crossed. And peering through my view-finder, I learned the skill of noticing more deeply; I felt a *thrill*—a new civil affinity budding in my dreams and in the brick-and-mortar city, simultaneously: that we, the people, were awakening to the truth that a bundle of twigs is inconceivably strong.

~

Justin and I drove north, to my parents' home, reentering the neighborhood of my childhood in the early afternoon. We rolled up my old road for Thanksgiving, the naked trees like gray skeletons, my fire from our moment at the Occupy encampment transmuting into shame—

A lone stick in a possible choir of voices, I'd witnessed the power of a movement; still I avoided retelling the pain of my assault. Not wanting to live that memory again, I'd been staring at the blinking cursor on my blank screen—wishing this hard history was not a story I needed to tell.

Parking against the curb outside my first house, I told Justin, "I want to be close with my parents again—"

"I didn't know you weren't." The car lights all switched off.

"But I think that publishing something about the rape would really upset them." I didn't want to undermine all the good progress I had made with them since hiking. Staring at the deflated balloons of dead magenta flowers on our rhododendron bush I used to hide in, playing, I lightly touched Justin's knee. "I once told my mom that when I grew up, I wanted to live next door to her forever."

He held my hand down. "But you're not doing this for them," he said calmly. Then I saw the front door open—my parents were looking at us.

"I know," I said. And he was right. They both waved and came outside to greet us. "But I don't feel comfortable writing it until I at least tell my mom."

Justin ducked out of the car; I followed. "Talk to her this weekend, if you want to," he told me as we grabbed our backpacks. "But you know how she gets. You don't need her permission."

Inside, we joined the festivities. Walter and Lucy had flown in from California, fusing with my family for a grand Thanksgiving dinner, a dozen of us total, our table crowded with food, a circus of warm dishes. They chewed with faraway smiles, half-dazed by the commotion of the meal. "Very nice," my in-laws said of everything they tasted.

Knowing my turkey preference, my dad passed me the huge platter of carved white meat; and he inquired about The New School. "How are you liking it?" he asked, his tone hopeful.

It was easy to tell him I loved it, which made my mother smile. Excited, I detailed each class, describing my professors and their different teaching styles. "In my history of blues class, the professor says that every ballad is an allegory." I paused to accept a bowl of glistening cranberry sauce from my mom, cool in my palms.

My dad was drumming his thumb against his plate. "These songs were the newspapers of the poor," he spoke—opening the door to a discussion about music as a medium for protest and an access to freedom, a conversation that extended through the remainder of the meal.

In a lull, I asked Justin about his volunteer tutoring in front of everyone—I was proud of him. Modest, he admitted he enjoyed it. Then my husband brought up our attendance at Occupy Wall Street; excited, he said that, having worked in finance, he intimately knew the industry's shortsightedness, the quarterly "success" of a given stock at odds with the stability and health of greater society.

But my father questioned the potential effectiveness of this particular "movement," calling its intentions undefined—and I feared that he was right.

"How is your job search going?" my mom asked Justin. She was referring to jobs that paid—careers. Justin's parents both looked at him, clearly interested.

He smiled, composed, but his blue eyes seemed tense. "I'll let you know."

Hours later, as my mom gathered up the sticky tins of consumed apple pies and a half dozen empty pints of Ben & Jerry's ice cream, my mother-in-law whispered in my ear, "Drinking coffee and talking past midnight. Your parents are true intellectuals."

~

I undressed before my husband in the bedroom of my teen years, my old baby-blue walls one flat color, like cartoon water. They were dotted with watercolor paintings I made as a child, neatly framed. My curtains were the same lavender linen, the little pastel ballerinas dancing, my sheets, comforter, and oval throw-rug all matching them—I collapsed into bed. "Come to me," I said, wanting him close.

He was standing against my dresser, apparently staring at the wall. "Why did you stop racing?" Justin asked.

I sat up and realized where he was looking—directly at my illustrated Nordic ski poster from the state championship qualifier my junior year of high school, one of my biggest races. *Because of my coach*, I almost admitted, the truth. Instead I told him, "No real reason. I just grew out of it."

That first night back home, I couldn't fall asleep. Too full and wide awake, I stared blankly at the dim rectangle of the poster in the darkness—and, for an instant, I felt the exhilaration of flying through boundless whiteness, skiing.

Lying awake, I checked my email, Justin passed out in a peaceful curl beside me. To my surprise, Nic had sent a 3:00 a.m. message with the intriguing subject "This might help . . ." Her twin in wakefulness, I was flattered to know that she was thinking about me on this holiday night. Opening it, I saw an article by a college sophomore, relaying her horrific experience in the justiceless aftermath of being raped at school. The essence of the young woman's account was commonplace, not exotic. Her story was as familiar as the houses on frat row.

Reading, I stomached every sentence, recognizing her pain. I saw myself in glimpses of her green campus.

And lying in my quiet bedroom, feeling connected to this faraway young woman, less alone, I understood the potential power intrinsic in my own buried memory. I pictured unseen people *I* could share my words with—and possibly *help*.

I dressed and slipped out of the room—inspired to write. Tiptoeing over creaking floorboards, I descended wooden stairs, not wanting to disturb the peace at home.

I opened a Diet Coke, settling at the kitchen table. Thinking about the second day of my freshman year at Colorado College, I returned to that horrible night, eighteen years old, naive and conspicuous as a neon butterfly. I typed:

> *. . . before classes began and even before I'd removed my yellow and blue construction paper nametag from my door, I invited three other freshmen to my room. A fawn-eyed girl I'd met that day and two new boys. I was 18. It was a warm late August evening. We all watched* The Breakfast Club. *A boy rolled a joint, I put it in my lips.*

> *The movie ended and two of the kids left. I was wearing pale pink linen shorts. I felt quite pretty. When the boy who remained in the room turned to me, I'd smiled at his red hair; I happily kissed him. He seemed easygoing, poised. But then he gripped my thigh. My voice wavered as I said "bye." Suddenly frightened, I didn't want him to stay, but he became deaf. The slice of sky in my cracked window glowed black, dense as a bomb.*

When I woke alone six hours later, the sky was a sheer flawless
blue. Two red-black stains of blood marked my white cotton
underwear. The bright sky defied the violence of the past night.
In its glaring emptiness, I lay still.

Footsteps on the stairs startled me. I pressed my laptop closed, unnerved to find that the sky was now a clear day-blue. My mom appeared in a navy and forest plaid cotton nightgown, looking happy. "Oh! You're up early," she said, as she heated water for a pot of coffee; and disoriented, I stood to give her a hug. "Did you get any sleep?"

"Not really, for some reason." I sat back down. I wanted to tell her that I'd been writing about my assault—to ask for her blessing. But all I said was "Thank you for cooking for everyone."

Filling two mugs, she joined me at the table. "Walter and Lucy are sweet people," she said.

I nodded. "Definitely." My laptop still between us, I pushed it away, safe from the coffee. "One of my professors is helping me write an essay about hiking the Pacific Crest Trail," I said out of the blue. I paused, perhaps too dramatically. "And what happened before . . . my reason for walking." I stopped, waiting for my mom to say something.

She seemed to be studying the grain of the wooden table. "I think it's best not to dwell . . . ," my mother finally spoke, trailed off.

Blood rising to my cheeks, I stared at a small brown bird on a low bush through the bay window. Again, I felt like she was silencing me. My mom had donated $1,060 to the Rape, Abuse & Incest National Network—on the condition that my own family, the people I most trusted and most loved, not find out that *I* had been raped. She'd worried that my secret shame would shame our family, and now I realized how much pain her "contribution" caused me. Really, my mother wanted as few people to know about what had happened as possible. Justin was right—if I waited for her permission to write this story, it would never be told.

~

The night Justin and I returned to New York, I went directly to a twenty-four-hour diner on the Avenue of the Americas. Watching two young women wearing matching purple New York University sweat-shirts walk in, laughing, I ordered a cappuccino, settling at a red linoleum tabletop, my booth.

Lost at that table in the sleepy Waverly Diner, returning to the hike, I saw that I'd walked the trail with the hope of literally, physically reclaiming my body. Prior to beginning that great excursion, I'd felt the air inside my heart, stolen. I needed to discover in my bones that I was safe in the world in the body in which I must keep living—I had wanted to prove my great strength, first to myself.

Deep in pink sleeplessness, I conjured my darkest past, channeling details of the night and year that followed, remembering as I breathed. Finished with my cappuccino, I saved my work, the sky becoming blue with a new sun.

Then I walked east, buildings gold with sunrise, the yellow cabs awake; and at a copy shop on the north side of Washington Square Park, I printed my freshly revised essay.

Jogging up Professor Solomon's granite steps, I left the new piece with her doorman, my jackrabbit heart thumping as if I'd run a thousand miles to tell her the truth.

7

A Hiker's Guide to Healing

Pressing the skin below my open eye downward with his firm thumb, Justin put in my contact lens; and then the other. He didn't do this daily, just when I asked him—otherwise, I wore glasses—but he'd told me that tonight was "a special occasion." He said he wanted to take me out to dinner to celebrate my bravery. "Wear running shoes."

Outside, the midday air looked almost silver, and holding hands, we descended into the subway—popping out at the edge of emerald Central Park, an urban sanctuary peppered with gold-leafed trees. The warm colors gleamed so brightly, as if autumn had stricken this pocket of the city more acutely.

Wordless, we wandered through a hundred rows of color-coded blossoms, vibrant as the bright strokes of an oil painting, the secret garden of a daydream. Moving through this sudden patch, grasping Justin's fingers, I became nervous, thinking of Professor Solomon's eyes on my words; everything felt heightened. And it was as if I could see the flowers breathe.

As we circled a pale stone fountain, a birdsong by the pond ahead alluring, the singer unseen, I finally spoke: "I'm scared about people knowing."

Behind a yellow rose bush, he placed a warm palm on the exposed back of my neck. "This is important," he said. "It isn't something to be afraid of." Absorbing his words, I relaxed into myself, falling in new love as he gave credence to my story.

He'd been unconditionally supportive since the long-ago impulsive moment I had first revealed the sexual assault—back on the trail, my lips against his neck, I'd softly told him. In response, he readjusted his body, wrapping himself around me without words. He held me, and I leaned into him deeply. That night, I slept inside his safe embrace.

Now my limbs felt lighter, my heaviness released, as I let my husband lead me down a broad sun-dappled footpath. His bouncy gait seemed happy—untroubled, too.

At 104th Street, a hidden rose patch blinked pink-green from behind rust-red foliage. Witch hazel and the magenta cones of butterfly bush appeared beneath the graceful boughs of maples shadowing empty gray-wood benches. Beside an erupting marble fountain, every petal looked animate and friendly.

Resting together on a lonely bench, I asked Justin for his thumb. I doodled a strange constellation made of five star-swirls over the raised veins on the back of his hand with a blue pen.

"This is kind of morbid," he said, looking at the navy design, "but if you died today, I would have to get this as a tattoo." Flattered for a moment by his perverse words of devotion, I felt my arm begin to tingle.

Periwinkle clouds fringed with luminous peach light drifted, afloat in cobalt sky as Justin led me back under the ground. We resurfaced onto a strange street of manic lights, red and purple and yellow neon signs all layered on top of each other up the fronts of buildings, tinting the shaded brick facades in foreign tones. Much of the lettering was in a language I didn't know. "Where are we?" I asked him. The many streaming colors disoriented me.

Entering a lanky beige-stone restaurant, holding the red door open, he told me, "Koreatown."

The room felt like a dim cosmopolitan treehouse. All the walls were draped with green fishnet, every inch of the interior covered, the netting forming a cozy tent around us; the ceiling twinkled with a thousand tiny hanging blue-hued lights on strings, like distant stars.

At a table made from a repurposed oil drum, my husband ordered a watermelon cocktail, his voice barely audible over blaring K-pop music. "Get whatever you want," he spoke into my ear, and I ordered us spicy tofu stew, family style.

A hollowed-out half watermelon arrived, filled to the brim with ice, fruit puree, Sprite, and the Korean spirit soju, and the server left us two bowls and a ladle. Sipping pink liquor, I felt a buzz—a text message from Professor Solomon: "I read your revision. Want to walk at eleven?"

Hands shaking with strong nerves, I answered yes.

~

Walking with Nic, tipsy, the night air was like dark water, thicker, and stepping over a spill of glinting starlight on the sidewalk, a dozen abandoned pennies, she called my essay "intense and brave."

A flutter of bliss kissed my heart, bright like good wine—I was floating down the sidewalk, through the familiar crowd of Village streets. Reaching the periphery of Washington Square Park, we passed a white-faced mime with a red ball-nose and an a cappella group singing "Take on Me" in yellow lamplight. "You liked it?" I asked, stunned— she was so blunt and honest that when she gave a compliment, it meant something.

She glanced at me, her eyes narrowed in a smile. "It's going to be fantastic," she answered. "And, truthfully, I think it's a Modern Love." She was referring to the famous weekly column. "The readership is over a million people each Sunday in the *New York Times*."

I was terrified by the thought of a million eyes scrutinizing my deepest shame. "Oh wow." Her confidence felt empowering, but also frightening.

Nic stopped abruptly to stretch her calf on the black metal fence that lined the park's edge. Then she handed back my paper, white pages marked all over with red notes. She looked right at my pupils. "You may want to tone down all the stuff about your mother," she told me. "If you're going to write something negative about someone, make sure we love them first."

I nodded, surprised by this interpretation. "She comes off badly?"

"If we care about them," Nic went on, "it's even more devastating when they hurt you."

When we said goodbye, it was nearly one o'clock in the morning, but I couldn't wait to read through all her feedback. Across the street from my apartment, I sat down at a small round table of ancient wood imprinted with a thousand scuffs inside old Caffe Reggio, an eclectic dark-walled Italian restaurant with renaissance paintings of soft nude women covering its walls; tense, I reread my account, my black and white confession absolutely covered with Nic's ruby markings.

Studying her crossed-out words and curt notes in the margin—"tighten this thought; tone this scene down"—I realized I had been very, very hard on my mother, criticizing how she'd initially reacted to learning of my rape at school. In my attempt to be honest, unfiltered, I had unconsciously painted my mother as the villain—seeing this now, I felt guilty.

But I wasn't quite sure how to "tone down" what I saw as *truth*. Or if exhibiting my family as a story—sharing our private history so openly—was compassionate, even as I could be impacting so many strangers positively. Conflicted, I didn't know if it was worth it.

Perseverating, I overheard two girls at the table behind me, their energetic voices distracting. One was saying to the other that she had moved to New York City to become a photographer and writer but was still a waitress, exhausted by having no money. She told her friend she was planning to leave the city, to buy her bus ticket next week.

Possessed by some strange longing, I twisted and interrupted, "Do not leave New York!" I apologized for my intrusion and told the girl that I was also a writer. "I moved here for the same reason," I said, my half-rotated torso awkward.

The writer girl was pretty, slight with pale skin. Voice softer, she introduced herself as Corrina.

Rising to her feet, her friend told us she needed to be up early, and I feared I'd scared her away. But Corrina stayed.

We talked for hours, trading stories of the city and our paths here. Leaning close, we tracked the rivers of our lives. How did we end in New York? Corrina had circumvented the world, escaping a brutal war in Moldova, as a child. She was graceful as a princess, strawberry-blonde hair shining and long down her back, worn ballet flats for shoes. Her cheeks adorned with subtle freckles that she had acquired in the heat of the sunflower fields of her first country.

Enchanted by this serendipitous meeting—this city of surprises—I invited Corrina over, just a hundred feet down MacDougal Street, when the café closed at 4:00 a.m.

Treading softly, trying not to wake Justin, I made her a cup of tea as the sky lightened, fresh sunrise celestial salmon. Whispering, emboldened, I described the state of my young love for New York to her: opaque and so thick and cloudy with suspended matter that the adoration made water appear solid as silver.

"Cities, like people, have personalities and energies," Corrina told me. "Different ones will welcome different souls."

Hearing that she hadn't found her place here, I explained that I was taking a magical course taught by a literary luminary. "The biggest newspaper and magazine editors in the city come, and we get to pitch our stories," I told her. "You *have to* stay in New York and take this class." Her sea-foam eyes glinted warmer with excitement.

Luckily Corrina's faded-denim backpack happened to have her toiletries in it—

She stayed over that night, though we didn't sleep a second. And the next night we talked in the living room until three in the morning. On the third consecutive day of these impromptu sleepovers, Justin cleared out a shelf in the medicine cabinet for Corrina's toiletries. He saw that she was special to me, my first friend in New York. He told her, "Stay here anytime."

~

Nic gave us a different assignment each week—a profile piece; an impassioned op-ed about some systematic wrongdoing that made us angry—but each class, I just kept on bringing back my same "humiliation essay," revised once again, ignoring all new coursework. Nic's reaction to this defiance was usually just a slight nod, conspiratorial; I sensed that she approved of my obsession.

So over the next weeks, working with intention, Joe Coffee became my office. The huge windows were rickety and charming, the West Village café a sun-filled box like a golden cube. I would tinker for hours, determined to make my essay a fable of self-salvation, a story both uplifting and empowering for the reader. I worked as if I were speaking to my younger self. For the title, I chose "I Walked Off Rape," hoping it sounded provocative.

In the margin of my fifth draft, my professor's thick ink handwriting suggested that I might be evading the root causes of my apparent resentment toward my mother: "Look at your childhood?"

Though I was reluctant to dig into old history, I trusted Professor Solomon. And guided by her perceptive questions, ever-probing, each draft came back with slightly fewer notes and markings.

One day when I arrived at class, Nic waved at me, beaming. She was sitting at the front of the room, as always, but far more students were present than usual, and I weaved through the room to hand her my fresh edit.

Talking fast, she introduced her guest speaker: "This is the Modern Love column's celebrated creator, editor Daniel Jones."

The smiling man beside Nic was unassuming, awkwardly waving at the classroom. Soft-spoken, he told us that Modern Love was "a series in Sunday Styles, a weekly column exploring the joys and tribulations of contemporary human love," explaining that each chosen essay ran as a full page in the *New York Times*. "I invite you all to submit," he said, "but also keep in mind that I get hundreds of submissions each week, and I can only choose one."

After Mr. Jones finished his introduction, Nic let us each ask him one question. When my turn came, I inquired, "What's something you've learned, getting all these love stories from strangers?"

He stared out the dark window for a moment. "I've learned that no one gets a free ride through this life."

A few weeks later, on my nineteenth draft, Professor Solomon returned my paper—the only red-pen mark the giant words "Submit this." I was overjoyed, the golden ticket!

Back home that night, Justin asked if I wanted to curl up and watch a documentary. He had been alone all day, I thought I should spend time with him—and hugging my laptop against my chest, adrenaline spiking like a drug, I told myself that when the movie was over, I would send my writing off to Mr. Jones. I hadn't shown Nic's stamp of approval to Justin, a remnant of secrecy.

The documentary was the story of a lovely British actress who had died young in her apartment in London—and though she was "beautiful and beloved," no one had missed her. No one knew her personally. Her absence was not reported until her body was found six and a half months later—decomposed, only a skeleton.

When the film ended, I had a wave of dread—after all this effort, I suddenly felt sharply ambivalent about my essay. A nightmare for so long, I didn't yet know if sharing this personal past was actually my dream.

Pacing inside my turquoise walls, I couldn't imagine my *grandma* reading about my rape. I didn't want to be marked by this story. I had been so fearful with Nic my only reader, I couldn't even imagine strangers knowing such an intimate aspect of my formation. Feeling the hot residue of shame, I didn't even want Justin to read it.

Nic had once told me that I was "not a PR machine" for my family— that this was my past, my story to tell. Still, I worried about how the release of this essay would impact the people who loved me, alter the nature of our relationship. The loss of trust. Though my words were honest, would it be fair to my mother to make my private feelings about her actions public?

As Justin brushed his teeth, I turned off my laptop. I went to bed that night without submitting, comfortable and warm as the scent of winter from the street below, frost-air and cinnamon, soothed me to sleep.

~

In the next weeks, the relief of my avoidance died away. Curled up one night, trying to fall asleep, a siren shrieked right outside, startling my heart; and my untold past magnified in my mind. If I locked this story away, abandoning it forever, then mine was the weakest whisper of an effort—showing no one, I'd be covering my opening mouth like a rosebud filling with snow. I would remain muted by fear of unknown summer—terror of what might happen if I spoke.

Quietly I wished to become braver. I visualized myself at eighteen and thought of the young women who would see themselves in me. I hoped that they might take some strength from my openness. Burying this past, deleting it, would be the easiest thing, an instant exit—but I couldn't. This issue was bigger, more essential, than my comfort. I had to try.

As Justin's restful body breathed deeply at my side, I wrote to Mr. Jones, hands hot and shaking—attaching my three pages of raw truth. But rereading my cover letter, my mind stalled on my name; "Deborah Parker" now felt wrong, and I erased it.

In elementary school, I had often introduced myself on the first day of the year as Sarah or Rebecca, confounding my new teachers. And a month after we'd moved to New York, I had started to call myself Aspen—I'd never felt like a Debby; I still didn't quite.

Adopting Justin's last name after all, I signed my message with the name I wished to have: "With gratitude, Aspen Matis."

~

A week passed, and the sky had been gray for five consecutive days; two weeks, waiting. Three; a month—no word, and all the electric anxiety, feeling torn, responsible to two masters, dissolved like the warm dimness of a sunrise, sheet-white before blue day. The growing chance of rejection an undeniable *relief*.

Thirty-four days and a response came, Daniel Jones's name a bold line in my inbox. My heart jumped with restless energy.

Mr. Jones called my essay "evocatively written and emotionally rich." Staring at his words, my long ambivalence evaporated, and I was too excited to sit still. Stunned, I couldn't stop smiling—my writing was going to appear in the *New York Times*!

Great Manhattan was a hedge-maze of desire that afternoon, I saw grace in every blade of grass and passing taxi. Gleeful, I was witness to a million passages and alleys: stepping-stones traversing parks to brick walkways beneath glassy high-rise headquarters, industrial lofts transformed into homes and powdered sugar I would never taste in bakeries I'd never enter, and fortune tellers I would not speak to—too many paths to ever walk them all.

And for the first time in my life, the road I walked appeared exactly as the road I'd choose. Every pipe dream I'd imagined felt five times more possible.

Wandering cobblestone streets, I glimpsed a metal staircase off West Fourteenth Street, rising from the center of the sidewalk, a shaded vision. Of course I climbed it, upward—to the top.

I found myself on a walkway in the sky, clouds surreal pink. A sculpture garden with benches, fountains and dusk-purple flowers—all elevated, above the grit of downtown. The place was trancelike, but as solid as my own body: the High Line, a sign told me. The perimeters of the park were glass walls, and through them I could see a hotel court-yard with its small blue ice-skating rink, still frozen even in temperate early April.

I felt wealthy with discovery—all the hundreds of breakthroughs I hadn't made yet. New York was mine, and I owned it in the same way I owned a beautiful sunset, or the Pacific Ocean: the city belonged to me because I belonged to it.

A little after dusk, Justin joined me at a fountain overlooking the Hudson River, though it was turned off by the time he arrived due to cold winds, the nighttime threat of icing. The city below us glittered like a black sequined dress, and we sat on the frosted walkway's stone edge, kissing, each breath visible as pale milk clouds in a fresh mug of coffee, opaque—vanishing in a blink.

Slicing honeydew for breakfast a week later, I got a call from Daniel Jones. The sky was overcast, but our apartment was strangely hot, and I sensed this wild-luck break was ending, bad news coming. On the phone, Mr. Jones asked me if Aspen Matis was my real name.

I had to tell him no. I had been born Deborah Parker, and legally, I still was.

"As the *New York Times* is nonfiction," he told me, "we need to use your legal name."

Distracted, I grasped the handle of a pan in the oven with my bare hand, burning my palm. Holding the pain under cold water, I told him I understood. The throbbing sharp, I decided to formally change my name before my publication day.

The next morning, I put on a tweed suit—a gift from my mother I'd never needed, until this moment. At a courthouse downtown, a large room of wooden benches and a low stage, I paid $200, a translucent blister forming on my palm.

Justin and I were two of only a handful of native English speakers. Most of the eighty or so people waiting were Asian immigrants, hoping for more-American names. A willowy middle-aged woman with long white hair became a Tiffany. A young couple's three small children were now James, Grace, and Peter.

I vowed before a judge that I owed no one child support and that I was not a felon. As I disappeared my younger self like the past skin of a snake, Justin was the only person I knew, present.

From that day forward, I had a new name, first and last. I would be Aspen. I was erasing my past—Debby Parker—for reasons I didn't confess to the justice.

When I sent my proof-of-name-change to the *New York Times*, a reply informed me that my essay had also been more elegantly renamed: "A Hiker's Guide to Healing."

8

Dark Pearl

Justin woke me with a playful pinch, soft like a squeeze—the *New York Times* held close above my nose. The paper was thick and smelled of carbon ink, fresh morning newsprint. He pulled it away, pretended he was reading, and I sat upright on our mattress. "Lemme see!" I said, still half-dreaming.

Opening to my article, I saw the beautiful full-page spread—the illustration whimsical, its lilac tones evoking an enchanting purple sunset enveloping a tent and sparse pine trees. Proud, I noticed that the air in our apartment tasted sweet and buttery, like a bakery.

Justin took my hand and led me to the other room—he had made us biscuits from scratch, the warm vanilla hit my senses, and two perfect poached eggs rested on a porcelain plate. A hexagonal glass jar trapping the sun held glistening apricot jam.

"It's Modern Love brunch," my husband said. He kissed my forehead as the apartment buzzer rang.

A man's voice spoke through the intercom: "I have a delivery for Aspen Matis."

Flowers—huge peach and red and smooth purple-pink roses, periwinkle hydrangea blossoms, and sprout-green orchids with striking wine edges, as if tear-dropped with red ink. The whole arrangement was presented in a woven wicker basket, unified with big beautiful oak leaves, shiny and forest jade. Admiring the ribbon-striped card, I saw a note signed by my parents.

Yet of course they had ordered the present before they'd seen the piece. Now I imagined my mother's horror, reading the story of my rape—and my critical words about her—printed in the morning paper.

Then an email caught my attention from a woman named Bella, someone I didn't know. She shared the story of how, at nineteen, "running away to California to be free of my lack of self-esteem," she'd met two "cool-looking guys" on the Berkeley campus who befriended her and then drugged her with a horse tranquilizer. "The next thing I know I am lying on a bed and one guy was massaging my breasts while the other was trying to penetrate me. I was confused and out of it," she wrote. "I never did anything about it. I was depressed my whole life. I am 60, and I've never told anyone until now." She thanked me for sharing my story and listening to hers.

I was mesmerized by this confessional message—she had held her brutal assault as a terrible secret inside, a dark pearl within her for so long, occupying her. Imagining the pain, her body cramping around the tremendous weight of this hidden shame, consuming her vitality and joy, my eyes welled. I felt a scratchy tickle in my throat, as if a new virus were blooming—horrified and touched.

Another new email appeared; I clicked—a mother named Randy shared that her daughter was also raped in college, and was now using Israel as her "escape route." She expressed, "Sadly, my daughter has not fully come to terms with her experience. I am hoping that your story will inspire her." Studying this missive, I felt this mother was missing something fundamental, her tone lacking compassion, subtly critical, as if her daughter should *just get over it*, faster. As if she should just "fully come to terms with her experience," already. Perhaps this "escape route" was really her child's chosen and instinctive path to healing.

The influx ceaseless, I heard from too many women who had been sexually assaulted during college, many of whom noted that—in the aftermath, a foggy malaise of guilt and shame—they had also dropped out. By dusk I had received more than a hundred personal stories—heartbreaking. Upsetting as they were, I couldn't look away.

My hot cheeks streaked with tears, Justin took my hand and kissed it. He placed a biscuit smeared with amber jam into my calloused palm. "Enjoy this," he said. "Take a break."

Resting my head on his arm, grateful for my love's presence today, I took a giant bite.

Then I noticed one message in particular, different from the others. Someone named Andrew Blauner who congratulated me on the publication and wrote, "I can't help but wonder and ask: Have you thought about writing a book about your journey?" From his sign-off, I saw he was a literary agent.

Excited, I called out, "Charlie!" my pet name for my husband, showing him my screen. Grinning, he squeezed my shoulder; and I emailed Nic, hands quivering, asking what I should say.

Immediately, Nic answered me: "Say YES!"

Nervous, I responded to Mr. Blauner, "Yes. I am writing a memoir about the wilderness adventure that helped me heal from the pain of my rape."

Waiting for his reply, I googled "Andrew Blauner," fast-finding that he was a respected literary agent who represented several bestselling authors and winners of the Pulitzer Prize.

An hour later, Mr. Blauner wrote back: "If you do not already have an agent, I'd love to explore the possibility of working with you on it." He asked me if I had a book proposal.

My phone lit up—my mother. Silencing the call, I let her go straight to my voicemail. I felt unready to hear what she might think and say about the piece, not wanting her critical words to taint this joy. I decided I wouldn't call her back until tomorrow.

Uncertain, I bothered Nic again: "Should I write a book proposal? WHAT IS A BOOK PROPOSAL?" She told me it was a sales tool used to help find a publisher, typically fifty to one hundred pages—which seemed to me like a lot of work for something that only a few people would read. I emailed Nic right back, "Do I even need an agent?"

Not half a minute later, Nic said, "YES!!!! You need an agent. That's how you sell a book." She told me to stop screwing around.

Writing Mr. Blauner back, jittery, I told him I was indeed working on a proposal and that, when it was complete, he would be the first to have it.

Pulling me to my feet, Justin spun me in a neat circle. Holding me close, he said, "This is why I brought you to New York."

~

On the last day of the school year, I rushed home from my final class, excited. At last free of coursework, I felt poised to finish the proposal for Mr. Blauner by the start of fall.

When I stepped into the apartment, a package the size of a milk crate sat on our kitchen floorboards, addressed from my parents' house; and I had a nervous feeling. I used a butter knife to slit it open.

Inside, I found five one-liter bottles of my favorite shampoo and seven of the conditioner I used, also huge; and sixteen pairs of new socks, the ultrathin black knee-high style I liked the best, each patterned with tiny purple polka dots. Folded in thirds like a letter at the bottom of the box was a page from a yellow legal pad that read only "Love, Mom."

"This is nice," I said to Justin, who was watching from the futon—but I could see that his face disagreed. I still hadn't called my mother back, though it had been weeks since my personal essay was published. "I feel a little bad."

Justin stood, smiling. "You have nothing to feel bad about," he told me. To my surprise, he kicked the package lightly, and it jumped. "*She* does." Then he gave me a hug; and I breathed more deeply, held in his embrace.

"Okay," I said, my face against his shoulder. "But maybe I should call her."

He let his arms fall from me. Backing away, he lay down on the futon, expression blank. "I'm renting the place out for the summer," he said softly. "Let's go hiking." He told me that after a long year in New York, he needed an adventure.

I was sure that forested mountains would not be the most natural environment for smooth writing, but this man had done so much for me; and compromising this season to alleviate my husband's urban restlessness felt important. He simply craved the wild, which seemed harmless. Following him to the futon, I cuddled up against him, acting playful. "So where are we going?"

~

Vacating the city, we disappeared from the mad island of Manhattan, returning to the Appalachian Trail.

The footpath snaked through woodlands, leading high above old towns to ancient mountains the soft-blue color of ice. After a metropolis, the trail appeared somehow different than I remembered, greener and more festive. On pace with a dense pack of other backpackers, we found that this hike was more communal than the Pacific Crest Trail, a drifting party coalescing around great nightly bonfires. But we did not merge with the lighthearted energy, preoccupied by a private mission.

Evenings in our tent, isolated from raucous laughter, I attempted to compose a book proposal. I typed disjointed memories, fragments of scenes and sentences, into Justin's shiny iPad, which he carried for me, protected from the elements by a plastic Ziploc baggie.

After a week of hiking, we stopped in a wooded village in Connecticut to resupply and rest. Beech trees closing in on little white houses, thick mountain mist cast silver in the setting sun, we approached the town's red diner. Recharging our batteries at a booth, I emailed my new writing to myself to prevent loss.

The reception good here, I saw a two-day-old voicemail from my mother. And breath caught by dread, I listened to her message—my mom was crying, asking through soft sobs what she had done. Saying how she loved me and she didn't understand.

Tears stung my eyes. "She sounds really sad," I said to Justin. She didn't even know that we were on the trail. "Maybe I should tell her I'm okay."

Justin was studying a pale blue paper map, the trail ahead. "Do you *want* to talk to her?" Sitting in the mute space following his question, I couldn't recall the last time he had called his family, lately resenting his parents when they'd phone—an odd shift from our sweet time back in Berkeley.

"Not really," I said. I wasn't ready to hear her condemnation of my public oversharing. Feeling a little guilty, I picked at a blister on my heel, peeling away the scab too soon, destroying its healing. Raw again, I began to bleed.

"Let's just focus on the miles ahead of us," my husband answered me. And for the next six weeks, we hiked without mentioning or contacting either of our families.

Crossing into Maine in late July, I twisted my ankle, pain shooting like an arrow as I stumbled forward, and it was as if I didn't belong here in the woodlands anymore—as if my body were telling me, *you should be somewhere else.*

Supportive, Justin left the trail as well, staying with me, not ever reaching the blue-green mountain summit at the great trail's end—abandoning our thru-hike with only 105 miles of the 2,200-mile footpath remaining. I imagined the view from the top must have been grand, the high blinding and pure.

~

In fall, balancing a full course load at The New School plus writing in my free time, my schedule devoid of a free moment, I found that I had little time with Justin. But I felt a sense of purpose and possibility—this temporary sacrifice of fun and freedom seemed necessary.

The agent had contacted me back in May, now I planned to finish the book proposal by the year's end, and I hoped he hadn't forgotten my story. In nights of electric blue ambition, my imagination fateful, I stayed up late in our apartment, typing with one fiery wish.

On October 29, 2012, sudden thunder and a flash of lightning startled Justin and me—the beginnings of the sky's violence before the infamous Manhattan blackout.

Hurricane Sandy hit: high winds and coastal flooding of the eastern United States, an estimated eight million people left powerless, in cold darkness. On that ominous day, we disobeyed the mayor's safety instructions for the rush of experiencing the wind more viscerally. Walking along the Hudson River, down an evacuated pier, we crossed into empty districts—the most dangerous edge of lower New York.

Pausing on a metal footbridge, the water below us jumped up through the grate, soaking our sneakers, high swells of steel-gray river energetic like we'd never before experienced. On that desolate periphery, he lifted me up. My tensed body raised in damp air, heart battering—I had the awful sudden sense that my strong husband would drop me.

And then my love threw his head back, face to the sky, and he howled at invisible stars, the island enveloped in russet clouds—lightning and warm wind. The most forceful storm was imminent, unimaginable still.

Wandering back inland, Justin wanted to check and make sure my friends were alright. So we got into his car and rolled up to a handful of apartments in the Greenwich Village area, buzzing to see if anyone was still around, ready to transport them north, to safety. After an hour of checking up on peers, Justin's eyes shined brighter. "What about Nic?" he asked me. "I have a feeling."

"Professor Solomon?" I thought that he was kidding. But I tried calling her—her phone was dead.

Minutes later, we showed up at my teacher's high-rise in his dinged-up silver sedan, unannounced.

The power was out in her building, the doormen all wearing head-lamps. When we arrived, Nic was an outline in the shadowed marble of the front lobby. She'd been trying to figure out how to get out, hoping to find a place to go—taxis were prohibited from driving in black-out areas and the subways were not running, flooded. The elevators in her apartment were not working either, no heat or light; the stairwells were dim and slippery, the place undergoing mandatory evacuation. Astonished to see us, Nic embraced me, relieved that we had come.

Justin and I drove Nic and her husband uptown, toward electricity and warmth. Navigating gridlock, we dialed hotel after hotel on our cells, draining dwindling phone batteries—each place apologizing: no remaining vacancy. Finally, crossing a nameless boundary into the spar-kling world of city lights in every color—Midtown Manhattan—Justin found a hotel with an available bed! The Radisson had just one remain-ing room, which happened to be an executive suite.

Nic offered us money for "rescuing" them; grinning with sweet triumph, Justin would not accept it. Then they offered to let us stay with them.

But Justin declined, a chill ran through me. Speaking for us both, he said we got a thrill out of the intensity of the rainfall—I restrained my tongue. And so my love and I coasted back down to the dark half of the island, loud downpour pounding the windshield, relentless.

Though our apartment was supposedly evacuated, we returned. And through the six-day blackout, my husband blessed the starkest hours of lower New York, lighting candles and holy wood incense—eventually making the hurricane fun, despite the freezing nights. We had no electricity, no heat, no light after sun vanished—but we whispered and sometimes giggled into those frigid shapeless hours.

On the second day, I contemplated calling my parents to tell them I was safe. Months had elapsed since I had spoken with them, our distance palpable. But Justin suggested I leave my phone off to "preserve battery."

Late that evening, my husband huddled up with me, pressing his palms to mine, keeping me warm. By the light of six yahrzeit candles he'd found for us with mystical resourcefulness, I said, "Thank you for taking such good care of me."

Leaning closer, Justin told me, "I love disaster."

I didn't grasp his words. Confused, I pulled away. "You love people getting hurt?"

The knit maroon throw-blanket we'd been cuddled inside together fell down to the mattress, a shadowed red pool in the sudden space between us. He didn't attempt to defend himself. His vision remained fixed on the window, which was fogged over.

"You want people to feel pain?" I pressed. It was as if he didn't want the hurricane to end—I couldn't understand him.

"No, no, that's not what I am saying," his voice returned. "I just want to be useful."

9

IMPOSSIBLE VALENTINE

In the early weeks of winter, of icy winds and snowfall, I would wake and go directly to Joe Coffee, drafting the blueprint of my possible book. Some mornings, I'd see the sun rise, the ashen blankness of the sky tinged with sudden ginger or smeared with a sharp gold. Others, the air was a shining, blinding sapphire, its chill biting—

One overcast afternoon Justin showed up at Joe, his posture straight, as if he were angry. Slowly sitting across the communal table from me, he said that he was crazy with cabin fever. "I like helping kids with math homework," he explained. "But it's getting a little repetitive."

I sipped my milky coffee, feeling his frustration. Touching his cool hand, I asked him, "What do you want to do?" A bronzed moth sat on the window like a freckle.

We sat for long seconds in labored silence, until he broke it: "I want to be a mentor." He explained that what he wanted more than anything was to help a child who he found "truly special," whose potential he could stoke. Describing his ideal pupil, it seemed that he was looking for an eleven-year-old version of himself.

Justin had fed my dreams, cultivating ambition—and thinking of how he fueled me, I grew joyful at the prospect of a young mentee whose future he would alter. Talking too loud, we were animated as if in our own living room.

~

Feeling bold one snowy January morning, frost sparkling on the bedroom's black windowsill, I sent my proposal to the prospective agent, filled with wonder. The whole world was the beautiful unknown—I woke Justin with a wrestling bear hug.

Together we stepped into the day, wandering the snowflake-powdered cobblestone alleys of Greenwich Village, the whole city suddenly my jewel, peeking into the butter-lit townhouses and wall-less lofts of open silver space, intoxicatingly luxurious.

Looking up to a home a story above, golden with the indistinct warmness of a crystal chandelier, Louis Armstrong playing and a man swaying a woman, I imagined my masked destiny, unpredictable as a daydream.

On a cold blue afternoon eight days later, we took the train uptown to meet Aaron Philip, a twelve-year-old boy from Antigua who had cerebral palsy. My cheek on Justin's shoulder, I worried that Mr. Blauner had somehow missed my proposal submission—it had been buried under a flurry of holiday messages, or worse, deleted.

Arriving on the fifth floor of a colorful primary school, we found the Blue Sky Room, a therapy space where Aaron developed his motor skills three times a week. Crowded with thick navy mats, padded pull-up rings, and big inflatable balls, the area resembled a compact gymnasium. We watched as Aaron's occupational therapist, a bold lady we'd serendipitously met at a café, completed a session with the little boy on grasping and releasing small objects, training his muscles to function so that he could hold a pencil to write and draw.

My love had come with a gift. He gave Aaron *Cosmos: A Personal Voyage*, a huge hardback illustrated inquiry into the history and nature of the universe. "My dad's an astrophysicist, and he gave me this book when I was about your age," Justin told him. "It opened my mind."

Aaron's eyes became bright with water. Then with his arm, he knocked the book open to the centerfold, twisted his torso to flip the page. "I *love* it." Bouncing a little, bumping—he was *dancing*. "When I read, the biggest moment pops up like a hologram in the sky," he said. "My mind is actually inside of the book, my body is just there, looking at it, and then my brain has to return to my body." As he spoke, his small elbow got trapped in the space between his lap-desk and his wheelchair; his therapist removed it. Justin and I shared a smile at his beautiful, surprising words, already impressed with this preteen's vibrance.

"What a creative way of explaining how reading feels to you," I said. I had never met such a poetic person, let alone a twelve-year-old.

My husband's face was vivified. Then he began telling Aaron about the stars and galaxies, answering his emerging questions. Seeing Justin in his element, I felt the warm flutter of affection.

Excited, Aaron opened his laptop, typing with just one finger, swooshing it from key to key—showing us *Aaronverse*, the Tumblr blog where he shared his experiences as a twelve-year-old kid with cerebral palsy. His posts were earnest, explosions of anguish and joy. His style was wholly original, mixing childish enthusiasm with candor and the metaphors he was constantly inventing.

"You're a talented writer," Justin told him. "You're very wise." I recognized this soft voice—he spoke to Aaron in the same tone of heartfelt conviction with which he had first inspired me. "Aspen's a writer too," he added. "Soon, she's going to have a book come out."

Mortified, I thought about Mr. Blauner's resounding silence. "We'll see," I mumbled. "Nothing is really certain—"

"No," Aaron cut me off. I could see a sparking confidence in Aaron's pupils, which seemed to be smiling. "You *will*. Remember to believe in yourself."

As we all became freer, more relaxed, Aaron opened up about how he and his father moved into a homeless shelter in Manhattan in 2010, where they lived until they were able to move to their Bronx home two years later. His healthy younger brother joined them in the new apartment, their mother remaining in Antigua. "My family are like a group of candles lighting a room. There are only three candles in the room, which light up the room partially," Aaron said. "In order to fully illuminate the room, we need a fourth candle. That fourth candle is my mother."

For a flicker, his longing made me think of my own mom and our different type of distance. I hadn't seen her in nearly a year—had barely considered spending time with her, though we were just a few hundred miles apart.

But hearing of Aaron's trials, I was grateful for my budding New York family. I focused on what was in front of me. And watching Justin engage Aaron, asking him questions about his life, interests, and dreams, I couldn't help but think: *He will be a great father.*

The following morning, I woke to a flood of sun, the aqua walls light-dappled as the sea—and a good feeling. Checking, I found a message from Blauner Books literary agency. Andrew wrote that he'd be thrilled to represent me. Immediately, I signed the attached contract, and, not wasting time, he sent the proposal for my memoir to eighteen publishing houses, simultaneously. He told them each that we were "closing on Valentine's Day, noon"—prospective editors would have only ten days to read the sixty-seven-page document and make a bid.

~

The night before our closing day, I didn't fall asleep. Justin lay, I watched his peaceful face, and frost glittered like fairy dust on the branches outside our window. Daybreak brightening, I snuck out.

February fourteenth was a bitter morning, icicles glinting on sidewalk maples along the length of Washington Square Park. My mindless westward wandering returned me to the pretty High Line overlook. Perhaps I was wishing that this park was lucky grounds. But ten o'clock came and went; and then eleven.

A few minutes after noon, I sat down on the walkway, pairs of feet stepping fast past me, the sudden fur of a jacket brushing my shoulder.

With all of Justin's support, Professor Solomon's guidance and connections, my kind new agent's industry savvy—this morning's standstill was as far as my story was going to go. The path here had been long—all my life, in a way—and there was no chance of negotiating back time.

At ten past noon, my cell brightened—but it was Justin. "Any news?" he asked, and I wished that I could lie. The park was no longer filled with flowers; winter had muted the rail-trail's springtime colors.

When Professor Solomon texted to check if the book had sold, I was standing in the middle of the elevated walkway, dejected. I stepped back down to the pavement at ground level, walking without focus, moving south.

Then my phone rang—Andrew's number. But I knew that he would call me either way, so I wasn't hopeful. When I answered I was somewhere in Tribeca, going nowhere.

He told me, "We have some very good news." He relayed that one publishing house had bid. Detailing the offer, he explained that this would be a paperback deal—"Do you want to move forward?"

I probably should have just said yes. But I remembered Nic had told me that hardcover deals were "better" than paperback. Possessed by some strange boldness, I told him, "I'd like the book to be a hardcover. Can we request that?"

His intonation flat, he told me he would ask.

I began walking north, toward Justin. Then, I was jogging. I couldn't wait to reach my love, to tell him. Yet minutes passed and I got closer—I was becoming nervous. My agent still silent by twelve thirty, I regretted my request, which had been needless.

But then my cell phone sounded and, hopped-up on nerves, I answered fast without first checking who was calling.

Andrew's voice was buoyant—they had agreed to my one term—and just like that, I had a book deal! My memoir's acquisition felt far-fetched, impossible.

When I called to tell Nic the news, the hardcover negotiation delighted her. She invited Justin and me to a Valentine's Day party at her apartment that evening, "an impromptu get-together for the candy holiday, nothing fancy."

~

Justin put my contacts in for me, torso bending, warm hands holding my face. I felt lucky to have this man who led me to New York and supported my vision in every way he was able.

The only item of makeup I owned was the sugarplum lip gloss from our wedding day, pink with a little sparkle; and I applied it, smiling.

At the party, Nic looked gorgeous, her black hair blown-out long and straight. She walked us through the packed room, telling her guests, "It was a gorgeous Modern Love that led to Aspen's book deal."

Sipping Malbec, mingling, I noticed all my friends from The New School, and Corrina—everyone I knew in New York. Then I understood, I was impossibly gullible—this was not a Valentine's Day gathering at all. It was a surprise party, for me. Woozy with bliss, I felt vast gratitude for Nic—my *mentor*—overwhelm every step and sentence of the evening; we were celebrating not sugar hearts and roses but the professional accomplishment of a girl, emerged from hiding in the woods.

10

GIRL IN THE WOODS

The manuscript was due by end of summer. I had just seven months to write a book, a mapless task.

Only twenty-three, perhaps not experienced enough to have "memoirs" of merit, I couldn't dismiss the feeling that I was green as spring—that I didn't quite know what I was doing. The morning after the deal, disoriented, my mind jumped with profound unknowns, and walking back and forth across my small apartment, still giddy with the energy of this happy validation, I found I didn't know where to begin.

Catching my frantic face in the kitchen mirror, I lingered, becoming stiller. I stopped pacing like a caged cub at the zoo. I had survived a rape, for God's sake, and walked alone into the Mojave Desert mountains; I'd hiked in dry and brutal heat, stepping over sun-basking rattlesnakes like harmless twigs.

I'd met black bears with their cubs, wonderstruck. For a thousand miles I slept in my tent's shelter, a girl alone.

Regaining calmer breath, I knew this sharp bewilderment wasn't the result of any authentic peril. Really, I wasn't scared. Rather, what I felt was invigoration, expansive and all-embracing, with the mesmerizing beauty of uncertainty.

Last night's frost still glittered on the windowsill like diamonds, yet the apartment felt very warm due to our building's central heating. Cracking the window, I thought about how an admission of uncertainty is so often, in our culture, seen as weakness. Yet it is only when a mind admits *I do not know* that it becomes open to unseen possibility, and honest inquiry. It's as if discovery becomes possible only when the fixed channels of one's mind become electric, charged with the untamed energy of wonder. In this way, humility is the necessary precondition for all *learning*.

When you believe you know everything, you can unearth nothing—

Dressing in only my husband's soft green shirt, I reveled in the sensation of utter ignorance: I didn't know anything about writing a book, yet. I made blueberry tea and poured it over a tall glass of ice, watching the bright cubes snap internally under the glassy indigo stream with an audible *crack*.

Years back, alone on the trail for the first time, I had learned the art of noticing footprints, the placement of the sun to tell the time of day. Researching meticulously, I discovered how to read the cryptic blue-green lines of a topographic map and the strange skill of triangulation to discern my location, from anywhere. And this new quest was no different, necessitating the mastery of a fresh set of abilities—

Again I tapped into the voices that predated me. Curled up with my computer on the futon in our snug living room–kitchen, I searched for conversations with great authors, seeking insight into the habits they'd cultivated to facilitate the creation of their beloved master-works—hoping to discover *my* best method.

Devouring an interview with Lili Saintcrow, glimpsing into her writing process, I read: "Discipline allows magic . . . You get into the habit of writing every day," and I was heartened. Putting in hours had always been my simple pleasure. This was clear advice I could imple-ment. The practice of consistency, she continued, exists "so that when [your Muse] shows up, you have the maximum chance of catching her."

Next, I read a theory by George R. R. Martin, a prolific writer of fantasy and science fiction. "I think there are two types of writers, the architects and the gardeners," he explained. "The architects plan everything ahead of time . . . They have the whole thing designed and blueprinted out before they even nail the first board up. The gardeners dig a hole, drop in a seed . . . as the plant comes up and they water it, they don't know how many branches it's going to have, they find out as it grows."

I studied this philosophy, rereading it—trying to discern if I was an architect or a gardener, or something foreign to both spheres.

~

Undefined, inspired, I would spend that humid springtime writing eight hours each day with joy and ardor. It was the season of caffeine and endless cherries and ice, cool breeze elation. Still a student, my deepest occupation was my manuscript, which now had a title: *Girl in the Woods.*

And the book was progressing slow and steady: daily, I would try to write a minimum of three hundred words—one page. In lucky spells, a gale of unconscious power would flow through me, and I would produce a thousand words in just an hour or two; and the day would become a vessel for conception. I found that recreating stories from the Pacific Crest Trail was fun and exciting, represencing the happy beauty of the forest. Writing the beginning of the story—the sexual assault, the apathy of the Colorado College administration—was, by contrast, very hard.

Slyly, I would jump ahead and compose memories and snapshots from the blissful ending: finding Justin, merging our twin paths. I was so lucky to be with him, and I savored writing of our budding love; it brought me back to the summer we'd met and made me feel close to him, blushing again.

Through that era of creation, damp heat descending like a haze, slowing the urban pace, Justin mentored Aaron and completely stopped all other tutoring. He encouraged the twelve-year-old's self-expression, recommending diverse books. Offering writing prompts, my husband inquired, "What's your biggest challenge?" and "What is the greatest gift your dad has given you?"

The innocence of Aaron's voice flowed out from a raw and tender heart. His responses were all personal stories. When Justin and I read about how, though he saw his mother every day via Skype, he hadn't hugged her in seven years, I began to cry.

I still hadn't told my parents about the book deal.

I noticed that whenever Justin wasn't working with Aaron, he spent more and more time in our bedroom, very focused on his computer. Also becoming a homebody, I wrote and wrote, more locked-in than ever, sometimes neglecting sleep.

One summer evening, Justin and I finally decided to come out of our blue cave and "go out" in the night-world of the living. Inviting Corrina to join, he and I dressed in a button-down and heels, respectively, and met up with Professor Solomon and a handful of her former students, attending the Lower East Side's famous Lit Crawl as a little pack. Like a pub crawl, the event occurred at dozens of bars, art galleries, and late-night cafés, simultaneously.

Nic was the director of our group, declaring which locale we would next head to, Justin our crew's navigator. Using the event's program booklet, my husband led us from poetry reading to cabaret party to publishing industry discussion, smoothly guiding everyone, the automatic leader. Seeing him in this map-reading role again was exciting, a fun echo of the trail.

Weaving through a crowded East Village sidewalk between events, Corrina asked me how the book was going.

I didn't know how to answer—headway felt gradual but constant, when I could focus. "Facebook is distracting," I joked, deflecting deeper consideration of the question.

Edison, a gay comedian I'd bonded with back in Nic's class, draped his arm over my shoulder, stepping in sync with my stride. "Yeah, that's why I'm off Facebook," he said to Corrina and me. "That junk's crack." We caught up to Justin, who was waiting for us at the corner before turning.

I laughed at my friend's crudeness. "Yeah, Justin barely uses it too," I told Edison. "He only has like seven friends." Entering a green-walled pub where contemporary novelists were reading from literary classics, we ordered a few drinks and toasted summer.

Later that night, walking home just the two of us again, Justin barely spoke, not engaging my chatter, reflections on the night. "Is something the matter?" I finally asked him.

He walked faster, ahead of me. I didn't know what might be wrong. "Did I *do* something?" I called after him, following.

Eventually we were back home, in our familiar walls, and I sat beside him on the pleather futon, which had grown shabby. "What is it? Please tell me," I said softly. "I can't read minds. I really wish I could." I winked at him, trying to be playful, but he didn't even smile. "I'm sorry," I said, truly lost, just hoping these words might help.

At last he spoke, his voice throaty with emotion. "You were telling people I don't have any friends." I squinted, perplexed. "The Facebook thing. I heard you."

I promised him that wasn't what I'd meant. "But I'm really sorry."

Then he nodded and we hugged, stiffly. He rose up and took his laptop into the other room; and I got back to work.

~

On a muggy Tuesday afternoon, a hot wind gusting through New York, Aaron's father was granted American citizenship. So we all went to Lucien, a lighthearted French bistro with yellow walls and flickering candles.

Aaron said he felt a little more secure in New York City. "We are nearly a joined puzzle," he told us, eyes fierce with hope. "Now the only one we need is *Mom*." The child's words were followed by a silence, no one knowing what to say for a moment.

Walking back home after dinner, my eyes blurred with stinging water. I wasn't exactly sure why, and I tried to hide my face inside my hair, which was unruly in the humid summer wind.

"We need an adventure," Justin announced to the sky. Looking above and not at me, he sensed my longing. "A place where you can write, focused, and we can have some fun."

"Somewhere beautiful," I said. I wiped my streaked face with my sleeve, liking this idea—to get away. The thought of escaping to an oasis where I could sprint to meet my September 15 deadline, which I was absolutely determined to hit, calmed my mind's chaos.

Like momentary rain, my tears had stopped.

11

Breeding Ground for Sharks

When the dog days of August descended on New York City, the black pavement becoming hot as a breathing body, Justin and I flew. Slicing through clouds, we escaped the auburn smog, disappearing to a little cabin on the Caribbean island of Vieques.

Landing in the jungle, we boarded a boat, watching the emerald mainland shrink to a misted strip of lavender. Up at the tourism port, we rented a big white Jeep and threaded a slim paved road, the green walls of a wildlife preserve pressing in.

Justin drove, his shoulders leaning forward with intense energy. We bumped up a rocky dirt path, grown narrow with tropical bushes, pink flowers like confetti dangling in the sun-dappled dark greens. Circumventing a huge dirt pothole the size of an open grave, we pulled into a stony driveway, stopping outside a small house that rested atop a lush hill that overlooked Puerto Rico's turquoise waters. The island seemed the perfect climate for seclusion. We planned to stay for a month and a half, happily isolated—until a whole draft of the manuscript was complete.

The home was a tiny two-story nest on a dried-mud street that rolled like the swells of an upset sea. Exploring, we found an outdoor shower, wild horses running the pebble roads of the rainforest below—poking their long gray and butterscotch noses into our open kitchen door, wanting sugar cubes and overgrown carrots. We could see both the Caribbean Sea and the Atlantic from every room in the house, the two green-blue bodies separated by an invisible border that was only nominal, nothing solid—just tropic beauty encasing us, boundless and *mythic*.

The front porch had two rope-swings, and Justin pushed me. Pumping my legs to gain momentum, I swung out over the treetops below the house—out; out; out, the cyan water winking in the sun like a great precious stone, far below.

Our first evening, Justin found something intriguing in the kitchen: a tin of mosaicked sea-glass in every color. Folded up inside, he discovered a whimsical treasure map, which indicated the existence of a trap-door that led to the roof.

I pulled a rope to produce an opening in the ceiling, a rickety wooden ladder unfolding. Lying on our backs on the flat crown of the house, moon-gazing, we fell into our place in the Milky Way. This concrete rooftop felt like the summit of the jungle, and I wished on smoky stars like distant pearls.

Studying the secret island atlas we'd found, squinting in weak moonlight, we learned that the black pool that glinted in the canopy far below us was actually a legendary bioluminescent bay, an inky cove known far beyond the region—famous because, in the nights, the water lights up upon any living contact, the disruptive motion of a blowfish or a human finger. Each passing creature appears silver-blue, a glow light. Also a nursery for sharks, dense with young predators, with nightfall the ebony water becomes like an animate galaxy, the species of the sea transmuting into shooting stars in ocean's obsidian.

"I can find the way there," Justin promised, tapping the yellowed map.

~

We thrived in the playground of our oasis hideaway. Days passed in smooth routine: Justin made French press coffee and the home became a treehouse-sized stamp of civilization, intertwined treetops shimmering in the sun, birds the loudest in the mornings, like wake-up bells; in evenings, we shared a knit blue hammock to watch sunsets on the porch outside our bedroom, reclined deep into each other's arms as pink sky faded.

Here at the outermost periphery of the Caribbean, Justin seemed happier and puckish, climbing coconut trees and snorkeling beyond the edges of the reef. I was enjoying rekindled intimacy, even taking some afternoons off writing to explore the island—still avoiding my memoir's painful sections.

One afternoon, sudden hands on my shoulders startled me. I looked up from my laptop in a lurch, twisted my neck to see my husband. "Mystic finally finished his masterpiece," he said.

After more than four years of "polishing," our friend had completed the Pacific Crest Trail Class of 2009 tribute video—which was not three to five minutes, as expected, but rather nearly forty minutes long. I followed Justin upstairs.

Together, we watched a thoughtfully ordered scrapbook of striking photographs Mystic had taken along the footpath, set to classical music. The film was transporting, stunning. He captured the desert flowers and the faces of the trail, the snowfields and the phases of the moon. Tuning back into the hike by way of Mystic's vision, a warm wave of vibrant nostalgia engulfed me. Justin and I watched, grinning and transfixed, pointing at the screen upon recognizing specific landmarks from our fateful first summer.

That night, I wrote a memoir scene I hadn't planned. I thought the story of meeting Mystic might belong:

I'd nearly stepped on his hand. He was just off the edge of the Pacific Crest Trail's dirt, crouched in the brush, handling tiny mirrors, leaning one against a tree's thick root, balancing another on a rock the size of a fist, carefully setting them up so they reflected the sky and the lake water in an intricate kaleidoscope pattern.

"Sorry," I said. I didn't want to mess him up. "That looks so cool."

He was focused, mumbled, "Thank you." He snapped a photo of his creation, another, cocked his head up and smiled. I was struck by his distinctive face. His eyes were strange, irises perfectly black, his cheekbones pushed outward, upward. He was boyish. "Come down here," he said to me. "You can see it better."

I squatted on the soil beside him. The woods smelled of pine and sage. The air was cool as fresh water. I looked into the small mirrors—windows of sky, the trees, the brilliant blue water far below; they reflected and fragmented everything.

I spent the next ten days writing morning 'til dusk, my passion invigorated.

But on September 8, the deadline a week away, I had to face the reality I'd spent the summer denying: I was behind. For weeks, I'd kept telling myself I would catch up, I'd write one hundred pages *this* week, but found again and again that I couldn't rush, as each attempt to do so inevitably compromised the quality of the work. Now, compiling all my scattered chapters into one document—bits of beauty, pages I was proud of—I saw that not even half the book was complete.

Panicked, I remembered one of my professors quoting prolific author Douglas Adams in class: "I love deadlines. I love the whooshing noise they make as they go by." I considered that missing due dates was common in the arts—except I would need months, not weeks, to finish. Pulse speeding, I composed a message to my editor, requesting extra time.

That night on the roof, we heard something: in the distance, far-off rhythmic chants, and human howling. The sky was moonless, and I imagined the strange sounds were a religious service, a tribe of faces in the leaves, a subversive community of people who had left their families, searching for something profound.

At midnight, the distant calls of harmonized people abruptly stopped—and, still jittery with anticipation, I told Justin about my request for an extension. I wiped my nose on my shoulder, worried he would be angry.

He shifted his body, crossing his legs. "Wanna go and see some sharks?" he asked me. He said he'd found the location of Mosquito Bay. "It's the brightest-glowing bioluminescent bay in the world," he told me, "and a breeding ground for tiger sharks."

In a surge of energy, we loaded the Jeep with two kayaks and drove a muddy dirt road through the lightless underbrush, the dense world shades of coal—searching for that dangerous black pool in the rainfor-est, dark waters treacherous with infant sharks. Justin and I descended, careening through the thick and skyless jungle. "An American girl recently lost her calf in this bay," Justin said as we hit an unseen pothole, jolting. "So swimming's technically illegal. But wouldn't it be pretty fun?"

"You're joking," I said, sure he was only trying to scare me. And then something shone through the dark trees—glassy black water.

Justin and I took the little kayaks, making our own paths into the still pool. The disturbance of our oars created bands of metallic ripples, each jellyfish and bubble becoming electric silver-blue. We paddled deeper, a neon cobalt flash of light surrounding our slim boats. Drifting past the tangled limbs of red mangrove trees, spectacular exposed roots, we floated away from land. With each stroke, the water made an incredible light show, like a million tiny underwater fireflies. The sea of stars was alive, each bright fleck in reality a creature, tiny organisms. The bay lit up with the metallic shapes of every fish—we saw stingrays and a barracuda, then a baby shark.

Braced, I felt the thrill of floating above the glowing predators. Daring each other, watching for the shape of sapphire sharks, we dragged our fingers across this luminescent crystal ball.

A drizzle began, millions of little jumping sparkles, the water becoming a field of iridescent rings. Now the bay seemed a mirror to the velvet sky, both populous with their sprays of twinkling celestial bodies. Then I saw Justin removing all his clothing—

I gasped as my naked husband jumped, treading water amid three larger shining sharks—*the mothers,* I thought.

Shot by adrenaline, not thinking, I kayaked to land, shaking; I stepped down onto the damp dust of the shore that sunk like mud beneath my toes. Terrified, I couldn't stop squinting at the water, trying to see him; but the fog and rain and darkness now obscured everything. My eyes couldn't find him, the mute bay a black field.

I called out, "Justin!" And then harder: "*Just*-in!"

But I heard no human echo.

I thought about how to get help—I could drive the Jeep through the jungle, back to the waterfront bar that was still open; find a rescue person who could save him. Though my Spanish was poor, the situation would be simple to explain.

After about ten petrified minutes, he splashed, shiny with water, onto the squishy sand, dragging his boat like a toy wagon. He appeared unharmed. I was shaky, crying.

I asked him, "Are you trying to kill yourself?"

In his beaming blue stare I saw a man who believed he was invincible.

$\sim$

The next morning, I woke up with the shadow of dark water still fresh, uneasy. Trying to forget last night, opening my laptop to start writing, I saw I had a response from my editor. He had granted me an extension—three more months, the new deadline mid-December, winter's start.

Relieved, I was heartened. Grateful to not have lost the livelihood I wanted—that nothing horrible had happened. I thanked him and got right to work, vowing to the silent trees that I would hit this new deadline. I *must.*

A week later, his mood playful, Justin took me out to an open-air bistro with a bamboo roof and amber lanterns, banana leaves rustling in the clear night as we kissed across the table over colorful plates of mango-lime salad and fresh-fried empanadas.

"To three years of a marriage," he said, clinking his wine glass gently against mine, and I giggled at his understated toast.

12

A Long and Silent Prayer

We returned to our blue apartment in mid-September's cooler skies, fall coming. Reentering the city with renewed commitment to the book, I napped between fourteen-hour writing sessions, routinely consuming six cups of iced coffee a day. My only social interaction beyond waking up next to Justin was splitting pots of green tea with Corrina in the evenings, both of us writing.

One windy autumn night, hungry, I took a break. After making a dinner of ratatouille and brown-butter pasta, I called, "Food is ready."

Justin had been in the bedroom with his laptop, and he appeared, his movements slower. "There's something I have to tell you," he mumbled, not sitting to eat—I stopped serving, fearing what he might confess. "I have a gaming addiction," he told me, face clammy, fixing his gaze out the window. "That's what I've been doing." His tone was somber, confessional. "That's why I've been kind of hiding."

I stared at his face, at a loss. I had never heard of such a thing, confused. "You have?" I asked, mind blank. "Don't worry about it." I wanted to ease his pain—there was no need to feel embarrassed. Then, hoping to offer a solution, I suggested maybe if he got a job and had something else that was more stimulating in his life—a community, friendships, a place he looked forward to going—then that might get him out of the apartment. "Maybe that could help?"

"Maybe." He finally looked at me. Solemn, he explained that, living in New York years ago, alone, the same escape had been a problem. "I was addicted to the same game, *Grand Theft Auto*." He took a seat, and I placed a palm against the raised ridge of his spine, gently rubbed. "It's good I told you."

Suddenly, he started eating, his manner buoyant; and I sensed a weight I couldn't comprehend was lifted.

The next evening when I came home from Joe Coffee, the apartment smelled sharply of aerosol. Opening a window, Justin presented me with his "work," a wooden chair he had found on a sidewalk, tossed out; he'd spray-painted the seat a lovely periwinkle. "Try it out, it's dry by now," he said. Sitting down to feel its support, my husband told me he was going to "revitalize" our place.

Three days later I returned from class to find him building a gigantic wooden structure, measuring and nailing two-by-fours. In the two years and two months we'd lived in New York, we'd been sleeping on a thin foam mattress on the floorboards—now, for just seventeen dollars of cypress scraps, we had a large frame from fragment lumber: magically, a bed.

On Halloween, Justin showed up at Joe Coffee, where I was typing madly, waving at me with a purple bar of Swiss milk chocolate. Seeing him through the glass, I rushed into his arms; he lifted me onto the café's green porch bench and I kissed him.

"Aaron has big news," he whispered in my ear. He told me that the *Aaronverse* blog posts had caught the attention of Tumblr's CEO and that—despite his dread of public speaking—Aaron would be addressing the tech company's entire staff, speaking at their office about his life with cerebral palsy. "Tomorrow."

I held my love tightly. "I think you helped him."

High in New York's triangular Flatiron Building, Justin and I witnessed Aaron Philip, our adopted mentee, enrapture the audience of coders and designers, my heart pounding, enriched with fierce delight. *Good Morning America* was filming, capturing the boy's wisdom for millions.

The following day, when I came home from an inspired day of braver writing, the smell of burning evergreen incense was overpowering. Justin was lying face-up on the floor, his skin too pale.

Worried, I asked, "Are you sick?"

Flatly, he told me that Mystic was gone. He was dead.

Our first mutual friend's fun-loving nature returned to me. "That's not possible," I said. "He's only your age." I asked to know where he heard that, my mind violent with shock. The man who introduced us on the trail, integral to the formation of our life, was not actually *gone*.

"I know," Justin said calmly. Sitting down beside me on the futon, he showed me Mystic's Facebook page, which had become a memorial wall. Justin had already written:

> *Mystic, the man who sat on pancakes to win an eating challenge. Hitchhiking 100s of miles for a little love. Throwing a glass off a porch and walking away like it was no big deal. The mirrors you carried. Days hiking with you were some of the best of my life.*
>
> *Burning a stick of incense in your memory. RIP brother.*

I wrapped my arms around my husband, but he felt a little stiff—
A groundswell broke inside me like a terrible wave crashing. I held my right wrist in my left hand—it was hurting. I was sobbing without sound, like a devastated mime. My arm and my heart were throbbing in time, a frantic flutter.

"Don't you ever," I said through soundless inhales. "Don't you . . . ever feel . . . overwhelmed?" In the course of our entire relationship, more than four years, I had never once seen Justin show an outward sign of sadness. And he didn't seem to be reacting now, either.

He blinked at me, his turbulent blue eyes softening a little, almost imperceptibly, at their corners. "Not like you," he said, but the words were free of judgment. I was still hugging him, holding on, and at last his body relaxed in my grip. He slipped an arm around my waist, half-hugging me back. "When I was twelve, I had a friend, Peter. He lived pretty close, and we'd ride our bikes in the hills around our houses. One day we were riding and a car hit him. And he was killed."

I shivered. "I can't even imagine," I said quietly. My breathing had calmed, but bright tears of salt still streamed down, falling on us like a leak in the ceiling. I realized his close friend's senseless death must have occurred in the months after the fire.

"I cried at Peter's funeral," Justin told me, "and I never cried since."

That dismal overcast evening, gripping the peeling paint of railings, my husband and I climbed the rickety cast-iron fire escape of our apartment—

Lying on the roof in mild night, the sky appeared not charcoal black but pale slate gray, soft with city lights. Watching the hazy field of air, waiting for the faint etching of the first shooting star, we noticed a vibrant golden ring around the moon. It was a halo, wild metallic yellow, glowing like an aura. Holding both hands on the dark rooftop of our city, our New York, we shared a long and silent prayer.

13

VORTEX

Day 1

On a gray day in November, Justin wakes me with a soft kiss on the mouth at five o'clock in the morning—he is heading to New Hampshire to attend Mystic's untimely funeral. The air is bleak with mist.

"Come with me?" my husband whispers in my ear, asking one final time.

I roll over, facing him sideways. "You go, I should work," I mumble. "*Love* you." I'd never imagined losing someone so young, so close to me, my first friend to die. On this terrible day of mourning, I want to circumvent the pain of the burial.

Minutes later, drifting off, I hear the door click shut, Justin leaving alone.

But in class, I only sit in unrest, my poetry professor's words slow rhythmic gibberish. I cannot focus, though I am present. Mystic has departed our world at only thirty-three; and my mind's eye becomes brutal, wondering how he died. In rising grief, right there in class, I open my laptop and post a message to his parents, who survive him:

I'm so sorry for your loss. I met Mystic on the PCT in 2009, and he brightened my hike—he was so kind, funny, and charming. I loved his stories. He also led me to a hiker named Dash, the man who would become my husband. Mystic changed the course of my life, and he touched many people.

When I drift back from class at dusk, all haze has cleared. The leaves like red flames and the air sharp blue, our vibrant turquoise walls are shadows in the dark. Walking the space like a ghost, all I need is a hug from my husband; but I do not find Justin. He must be stuck in traffic, I assume, still coasting south from the funeral I know I should have attended. I wait for him to return to the city, our apartment quiet.

Yet by midnight, my husband still hasn't come home. Trying to suppress deep rising panic, I call him—his phone doesn't ring but cuts directly to voicemail. Stunned, I sit in the silence that outlasts the end-beep of the familiar automated message telling me his voicemail box is full; and I send a frantic text. Eventually, darkness swallowing our room, I go to bed alone.

But lying still, worried, I cannot sleep. Rising again, restless, I undress in front of our black fifth-story window. Buried away in my dresser is the garment I've kept pristine for three years: the mermaid bra I wore under my wedding dress, strapless and white. I put it on. I feel nervous and pretty, hooked in the fabric I married him wearing. That night, I sleep in it, my heart held tightly.

Day 2

I wake to a pale and glowing dawn, the off-white sky in my window too pallid, it appears almost snowy. But the first flakes of the coldest season have not yet fallen; and the bed remains empty beside me—still no Justin.

I notice his cherished belongings in the apartment—his grand-father's WWII wallet, a great treasure embossed in gold, and his iPad both remain on our bedside table. Wherever he is, he clearly planned to return. All the colors in my apartment appear to me tinged with sandy copper, as if the room is dusted in the faintest film of pollen.

Eyes unfocused, drunk on fear, I call my husband's parents. The digital bell is faint, mechanical in my ear, *ring-ring*. My thumbs feel stiff. So early on the West Coast, I am not expecting an answer. But I hear, "Hello?" His mother's voice.

"Hi," I say. I realize I don't know how to express her son's absence. "This is kind of a strange question, but have you heard from Justin?" Saying the words to my mother-in-law, I feel raw nerves. I am present to the tenderness of our affection. "Our friend Mystic died recently. And the funeral was yesterday, and Justin went, and he hasn't come home . . ."

I hear no sound from Lucy for a moment. Then she clears her throat. "Oh no," she says calmly. "I am so sorry, dear." Her tone is not frenzied or even upset—not what I had expected. "Have you tried call-ing him?" she asks.

I exhale audibly. "There's no answer," I tell her. "Can you try?" I am becoming confused, almost angry. Wanting her to feel the severity of the situation, hoping to wake up a lion in her heart—her son has *disappeared*—I ask her, "Actually. Should we maybe call the police?"

Lucy laughs, uneasy. "It wouldn't be good for anyone if we called the police," she tells me. "I know this is upsetting, but it's all going to work out. Trust me, he's okay, wherever he is."

When Lucy and I say goodbye, the room is hot with sun, the green-house effect making me sweat—the metallic tint persisting.

At 7:00 p.m., I leave the apartment for the first time.

Still perplexed by the strange interaction, I pace the sidewalks of our New York neighborhood, passing familiar lines of street-parked cars. Justin's silver sedan is missing from its usual spot. Gone—as if there are one-too-few faces in the navy dusk, but no one even knows. It makes no difference to the city that Justin is not here tonight—work still started this morning, anonymous taxis honking as they carry strangers home.

I feel the infrastructure of my world cracking at its foundation, and I can't grasp why. I wish on a passing bicycle with spinning golden lights as if it were a shooting star: *Bring him home.*

A young brunette couple passes me on the sidewalk, clasping hands. They are both wearing worn blue jeans. They might have been us. I take out my phone, slippery in my clammy fingers. I call my husband. This time it rings five times—his phone is on!—but terminates in his non-existent voicemail; silence.

A sudden siren screeches, burning my ears—a cop car passing in the night. In a fierce flash, it occurs to me: *Just call the police.* My husband is technically a missing person, as much as I hate to think so.

But Lucy's words persist—and the action feels too dramatic, like something people do in movies. My instinct tells me not to dial, sensing he will soon walk through our door.

Day 3

In morning, waking from anxious dreams, I discover under my covers—eyes still closed—that, overnight, my cheeks have become rough. With my fingers, I explore my face, feeling blotches, their texture delicate and abrasive as sand.

In the mirror, pale markings on the sides of my eyes startle me. I splash myself with cold water, my cheeks become smooth again—and I realize what I've washed away: salt crystals stuck crusted on me, dried tears in sleep.

Stretching, my soft abdomen is impossibly sore, as if I have done tension exercises, crunches or long and rigorous planks.

Lying back down I see the emptiness in my bed—I remember my husband's absence.

Above the bedside table hangs a picture he gave me as a gift, just a week ago: an illustrated map of several Caribbean islands set inside a pretty gilt frame. Among the islands is the intricate outline of Vieques. The island sits silently there, a grayish mole.

Out the window, rain falls audibly onto the black sill. No matter how hard I throw my mind onto comforting reveries of him returning, my heart always sinks again back into my aloneness, the strange reality of this wordless dawn.

I close my eyes once more, bargaining with the stars against the impossible.

Day 4

In class, a girl I am friendly with asks me if I want to come to a brewery in Alphabet City tonight. Excited, she is pretty, her hair long shiny blonde, stick straight with lilac tips. "And bring Justin!"

"Ooh, fun!" I say. Then I lie, telling her that my husband is "on a trip for a few days in Maine. I wish I could have gone away with him."

I slip out of the classroom, ditching—skipping the remainder of my school day. Drifting west to a wine bar under the High Line where I know no one, I drink without him, the distraction of intoxication offering some refuge.

Day 5

I take a late-night walk with Nic around the periphery of Washington Square Park. A dingy dog appears to be unattended, crossing the black lawn of shadows, stony shades of darkness—then it's gone. Nic is talking quickly, answering a question I've already forgotten; I am not hearing well, my ears ringing—which scares me. "What?" I ask, interrupting, and her smooth river of words falters.

But Nic responds with the blunt question, "Have you told your parents yet?" I cannot meet her eyes, but her nose and lips seem lovely and simple, delicate like a familiar postage stamp of a woman in profile, my comfort in the dim anonymous city.

Washington Square Park has never looked so bleak, the streetlights yellowed. A little boy with a Yankees cap is playing an African drum, begging for dollars from strangers as he squats at his father's feet in the grim night. In the soundless gap following Nic's sharp question, I realize how alone I am, how private I've become.

"I haven't told them," I answer, uncomfortable with this truth. As we pass a streetlamp, the silhouette of her eyes narrows, and I promise my mentor, "But I will."

"Good," Nic says. Then she suggests I focus my attention on the book. I don't tell her I haven't written a word since the day before the burial.

Day 6

I ring my parents for the first time in over a year—my father picks up. He tells me that Mom's traveling in Morocco.

I tell him that Justin is gone. "I don't know where he is."

My dad says that he'll drive down to New York, tonight.

Six hours later, my buzzer rings, the young evening cold and clear, bitter as ice. My father surveys the apartment and helps me compile all of Justin's abandoned belongings, examining them. I want my dad to make sense of the objects, to decipher this loss for me. We treat each other gently, with extra care, given the circumstance.

"How's Mom doing?" I ask, feeling softened, really wanting to know.

He says she still misses me, contorting his face into a polite smile. Then, searching for understanding, he asks about Justin. "What do you think happened?"

I explain how he just vanished without a word—"I don't know why." The air in the apartment feels too warm, the heater clicking and humming its strange music, and my father cracks open a window. A cold gust chills us. "I don't know if he's even still alive," I tell him—frightening us both.

We walk in silence to a Fresh Greens deli. Ordering us a build-your-own salad, I say yes to every ingredient, thoughtless, creating something gigantic and clashing in its flavors.

At home, my dad and I divide the salad on white porcelain plates that Justin and I had purchased together for cheap the week we'd first moved here. Needing reassurance, I ask, "Dad, what if he never comes back? And he's gone."

"Then you'll be alright. You will." My father's presence is a comfort, exactly what I need. Then he tells me he's rented a hotel room less than a mile from my place so he can be here for me. Together we eat the twin salads, tears dripping into my lettuce.

Day 7

A freak snowstorm dusts the city with silver glitter, the gray bark of the bare trees in Washington Square Park shimmering with frost. As I trudge through the cold, my mouth feels dry—a rough texture, my parched tongue rubbing against its roof, abrasive. I am perpetually dehydrated, thirsty beyond reason.

Each morning I've taken two aspirin for a dull headache, drinking coconut water to replenish water lost by tears; today becomes yesterday.

A week has passed—no word.

Unsettled, feeling drunk on the shimmering air and on the wine I sipped an hour ago with my friend Edison at a Village café, I call Justin's older brother.

Jeffrey answers after several rings—"Debby?" He's forgotten my new name.

"Hey, Jeffrey," I say, filling with quick adrenaline. I do not know him well. "This is a little awkward—"

"What's up?" he cuts me off. He sounds surprised.

"Do you know where Justin is? The past six nights, he hasn't come home," I tell him, praying for the answer.

Jeffrey's tone becomes soft, sweeter. "He didn't?" He has not heard from his brother. "I'll call him," he promises me.

"I love him so much," I say, my voice breaking. I notice a girl in an ivory sequined jacket and metallic spandex is tap-dancing on what looks like the curved plate of a car windshield, dark and glassy. As if she has premeditated her outfit to match the sparkling world.

"Justin loves you too," he says. "Everything will be okay."

I stop walking. First Justin's mom, now his brother. I sense they must know something that I don't. "What do you mean?" I ask. The tap-dancing young woman's red lips are full and beautiful, stunning in contrast to the mute tones of starkness. "I think I should just call the police."

"He's probably just upset about something, don't do that," Jeffrey says. "Justin's like that sometimes. I'm sure he'll come back soon."

The question of my husband's location burns like insidious smoke, our shared life obscured in nothingness—and yet his family seems indifferent. Snow is falling again, an endless white curtain, and my heart pounds with the howl of spirit, my void.

Day 10

I wake up very hungry, a spot of sunlight in my open palm. All I've eaten in the past days is watermelon, coconut water, and coffee. My stomach speaks deep rumbles, but the thought of savory food nauseates me. I have hunger but no appetite, strange hollowness. My life is empty—without my husband, my calendar hasn't a single happy mark.

I settle in at Joe, finally turning on my laptop. The new deadline now just a month away, I have to face the painful task: writing about falling for Justin—in his absence. Yet not knowing where he is, or if he is okay, I can't even imagine composing our love story.

After hours of blinking at my white screen, useless, this history stuck, I email my editor again, sharing that Justin is gone. I know that if I don't follow through on *Girl in the Woods*, I will have to somehow pay back my advance—which is dwindling. And I'll need the money that remains in order to pay my next month's rent.

Still, I ask for a second extension and click Send.

~

I need something, or I am going to faint. Light-headed in sunshine, I walk up Sixth Avenue. I wander to a bodega to get some real food. I have become so weak I strain my bicep pulling the heavy door open. The idea of meat and cheese sickens me, but I know that I need nourishment.

Inside, odors of garlic and parmesan and curry make me woozy. I find the plainest things: steamed broccoli, fresh pea sprouts, plain baked chicken with fire-roasted carrots. I load them into a pay-when-you-go cardboard carton at the salad bar—$8.99 per pound. By now, I must have collected more than two pounds of food, my flimsy container heavy in my hands.

By the lettuce, a couple is touching. He kisses her cheek. How sweetly he carries her milk and a can of golden peaches. I see the sunny hue of kind love, vividly.

I pick a soft pear from a black crate, place it on top of my salad—and then strut through a propped-open exit, out onto the sunlit shark-gray sidewalk, like I am invisible. I have walked out without paying a dime.

I touch the pear to my lips and break its thin skin with the soft snap of a bite.

Day 11

My phone rings. The tinkle of sound is sudden, like a windblown feather arriving. It is three o'clock in the morning but I am not sleeping, just lying on my back on our mattress, the ceiling a still sky of grayness in the dark. I have memorized every scuff-cloud and hairline paint crack. It's a number I don't recognize. I answer the call—hoping.

But Michaela, Mystic's girlfriend, greets me. Her voice is a milky alto, lovely and smooth despite molasses-tempo. "How are you, Aspen?" she asks, and I sit upright. "Is it too late?"

It takes me a moment to realize she's referring to the time of day, and not something deeper. "No no!" I say. "Now's good. *Of course* I can talk." I feel a pang of embarrassment, as if she'd seen me steal the pear and broccoli. I want to explain that I'd never stolen before my husband vanished.

"I feel guilty," she says, slowly, as if through water. She tells me she's afraid that Mystic's parents blame her for his death. "Aspen, I had just broken up with him. He killed himself."

I inhale sadness. Michaela is opening herself like the arms of a frightened child, needing to be lifted. I stare at the black-blue block of sky, the moon an ashen bulb.

Delicately, I tell her, "This was not your fault. You didn't cause this." I get a chill like a sudden wetness on my heart—wordless lovesickness. I have the thought to ask if she had seen my husband at the funeral, wanting to tell her that I lost Justin when she lost Mystic—but I don't want to augment her suffering in any way. Seeking comfort in her right now would be inappropriate. I only repeat, "I hope you understand that this is not your fault."

"He had so much potential," she says. Her voice cracks like an egg, raw soft heart spilling. I imagine her eyes welling. "He was an amazing photographer. A great musician also. He could have done anything, but he never let himself try."

"He was talented," I whisper. "I am so sorry."

She then tells me that when he ended his life he hadn't slept in five days and five nights. "His mother found him. He hanged himself in his bedroom."

Pacing my apartment, horrified, I picture sweet young Mystic, eyes bloodshot and hair greasy, tortured by exhaustion. So tired, and yet unable to fall asleep—desperate for the sweet relief of rest. Longing for sleep myself, I breathe with the tempo of my steps, hot and claustrophobic.

"He'd been drinking too much, he had been so stuck," she continues, and her tone seems tightened, as if building to a confession. "I asked him to stop smoking weed, escaping. It got to a point where I needed to end it—and he told me if I left him, he would kill himself. But I didn't think—"

Tears are dripping into my phone, interfering with our connection. "That wasn't fair of him." I exhale sharply, my rhythm still unnatural, forced calm. She doesn't say anything back. I wait, uneasy, and Michaela's gentle sobs become audible. "Suicide was his action, not yours. *His* choice," I finally say. "What he did was cowardly and unkind. Do you understand?"

"I understand, I know," she says quickly. But then she says she has to go. "Thanks for answering."

I climb back into bed. The sky is lightening in the east, the translucent purple and yellow of deep bruising. I inhale Justin's sky-blue shirt and wear it in our bed he built, wishing to see him. I think about our vows, *'Til death do us part,* and I wonder about what the words really mean.

Day 14

The air I inhabit is a dim haze—of longing; of the regret that I had not gone north with Justin to Mystic's funeral. Childish, I'd wished to bypass sorrow.

Now, the dense cloud of remorse swallows me up. I am still home. I haven't left since speaking to Michaela. I missed classes yesterday, again today.

I open Facebook. Seeing a picture I posted more than a year ago of the Modern Love breakfast he made me, apricot marmalade gleaming, I remember the warm taste of the biscuits, the rich yolks of eggs he poached me. Like a gust of holy valley wind, love calms me—I am struck by the vivid impression that Justin's disappearance is an illusion, that it is temporary, this loss not actually even *real*.

I study our visual history, my smiles he caused—each digital snapshot enduring in this quiet living room where I now sit. These photographs are what is true, not my aloneness. I was married—I still *am*.

Every blessing in my present world begins with him—and persists. My writing still appeared in the *New York Times*, nothing can take that away. I got a book deal, and I still have it. I have a mentor, a community, a life—precisely the life that we dreamed up, together.

Still, two weeks gone, my husband is an echo: the memory of that single goodbye kiss.

I look through our online wedding album. With an innocent click, I slip back to the past, a beautiful vortex. With all my powers of will, I have avoided this fruitless comfort, until now—

In photographs of the day, I am twenty and ever-smiling. In one, my maid of honor slides an ivory dress over my head. It is heavy on my body; I feel light. She zips the gown's long back, the linen bare and pure, clinging to me like a second, expensive skin. Chestnut eyeshadow accentuates my honey-colored irises, and I look elegant. In another, I clasp a turquoise necklace my father gave me. It is made of polished nuts that look like stones. He'd found it in Ecuador and had given it to me at the rehearsal. I hadn't told him that I was going to wear it, a sweet surprise. I thought it might mean something to him.

Justin and I were not allowed to kiss before the ceremony, a rule we'd made the day before. But I recall how he'd pecked me on the forehead and I released the tension of all doubt.

I'd looked up to him, then. Even in four-inch heels I was half a head shorter. "Justin," I whispered, "know when they say, 'You may kiss the bride?' Maybe can we Eskimo kiss before we kiss for real?" I told him it seemed sweet to me.

His lip had curled—smirking, his eyes brilliant lake blue. He smiled, his nose drifting toward mine, nuzzling. I was blushing. "Okay," he whispered. "Cute."

I disappear deep into pictures of that drizzly afternoon: Justin and I on a rocky platform lined with lilies, a fog of mountain clouds erasing the faint path in the grass, swallowing our stage; reading our vows to each other beneath a blotched canopy of blood-orange blossoms quivering in hot wind; exchanging simple white-gold and tungsten wedding rings, lightning flashing like a camera.

I close the pictures, sick with hot blue homesickness for a nameless *elsewhere*. Our place is dark, night mirroring my heart.

Lonely, desperate for some opening—even just a fleck of clear-cut insight—I begin clicking through profiles of other long-distance hikers. I Facebook message a mutual acquaintance from the trail where we'd met: "Have you heard from Dash?"; then another. I am trying to think of all possible people, scouring our contacts.

His vanishing confounding, no trace of Justin has been found in a credit card payment or an accident report, no hint of him.

Day 15

One by one, responses fill my message box: no one has seen him. It is as if I am trying to summon an apparition.

Day 18

I sit with Corrina at Caffe Reggio, sipping Merlot. Now my closest friend, she sips her jasmine tea. (She doesn't drink.) I call her Corrina Ballerina, for her elegance. Since Justin, I have been drinking more; I crave companionship like I wish for peace of mind, the two sweet states conflated in my heart.

The Ballerina and I speak in the carroty glow of beeswax candle-light. With milky grace, she takes my hands. Her palms are pale and delicate as petals, soft; and she tells me, "You were one of those couples I thought would be together forever." She is shocked, especially because just weeks ago we had told her about carrying each other in the bright teal waters of Vieques. Now she asks me, "Could he have just left?" her gentle voice wavering.

Her directness surprises me, attracts my interest. I feel we are at the beginning of a trail that leads somewhere worth going—a hunt for the truth, an answer.

We sit in silence, wondering. "I really can't imagine that," I tell her, my tone too sharp. "Also, he left his iPad and all his clothes." She reaches out her hand again, lifts mine up. "What could have happened is—" I begin, again. "Do *you* think he could have left?"

Day 20

Sitting at Joe Coffee, I hear back—a kind note of condolence from my editor, but no information on whether I'll be granted an additional extension. He has already given me three extra months. He says we'll set up a call soon to find the best path forward.

My stomach growls, but without Justin bringing me home food, I routinely forget the need to eat. Outside, the West Village town-homes rest in the midday sun, white and rose-red painted bricks and the perfect sky clean blue. At a corner store with a dimpled spring-green awning, I see a little black plum I imagine is sweet. Examining it, I remember the firm grip of my husband's hand, holding mine on this exact spot of sidewalk.

I slip the dark fruit in my bag.

Day 25

I wake up from a nightmare—Justin hanged himself in an attic, in front of me and his mother. Brittle, I become a trembling leaf in wind, my mouth terribly dry.

Instinctively, I reach over to his side of the bed to make sure he's okay; but I feel nothing. Opening my eyes, remembering my life, I cannot shake the vision: the attic of a weird industrial loft smelling of paint thinner, Justin's white face lifeless.

Haunted, I know who I need to talk to—

Brave before sunrise, I ring Coyote—we have not spoken in years. Her real name is Sarah, but I've never called her by it. She'd been Mystic's girlfriend a few years back, lovely and fierce.

I knew them by their trail names, Mystic and Coyote, exotic, but in the real world they are Michael and Sarah. At nineteen, I'd viewed them as our parallel: Coyote and Mystic had met on the Pacific Crest Trail the same summer Justin and I had, when she was a wilderness firefighter, stationed at a lookout tower in the Oregon woods.

When I met Mystic on the footpath, he had been gregarious and bubbly, couldn't stop smiling about Coyote, the gorgeous girl he'd met at Crater Lake. He was sure that something real would blossom from their brief connection. Beside a campfire two days after they'd first met, he'd told me that he loved her.

Coyote answers the call, "Wild Child!" and I am heartened. She still remembers my trail name. I try to picture her delicate features, cute as a pixie, her blonde hair always tied back in a tiny ponytail.

After some stiff minutes of ancient stories and inside jokes, bitter-sweet memories of Mystic, the line goes quiet for a moment.

Nervous, I tell her what has happened. "Dash is missing." A distant car honks, startling me—and, as if cued, a bird begins to sing. It is five o'clock in the morning where I am, still dark as midnight—two o'clock where she is, in the west.

"He just disappeared?" she asks, trying to understand. I nod, as if she could see. The invisible bird is still whistling, merry. "Had Dash been acting at all strange before the funeral?"

I consider her difficult question. "Not really," I say. Not wanting to think deeply about Justin, I ask about her relationship with Mystic. "Why did it end?"

"He was drinking and smoking weed every night," she answers bluntly. "And he became super reclusive. Just stuck in a funk."

Absorbing her words, I think about how, as I devoted myself to my manuscript, Justin had become isolated, too. Often he played computer games in our bedroom, all the lights off. "Maybe Justin got into a little funk too," I say softly. "But our marriage was still happy."

Coyote tells me that Mystic had been physical, so affectionate in the beginning. But he'd completely lost his sex drive. "In the end, he never wanted to."

"Actually," I say, "this is embarrassing to admit, but we'd been way less intimate lately, and it wasn't that *I* didn't want him." I stop, face flushing. Then I qualify my statement, wishing I could erase time. "That's really just how relationships are, though. They ebb and flow. I didn't think it was a sign of anything."

We sit in eerie silence for long moments. I'm struck by a terrible thought, worse than a car wreck or betrayal—maybe Coyote is having it, too, now—

That like Mystic, my husband killed himself.

Day 29

Corrina sleeps over for the third straight night, an angel. Lying on her side next to me in my bed, she notices the last bouquet Justin gave me "just because" only five days before he left, petals now dry and browning, a few fallen, the blooms all dead.

Drawing on my arm with a finger, she asks me, "Do you want me to throw those away?"

The flowers are drooping downward on my dresser like forgotten stalks of wheat, abandoned. Still, I tell her no.

Later, she looks for food, but finds nothing substantial in the refrigerator. Neglecting nutrition, I've lost fifteen pounds in four cold November weeks. Holding up a shiny tube, she asks me, "What is this? Cookie dough?"

Shortly before Justin disappeared, he purchased a cylindrical bar of imported yellow butter, wrapped in gold paper. I keep it in the fridge beside our coffee beans that remain, unmade.

I remember coming back to our sun-flooded home after class one afternoon and my husband saying, "Look!" He was standing over the sink, above the Teflon pan he'd made pancakes in that morning, and a bright film of rainbow swirled on the butter-water. He told me to blow on it, and I did, and the pink hopped to purple; yellow to blue. He explained to me the science of why—I don't remember that part. But I was happy.

Day 32

My editor calls—I dart out the front door of Joe to answer. "How are you doing?" he asks me, and I hold my shallow inhale. "I can't imagine how difficult this must be for you." His tone is sincere, compassionate.

Tears drip into the keypad of my flip-phone, creating soft static. "Have you been able to get back to the book yet, at all?"

My hand gripping the phone is squeezing, holding my fear still inside me. I answer him, "A little. It's been hard." While missed deadlines are normal in the literary sphere—creativity bound by no contractual timetable—it is already early December, and my publisher believes I am just ten days away from submitting the entire book. Yet it still feels like I'm underwater in the middle of the draft, leagues away from resurfacing with anything worth sharing, much less a pearl.

Treading the curved arm of the alley alongside Joe, old Gay Street, I softly ask him for an extra hundred days. "Would that be possible?" I quickly add, presenting confidence, "The final chapters are really coming together beautifully."

Sweet and understanding, my editor grants me this second big extension—I now have a March 17 due date, nearly springtime.

The sun rests on a metal pub roof as we say goodbye. Standing in silence in the alley, daylight glaring, I feel entrapped—the extension also greatly extends the dreadful era of this task.

Day 35

Caffeine and wine make sleep tonight elusive. Time precious, I don't rest, staring at my homework, an essay about the liberating nature of folk art, due tomorrow, my laptop producing blue light like an oracle in the dark city. Hands unsteady—the consequence of five and a half mugs of black Ethiopian coffee—I have reached an impasse, feeling windblown and overpowered, transient as a red spark falling to its ash.

Typing my conclusion, sky blushing in the east, ruby and silver, I consider leaving college, once again.

Day 39

Chilly air stings my cheeks like needles. Nic doesn't slow, unaffected by bad weather. The world is getting colder. Gold and emerald Christmas lights twinkle in the gigantic evergreen at the northern entrance of the park, and we admire the decor, our festive metropolis caught in the holiday spirit.

"They gave me another three-month extension," I tell my mentor, this early-evening walk breaking my stagnancy. The sidewalks along Washington Square Park are crowded with New York University students, the frosty ground purple and white with fallen confetti from some rogue celebration. "But I don't know if I can live in our past right now. It's too heartbreaking."

Nic doesn't hesitate. "You absolutely *can* do it, this is your story. You're strong without him." A young couple passes in the opposite direction, the man wearing a huge cherry Santa cap with a soft white puff on top.

Feeling raw, I confess, "I've been stealing food, *shoplifting*. I don't feel very strong."

She tells me I have to stop, immediately. "If you don't, you're going to end up on Rikers Island." She stops walking, her dark eyes furious. "You're wildly talented and completely able. But if you choke on your first book deal, you don't get a second one."

No longer caring about her opinion, I feel self-destructive. I tell her, "Then I have to leave college."

Nic seems to be distracted, glancing sideways at a sudden patch of sapphire bud-lights glittering on the park's coniferous hedges. "Don't be dramatic."

"I'm dropping out, Nic," I say, wanting her attention.

"You're not dropping out," she tells me. "It's a sabbatical. Your book is your job now."

Day 43

For forty-three days, I haven't known where my husband is, no hint. Until a dawn moment in mid-December, the day cold, like any other. Lying in bed, I check my email—and his name is there, in bold:

FROM: Justin Matis.

Seeing "Justin," I feel a pang of yearning.

> *Hey, I hope you are doing well. Can you mail me my out-door gear? What I have isn't cutting it for the snow and ice. —Justin.*

I read it again. Just this nothing-message. A missive like a cut. So he is fine; just gone.

PART II

ABSENCE

The cure for pain is in the pain.

—Rumi

14

ROAD TRIP

A cold wind breathed through the window, which was cracked open despite the season, fresh air my preference. I stared at Justin's email, baffled as a stranger—uncertain what to make of his indifferent words. He wanted me to mail him his climbing ropes and ice ax? But he gave no home address. I typed back to my missing husband: "Oh sure yeah. I just attached them to this email."

I flushed, enraged—clicked Send.

Unable to grasp the essence of what had happened, I remembered how, trapped in the snowy Cascades, he'd saved my life. How I'd awoken with him wrapped around me, warm.

Now, I couldn't make sense of that tremendous selfless bravery.

Thoughts barraging, I strained to find some hidden rift, our fracture. A hairline crack, the clue I'd never noticed. Something of the past, to hint this void. Of course we didn't agree on absolutely everything, both wanting adventure but defining the word in our own languages.

But our bond had still appeared strong, at least to me. I felt flares of joy each day when I'd see him, home again from classes. I was his Frankie, he was my Charlie—pet names that meant everything, only to us. We had inside jokes about the mannerisms of quirky characters we encountered in our shared urban world, every distinctive face a mine for silliness. Nose and small cheek kisses were like symbols we'd created, meanings determined by the placement of our lips. He would wake me with these light pecks, poached eggs in bed; I'd leave him love notes hidden in books and in his wallet, tucked-away spaces. Eventually, he always found them.

And I knew him so intimately that I couldn't imagine there was another woman. I didn't want to wonder about that brand of betrayal. And yet—all I had was this empty bed he'd built, all questions.

Then my email pinged, Justin's name again thick black. My heart rate sped—I clicked:

> *sorry, what? Is that sarcasm? my life has become terrible in the last two months. a few things might make it a little better for Colorado winter. A trip to the post office is too much?*

How *dare* he? His life was terrible *because he left*. I hadn't heard from him in forty-three days, heart-sickened; here I remained, alone in our home, goosebumped—incensed, I wrote him back:

> *I wanted to have your children. I wanted to be your wife forever. I loved you. You chose having nothing over sharing a lifetime with me.*

His reply came immediately:

> *I've made so many choices to make you happy, that I wouldn't have made for myself. Why go to New York? Why bring home healthy food? Is this not love?*

Too jittery and upset to write back, I walked out—went to a bodega down the street. Hopped-up on adrenaline, I took a big bar of black cherry milk chocolate, not paying. I wanted the world to take care of me, like Justin had.

Then I ambled all the way to the dull-dark green-blue Hudson River, consuming square after square—reeling. I imagined what might have happened if I'd someday had his children and he had done this, then. I'd be alone, needing to care for and support them. When I reached the sun-skimmed water, I immediately turned back around, not pausing for a moment to enjoy.

On the way toward home, I stopped at a Fidelity. The green storefront of our honeymoon hit me with a sideways punch of grief. Inside, I withdrew everything from our joint account, which was now only $2,027.

Back at the apartment, Justin had sent another message. Hot breath stuck in my lungs, I opened up:

> *Do you know the pain of realizing that your problems are cyclic? The same thing happened years before.*

I slammed the laptop closed, furious. Dumbfounded—this cryptic message seemed to suggest that the "problem" of Justin's present isolated circumstance, which had been his own creation, was a "cyclic" issue, outside his control.

I couldn't write back to this. Infuriated, I thought about mailing all his belongings to his parents—he should call them, anyway. In spite of their composure, they had to be concerned, not knowing where he was or *how* he was.

My heart was snapping under the weight of this new exchange, a brittle fall leaf crushed in one careless hand. My love for him was still present here, alive and hurting—his tenderness remembered. Despite the fire of my rage, I felt myself still longing—holding on to our ghost family, a stillborn life. Little Winter and Marin.

Overwhelmed, I pulled the sheets over my head like a child making a fort. Half-protected from daylight, it struck me: my husband really had left me. There was no explaining this away.

Still, I couldn't stop my soul's dark imagination, seeking for the root of this terrible shift—his present tone so different from the Justin I had loved.

~

At a cozy café called the Tea Spot, shadowy and candlelit, the Ballerina requested we be given a table by the window. Time with her was beautiful and alive, not dead. She created a safety for me, deep comfort in her presence.

"Little love, what's next?" she asked. She sipped her herbal tea as I drank the cheapest wine. "Shall we go find him?" Corrina joked, and I smiled a hint.

In the yellowed light of our table I imagined actually hunting him down—renting a car with loud music belting and my favorite girl on the planet, our two faces floating west like light specks in the night, looking forward. Excited, a little drunk, I lifted my wine glass in a faux toast. "It'll be a road trip," I answered, grinning. Dizzy, I felt unsure if I was kidding. We could leave as soon as tomorrow afternoon, even— reach the snowy towns of sprawling Colorado by the weekend.

The room was spinning slowly, and in the wall of mirrors behind the bar I saw my mouth was darkened, stained scarlet. Confronting Justin might be empowering, offering closure.

The Ballerina and I whispered in the dim of the small hours, and she spoke of how we struggle for no reason. "You are the gift the water brings," she said softly. Her body leaned slightly, tilting toward my forehead. "When we remember to stop struggling, we rediscover we are floating. Trust the water, it will carry you." With gold-green eyes, she held my stare. Her gaze was straight and gentle as a leaf.

"I'm sick of struggling," I said.

Then in this open darkness, she confessed how she had been fighting for air, herself. Living paycheck-to-paycheck, she'd grown tired—she still fantasized of fleeing New York. "We could leave Friday night after my shift," Corrina said, beginning to plot our hypothetical road trip.

For a half-moment, I was excited. But then I remembered. "I wish I could. But I have something with my parents."

~

Saturday evening, up in New Hampshire, not far from the town where Mystic passed, the brilliant jazz musician David Lockwood would be performing his new album *Modern Love*, which was inspired by the *New York Times* column of the same name. Thus my love story with Justin had become a song; and I'd received a special invitation to the show— two free tickets, to be used by my missing love and me. Not wanting to go alone, I had decided to ask my parents. Rather than calling, I'd forwarded them the information.

They quickly responded, eager to join me.

In the car, my dad played wordless jazz. It had been over a year since I'd seen or spoken to my mom, withholding love with each passing day of avoidance. And as steady time without her had accumulated, my island-of-two with Justin quietly drowning, the idea of explaining my long silence became daunting—a terrible paradox. Each time I almost called her, a well of resentment stopped me cold from searching her name in my phone. We still hadn't even talked about my Modern Love, and soon we'd be watching a performance of it, side-by-side. Rolling through shadowed farmland, the palpable awkwardness of our rift went unacknowledged, Justin's absence taking precedence.

"He was a very sweet guy," my mother said. "But it was strange, he didn't seem to want to work." She had always liked Justin, finding him interesting and kind, for years holding out hope that he would eventually choose a lifelong career.

"Mom," I mumbled. "What you don't understand is that he never subscribed to the 'necessity' of doing meaningless work."

My mother was quiet for a moment. "The way he left was very bizarre."

Feeling cornered, I exhaled loudly. "Can we not talk about this right now?" Justin had always felt my mom's concern for our so-called wellbeing was oppressive, and now I feared that part of why he'd left me was to break free from my family.

My father turned up the music, and we coasted through the pained notes of a sad song.

Crossing Connecticut in dirt-brown dusk, our car slipping through new darkness like the light-flare of a falling star, my dad spoke, our first words in two states. "A man is not an island," he said over a quiet melody.

I turned, heartsick, my eyes glassy at the window. "Justin was," I finally said.

Fifty miles later, upon learning I couldn't dial the number seven, my dad insisted that they get me a working cell, "an early birthday present." My keypad had been faulty ever since the call with Mystic's Michaela—I'd broken my phone with tears. "I noticed Justin had a smartphone while you've had your cheap flip-phone," my dad observed; he did not like this "odd discrepancy." He felt it meant something.

Despite my tense reluctance to be indebted to my parents, I accepted this kind offer. So with two hours to kill before the concert, they took me to an Apple store in a bucolic New Hampshire village powdered with a shimmering coat of early snow.

The concert hall, a grand theater, filled with bodies. The lights dimmed on us, and I felt darkened. My mom and dad were seated to my left, enthusiastic; the space beside me was the empty seat for Justin.

On stage, David Lockwood's baritone voice was gorgeous in song and speech, his presence magnetic as a blue moon. His style was fun and conversational, the band playing with lightness and smooth grace, relating to each other teasingly—performing a funky song about a mother critiquing her daughter's choices in men called "He's Not Right for You." My dad loved modern jazz and melodic old folk that possessed a beating heart. Listening, he seemed transfixed, his eyes alight.

Watching my father's joyful air, for a moment I was happy.

The fifth song was ours—written from Justin's perspective. It was called "Come Back Here," a title that referred to Justin's and my return to the Cascade mountains, the same wilderness where we'd first met, to marry:

> And I will make a fire for you
> Set your tent up in the rain
> Hold you in my arms
> 'Til you're safe and warm again
> Wake you from your nightmare
> Wipe away your tears
> One day we will marry, come back here

The lyrics were Justin's sweetest gestures, the beauty of his strength exposed on the trail—salting my unspeakable wound. And to me the title, "Come Back Here," had unique meaning—a microphone to my mind, a plea. A sudden spotlight appeared on my face and the bucket seat beside me, which was empty. The song had ended. David Lockwood called into the mic, "Is Justin here?"

A silent moment passed, my breath stopping. "He's hiking!" I called back. I was empty, the shallow bowl of my heart in a drought that felt as total as the globe.

Weaving through the after-party at Lockwood's beautiful house, I dodged well-meaning questions, becoming drunk on red and white wine.

~

The new year nearing, an envelope came—mail from Justin's parents. Inside a pretty card read "A San Francisco Lover's Christmas." I opened it to discover a letter, in Lucy's hand, that ended:

> *I find it hard to write or even think about these last few months, it's been painful. I cannot imagine what it must be like for you. People I talk to have been understanding, offering comforting words. There is nothing in his past that would have predicted this.*
> *All our love,*
> *Walter and Lucy*

From this message, I sensed their tone relating to their son's absence had shifted—and I felt strangely comforted by this glimpse of solidarity. Yet I couldn't fully imagine what his parents must be feeling. He was their child. And the truth remained opaque, a state of fog.

Holding the sweet greeting card, all I could think of was this lost family—how they had been mine. I answered with a phone call—dialing my mother-in-law, nervous she'd broken up with me, as her son had. She picked up quickly. "Aspen! How are you, dear?"

I told her that I missed her. I still loved her. She told me it was so good to hear my voice, as well. She was glad I was still writing. She and Justin's dad hadn't heard from their son at all. Seven weeks had passed.

As I paced between turquoise walls, my apartment like a greenhouse in the sun, we spoke for over an hour. She told me that everything was going to work out, that this was not the end of our story.

15

BLACKOUT JANUARY

The moon was pallid yellow, a sickly crescent through my window. As the wisp of soft comfort from my talk with Lucy had fallen fast away into the silence, I was left longing strongly for the irretrievable past. Wanting to be a part of that Berkeley world once more, to feel welcome again in my chosen family—I missed feeling at ease with *any* family.

Outside, the snow had stopped, the sidewalks painted pastel, sparkling with fallen flakes. Weaving through the glittering neighborhoods of townhomes, gold porch lights casting stretched-tall shadows on the steps and cobblestones, I wanted more than anything the pure protection I'd felt when I was falling in love. Missing every mundane routine I'd taken for granted when we were married, all the sweet daily things he did for me, I was lonely—

I texted each friend in my phone, "You free tonight?"

The first reply was Edison. He'd been dating a younger guy, a handsome Italian college student—but hoping to make me feel "alive," he took me, just the two of us, to a black-lit gay bar with immaculate white sofas that glowed ultraviolet.

Shirtless bartenders wearing big silly bejeweled necklaces looked like sculpted ancient Roman gods. I was one of just a handful of women, and the only who wasn't joyously dancing like a duchess. Edison tried to move with me, grinding his body with abandon—I stiffened and told him "dancing is against my religion." I stood like a door with no handle, no swing in my bones and no desire to be touched. I only wanted intoxication.

Finally Edison led me to one of the plush couches in the corner, and I sunk into its white leather cradling a honeysuckle martini. He disappeared back into the crowd of raucous dancers. Thinking no one was watching, I let my forced smile fade and my eyes close.

I felt someone sit beside me and lean close to my shoulder, pressing against me. "What are you doing here?" he asked me in my ear, his warm breath sharp with gin. His tone was not condescending, but truly curious. I opened my eyes to floppy blond hair touching my neck, giving me goosebumps. The man was handsome, like pretty much everybody at this club.

"My husband and I—" I started. A pop song I didn't recognize was deafening. "I thought—" I said, yelling over thumping beats. "He disappeared, and I didn't know where he was, or—" I stopped myself again. The story seemed simpler now. "He left me."

"Why did he leave?"

Tears fell on my black tights, my glasses slipping down the bridge of my nose. Without Justin, I still couldn't wear contact lenses. I answered only, "I don't know."

Then the young man hugged me. "When my boyfriend left me last year," he spoke into my ear, "I tried to kill myself."

"You what?" I gulped the final sip of my pink drink and, needing room, lay down on the soft rug at the foot of the sofa. The next thing I could recall, Edison was kneeling over me, touching my shoulder to wake me up. I hadn't fainted—I had just closed my eyes, needing to shut down, wishing to be alone, or someone else.

"You're twenty-three! You are *gorgeous!*" Edison was explaining to me how this life was a blessing. "You live in New York City! You should be so happy," he was telling me. "This is a dream."

"But I thought—" I said, gasping for air and words. "*I thought* I was going to be married forever."

"You're *supposed* to be single in your twenties."

Sitting up on the soft black-lit white rug, glowing violet neon, I said I needed air.

Outside, the street names were all smudged, as if the signs were melting. Their meanings were obscured. Disoriented, I couldn't remember if I was in the Meatpacking District, or to the north, in rainbow-kissed Chelsea. Rain fell in silver sheets, the air thick with gleaming traffic, honking. Lost, I stumbled. My anger burned out, a fire in cooling drizzle, and I became curious—wondering about the blond-flopped man's question: *Why did Justin leave?*

The water had consumed the last crusted piles of snow, the streets shiny and black, reflecting colored stoplights. The rainfall became green, gold, red—and I was inebriated, lonely; alone—

I drunk-dialed my mentor. Sensing my desperation, she told me to come over.

~

Nic and I took a walk around Washington Square Park, the late-night midwinter air nipping our noses. The shine of rain on the streets was already becoming black ice.

In the din of Friday sidewalks, I wove through couples, rushing to keep up as Nic told me how she'd missed me in her classroom.

In short breaths, seeking out the warm embrace of sympathy, I detailed the humiliation of the concert. "They shined a spotlight on his empty chair." I grinned at her. Nic smiled too, her brown eyes empathetic, feeling my embarrassment. I added, "But I didn't tell anyone how he actually *left* me."

A flurry began to fall in tiny flakes, the peach-gold light of Village streetlamps shining. The snow specks like glitter in the air.

The sky a dusty deep gray, darkening the hue of her eyes—creating an illusion that her pupils were impossibly huge. "Justin is missing some essential fingers," she told me. "He is very smart in some ways, yet there were some simple, common things he couldn't grasp." She stared at me.

I asked her to elaborate. "What do you mean?" I wanted to understand what she was suggesting about my husband. But only shrugging, she didn't offer greater detail. Growing impatient, I told her, "He had all ten fingers."

But my mentor's lovely profile did not contort. Her face remained unmoved, no hint of smile. "Can I be honest with you?" she said quickly. She then told me, point-blank, "You wanted this." She kept walking, the same relentless rate—

Striding, a little unsteady, I touched her shoulder. "What?" I stopped walking, an abrupt rupture, stillness. "That's not what happened," I insisted, at a loss. Of course I did not *want* my husband to disappear. My heart pounded, quick with fury—"I can't do this."

Then I just left, fleeing the dark edge of the park. I walked away from her, abandoning Nic on our old path.

The next morning, skull pulsating, I woke with the sun hot on my cheeks—five 'til noon.

Hungover, I stole a hardboiled egg from my local bodega; then I met the Ballerina at Amelie, a French bistro in the West Village, under the pretense of "a writing session." Yet this spot was really not a café, but a dark and intimate wine bar. Modern chandeliers shaped like gigantic molecules—big white glowing balls connected by twiggy metal arms—reached down from the ceiling, hovering.

Poised to tell our waiter "just bread" and save my money, sharp hunger stopped me, a pang of emptiness. Scanning the menu, I ordered a cheese plate I could not responsibly afford. "And a flight of wine." Then I told Corrina, "Nic thinks *I* made Justin leave."

The Ballerina placed a small palm on my forearm. Softly, she assured me, "Beauty, people's beliefs say everything about them, nothing about you." She told me, "Only you know what is true."

Only I knew—yet I had no deeper insight, recalled so little. I drank; Corrina sipped gold jasmine tea. In fact, I *wanted* to forget; I gulped dark wine.

It wasn't sundown yet, too early for my buzz—I should have been making progress, working. In an effort to sober up, I nibbled on a crispy oval of baguette, spread thick with sweet whipped goat cheese. Yet swallowing deep sadness, I only felt drunker.

Then a miracle happened—by chance I looked up, glanced out the window just as a man passed by at a brisk clip. He was heading west on Eighth Street, wearing a blue hood.

I recognized that jacket—it was Justin's! I knew his profile, that buoyant gait.

In a burst of intense instinct, I stood—I ran out the door, my whole body thundering, awake. Unsteady on the street, I ran hard in the direction of the man. At first I didn't see him, but I felt sure that I would find him.

Jogging, following the sidewalk westward, I glimpsed his blue coat again. A shocking thought struck me: *Justin has been here, all along.* He was moving just as swiftly, his step familiar. Already dusk had come like the permissive shadow of a dream, the dim sky drizzling and misty. It started pouring just as I ran faster, trying to catch him.

When I finally reached him, I grabbed his swinging arm. It was as if I had materialized from sapphire air, and he gasped.

"Justin!" I said, trembling, triumphant.

He turned to look at me—his face all scrunched with fear—but his eyes and lips had shifted. He was no longer Justin. He had never been my husband, after all.

I released the man's arm, apologizing softly.

The lights were reflecting in the watery black concrete, like a carnival fun-home. Minutes passed, and I stayed there, on that dreary sidewalk. I was lost—frozen in falling rain. Longing after my blue-hooded man.

Slanted sheets of inky downpour and a streak of lightning returned me to the sky before Hurricane Sandy and the beginnings of the blackout. Huddling within our dark and heatless nest, he had transformed adversity into candlelight and laughter.

My warm recollection of the six-day darkness brightened the blue rains of my present lostness. Wandering in the deluge alone, I missed him. Now, thinking about Nic's shocking assertion, I wanted to understand what she'd been saying. To discover the heart in her harsh statement, which stung me.

~

The next few weeks unfolded like a muddy footpath, treacherous and dirty.

Hungover again, sprawled out on the cold hardwood floor of my apartment one afternoon, I couldn't remember how I had gotten home. My hair damp, shirtless, I could not stop shivering.

More and more frequently, I'd sleep on the ground—it reminded me of the hard tent floor, camping with my love. I turned onto my back, wrapping myself in both my heavy comforters. The white ceiling was gently turning, glaring like a salt field in the sun, my mind awakening from the blackout as if from a bad dream; a hole in my new life.

I desperately wanted today to be better. Hoping to sit and write for hours, I walked to McNally Jackson, a sunny café-bookstore in the fancy SoHo district. Not a regular there, the chance of seeing someone I knew, and thus getting caught up in a lengthy conversation about Broadway shows or the weather, was much slimmer.

Yet finally inside, I felt suddenly hazy. I didn't know how I was going to finish the book, and I was struck by the understanding that I no longer had an ending. My original plan for the final chapter—our wedding—now felt disingenuous, incomplete.

At the table next to me, a good-looking man with black hair was reading. I hadn't intended to start a conversation, but he caught me looking at him—and I glanced away at my laptop, my cursor blinking. "Nice place this is," the man said to me, his accent unfamiliar. I glanced back up to find him smiling, handsome.

"It is." I smiled back. "Where're you from?" My face heated, as if I had been flirting.

"Paris," he answered.

We kept talking, and I learned that he had lived in Manhattan for a decade, which explained the lovely subtlety of his foreign inflection. In our conversation, we both became confessional, too quickly. In a hushed voice, I shared stories about my husband, ending with his total disappearance.

The Parisian man lightly touched my undone hair. "You are lovely," he told me. The sun was high and bright, beaming its honeyed warmth through the big windows. "And I should know this. I am a photographer." He said he'd shot for *Vogue Paris*, but "stick models" were never his passion. He had a current exhibition at a new gallery in Brooklyn, where a candid shot he had captured of a woman he'd just kissed was on display.

"It's so amazing I'm meeting you, right now, because I am a student, and this semester am studying photography for the first time," I lied. Because I suddenly wanted him to want me. "I truly love it. Maybe you can teach me."

Late that night, the Frenchman and I went to get a drink in my neighborhood. The café was very red, the lighting behind a wall of Italian wines crimson. Soon, my hands unsteady, I unlocked the door, showing him inside the turquoise apartment, now only mine.

He cupped his hand over my mouth, very rough with my face. I had told him, "You can do anything you want." My wasted limbs filled with numbness, a chilling current.

After four years of soft kisses in places that made me smile—my nose, pecks on my lower forehead (the invisible third eye), playful squeezes that made me giggle and my husband's affectionate embraces—I was now naked below the body of a stranger. His muscles were harder than my love's, skin darker olive. The veins of his forearms were like the branches of a dead tree, stiff and twisted. And the strange scent of his hair and cologne too forceful, weird, not good. *What am I doing?* I wondered, drunken. The ceiling bruised, bluer in low moonlight.

The next morning the sun was dark, topaz with clouds. The foreign man was gone, my whole chest empty. I saw that he had texted: "Hey love I left my belt. Bring it to me?" His voice back in my head, I remembered how the night before, he had called me "love" as he directed me to be still, taking photos of my naked body. He had not asked for permission; yet I had not protested.

I never responded to his message. I threw his belt into the trash.

A week later, alone on my twenty-fourth birthday, I sipped ginger-mint drinks in long-stemmed glasses at a purple-blue cocktail bar in Murray Hill. Noticing a stranger's birthday party, I joined in. "Today's my birthday, *too*," I told a bartender. He gave me a shot of something, and I stuck my tongue into the liquid—the liquor burned it. I then took two clear shots, back to back. I woke to a coldness in the single-stall bathroom, my own tears dripping onto the hand I had been using as my pillow. Vision blurred, I found my glasses on the red linoleum floor.

Trying to walk back home, I removed my high-heeled boots to quicken my pace. Thinking I was close to my apartment, putting them back on, I fell into the bushes of Madison Square Park. My toes were numb from contact with cold concrete, my soles blackish.

Hobbling back to the blue apartment, streetlights burned my eyes. I wished for Justin to come and walk me home.

~

January blinked forward, the nights marred by lightless gaps. My memories were brief, like blurry wine-bar snapshots, underexposed and dark. Another drinking story, another sunlit headache in new day's shimmering snow. Cafés with Corrina; with men; with friends of friends I met and then forgot. A lively time in its own way; days began in late afternoon, cheerful spells of rapid discussion, drunken. Nights were smashed or sad, or both. Killing my time, I remained aware I had a job to do—but instead of producing pages, I was drinking, falling behind, no longer on pace to meet my publisher's March deadline, the chance slimmer.

The more I wrote, the more I had to feel; the more I drank, the more I bypassed all sensation—sidestepped myself.

One afternoon, my friend Val and I met up for an "emergency tea." Val was newer to my inner circle and a little older, a raven-haired twenty-eight-year-old aspiring writer. She was beautiful, bright blue-eyed, and half-Colombian, her black hair silky straight.

She started telling me about what happened last night while she was home watching her two-year-old son, Tanner. "I noticed a video on my husband's laptop that was saved as 'Tanner playing.' I clicked to watch—but it was a video of sex. And the woman in the bed looked just like me, for a second I thought it *was*—but then I realized it was another woman on top of my husband," she said, without visible emotion, shell-shocked.

I listened as my friend shared her horrific experience, still fresh. "Val, I'm so sorry. I can't imagine."

Tilting toward me, her nose six inches from mine, Val asked me if she could sleep over later. "I know it's last minute," she said. "I just can't be home tonight."

"Of course," I told her, lit up with rage and purpose, wanting to help this girl whose husband had betrayed her. "You can always stay with me." We made a plan that she'd text me when she was ready to come over.

Hours later, I was out drunk with a boy I'd met that morning at Joe Coffee. He came over to my apartment, the bluest nest, and I hadn't noticed that my phone screen was black, dead.

When I woke, I had faint memory of the cold night's final hours. Yet here I lay in bed beside a sleeping stranger, hating myself. Through foggy eyes, the plan returned to me: I was supposed to be there for my friend. But I had forgotten.

My heart raced as I read Val's final text message, sent after midnight, relaying her distress—"where are you??"

16

FUTURE SADNESS

"I'm an awful person," I whispered. Sobering from my blackout, beside Corrina, I confessed to her that I had forgotten about Val—someone who'd needed me. I felt that I deserved this throbbing melancholy, headache and all. I *deserved* this exhaustion of alcohol sickness and this fundamental, heartbreaking aloneness because I was, by my nature, very bad.

In the confusion of that cold day's sun, the Ballerina looked at me, lips upturned in the subtlest smile, her bright eyes squinting. Then she told me, "Love, you are *not* bad." She spoke the words in soft tones, as if talking to a child. "I promise, you're the opposite," she said.

"Really, you have no idea," I protested. I thought of everything she didn't know. "If you knew," I started, staring at the blue wall as I spoke, "if you knew all the things I've done and all the things I think and feel—" I didn't want to finish. "I can't even tell *you*," I said, "and you're my best friend."

Corrina listened, attentive as an angel. I refused to look at her directly; yet her sharp eyes studied me with trust and love. "I have hard secrets too." It was nearly five, and we had both eaten nothing all day—my sweet friend's stomach growled.

I slipped off the bed to the refrigerator and produced everything I had: hummus and carrot sticks, bodega celery, and a tall paper carton of coconut water. Corrina set the bedside "table," laying out long metal forks, and we ate in heavy silence. Chewing, I noticed a handmade fortune-teller I had given Justin, pinned to the corkboard on the wall like a paper dove. Something delicate that reminded me of joy, this day the sadder sister of the time in Colorado when I stayed in all day talking with Justin when I was twenty, smiling and crying into his chest, vulnerable as a lost lamb, as I confessed aloud for the first time, before he had said it to me, that I loved him.

The silver sun already falling, I read all eleven texts Val had sent me last night, disappointed. "I still can't believe I forgot her like that," I told Corrina. Wiping a loose curl out of my face, I felt my puffy eyes.

"Why do you think you did that?" she asked me. A frigid gasp of winter wind brushed our bodies, and I walked away to go and shut the window.

"No good reason," I said, climbing back onto the bed, joining her. "I was just drunk." A honey-milk candle sat on the bedside table, thick and near-translucent in the low light, and I flicked a match and lit it, creating a tiny pretty flame, a spot of gold with a friendly orange aura.

"I used to accept that my dad was like a stranger in my home," she told me, dark pupils fiery. With her fingertip, the Ballerina drew a heart on the worn white sheet. "I tried to wish away his heavy presence, to forget."

When I thought about my own dad, what I wanted most was to know him better, to connect with him more deeply. "You've never mentioned him," I said gently.

The apartment felt colder as she shared details of her private history, glimpses into how she came to be here. "We escaped the violence of Moldova when I was two," she said. She paused. Her eyes glittered with unfallen tears, bright in faint moonlight. "But it took nine more years to escape my father's violence."

Her exhale blew the candle out, and we sat in the new darkness, startled. I took her hands up in mine, squeezing. I wished I could give my sweet friend the comfort she gave me.

Then Corrina told me she had recently seen her father for the first time in almost a decade. "Sober now, he suggested I could move in with him at his new house in Texas," she said, voice soft. She pressed her lips together, making a flat line. "I could understand his wish to reverse time."

I was staring at her hands, which were now still, folded on the bed, wrists crisscrossed. Her dad was an abusive alcoholic—I suddenly felt guilty about how much I'd been drinking in front of her. "I'm so sorry," I whispered. I didn't know what more to say—I felt like I was letting people who cared about me down. "What if I'm like your dad," I finally said, ashamed.

We sat in long silence, Corrina drawing abstractions on my back with her fingernails. When she eventually stopped, she shifted, finding my eyes. "You don't have to be." Then she told me, a little louder, "Drinking to cope with sadness creates future sadness."

The Ballerina's cutting story of her absent father penetrated my hard armor of stony rationalization. I didn't want to devolve into his life. For years, I had been striving to become an actualized woman—but now, as I considered what I sought in alcohol, I saw the pain I'd been creating whenever I got drunk was much bigger than the pain that I was numbing.

My book deal had happened a full year ago, and I'd been immaturely assuming it was inevitable I'd finish—but I was barely writing, and the deadline was now just six and a half weeks away.

In an effort to save my livelihood—and my life—I vowed to quit drinking.

17

CONFESSIONS

Freshly sober, I felt unsettled. In the shadow of my walls, overwhelmed by self-loathing, I sat upright on the scuffed wood of my floor, feeling masochistic—I opened my laptop and created a new document:

Confessions~

I want to attribute the pain and feeling of disbelonging and isolation I feel to some specific thing—my rape, my husband leaving me—because it feels better to believe that than to consider that maybe I am more personally responsible for the bad things I do and my unhappiness and introversion—or that I am innately bad.

My greatest secret is that I am a liar. My lies are products of my insecurities and my desire for more attention. I love to be the center of attention. I want older men's attention. Maybe I felt unseen by my father. I want to be desired and told I am special and impressive, even when I don't believe I am in truth desirable. Growing up I was chubby and funny looking. I often lie about that. I pretend I've always been very beautiful.

I'm ashamed of my childhood self—her body, her social awkwardness. I don't want people to be able to see her in me. I want them to see a beautiful seductive brilliant rare gem of a woman. I don't feel like a beautiful seductive brilliant rare gem of a woman, and so the vision I'm trying to constantly conjure feels like a lie. Often I tell men whatever I suspect will make them desire me more intensely, even if it is a lie. I can relate to Cal Trask[1] more than I can relate to anyone. I want to be good. I desperately want to be as good as my friends believe I am. I lie and lie to them because I want to be good, and they believe I am good. I want to stop lying forever.

I feel terribly guilty about my lies. So often I am kept up at night by my guilt about lies I've told for attention, for affirmation, to seem sexier, more successful, accomplished, impressive, special. I desperately need to feel affirmed. I can't stand it when another girl with me gets more attention or seems more loved or more attractive to a man. I want every man to desire me, even if I don't desire him at all. I don't know why I want this. I don't want to want this.

I am perpetually so worried that my lies will get found out, so consistency is a huge part of my persona. If someone observes to me that I am a certain way—even if I am not typically that way—I will tell them yes, they are right, and make a great effort to always seem that way, to be consistent, to behave the way they expect me to behave rather than how I more truly am—so I will seem comprehensible to them, and they will not suspect I am a liar.

---

1   The protagonist of *East of Eden*, who believes he is evil but desperately wants to be good. He prays to God: *Make me good.*

149

I am terrified of aging. I am 24 now, and I know that I will never be more desirable than I am today. It's horribly sad and I feel powerless because it's also unavoidable. I've spent my whole life becoming more attractive—I was a very physically awkward teenager with no personal style and terribly low confidence—but now I am affirmed, affirmed, affirmed daily by homeless men, construction workers, doormen, waiters and men in bars and clubs and bookstores and everywhere, and I need it. It's everything I always wanted when I was invisible, or, worse, teased. I wore the wrong clothes growing up, the clothes my mother put me in, and girls talked about me behind my back and sometimes (especially in my bunk at camp at night) I overheard. I have ugly duckling syndrome. I'm too narcissistic. I want to be honest and kind, and to take pleasure in my friends' successes, and their happiness. I want to be honest about my intentions, and I don't want them to be malicious. I don't want to hurt people. I want to improve the lives of the people I encounter. I want to do more good in the world than bad.

I want to want to be in a loving relationship in which he and I are equals, I don't want to speak disparagingly of myself, to tell him how I can't do this, how I'm bad at that, how I need him; without him I would be lost. I want to behave in a way that displays my intelligence, not a way that masks it. I don't know why I tend to dumb myself down around men, to act like I need them to take care of me, to protect me, to help me, lead me, guide me, show me how. I act helpless until I become helpless. I don't know why. I would hate the girl I act like if I met her. Whenever I meet someone I actually might like to keep in my life, someone who seems honest and good and inspiring to me, I tend to quickly disparage myself in front of him, talk myself down, describe something I can't do/am bad at/have never done—I don't know why—even if it's a lie and I have in fact done/do know how to do/am in fact very capable of doing that thing. Maybe because I want him to teach me, to give him the power of having taught me. Maybe because I unconsciously want to create an unmountable wall between him and me, because I'm afraid that if he truly knew me and THEN rejected or hurt or left or lied to me, that would be so much worse.

I've always felt antisocial, and I've wished I were naturally social and extroverted and popular, and it makes me sad. I am very good at faking extroversion and charm among people I've just met for a short period of time. When I'm in that mood, wanting to get attention that way, behaving like the social butterfly I've always wanted to be, calling myself a social butterfly—people fully think I am and have always been a charming extrovert. If I tell them I am an introvert—which I am—I tell them to surprise them and gain their interest and attention—usually they can't believe it. They tell me I must not know what I am.

I am subversive. Whenever someone believes I am a certain way, I tend to try to either act exactly that way or exactly the opposite way—to be consistent and therefore implant/enforce the idea that I am very honest, or to shock them to gain their attention. I have a hard time fully anticipating my actions' consequences/effects on people, even people I love. But then I do feel horrible when I've hurt someone I love. I don't want to hurt people. I don't want to hurt people!!

I tend to tell new people I meet—especially those I am interested in—very intimate things very quickly, usually to hook them. I've had a dramatic and interesting life, and quick confessions are fairly unusual—and people tend to mistake this kind of forward dramatic openness for honesty, which I often reinforce by telling them I can't keep a secret to save my life, and/or that I'm a terrible liar.

I feel that there's an arbitrariness to a lot of the things that I do that I can't understand.

18

A Line of Small Black Dots

Without drinking, I was a lone sailor, looking in a mirrored café wall. I felt panic and energetic strength, my heart tender as if sunburned. I was now the captain, forced to experience directly the state of sky and water, the weather now mine to confront. Sitting in the neighborhood of my marriage's desolation, three days sober, I felt every storm and current I'd used alcohol to numb.

Now, instead of trying to forget it all, I had come to this espresso bar to capture memories to which I now had access. Typing, clear-eyed and exposed, I felt renewed confidence—this time I was going to meet my deadline, hell or high water.

Sitting on a red stool, I wrote the story of my first miles walking with Justin in remote mountains, when he offered me his best food, impossibly generous. I conjured my handsome bearded stranger giving me mac and cheese under fierce stars; my grand dreams that emerged in our first nights up late talking; our whispers of skiing cold mountains, gliding down the powder together—him promising to someday visit me in Colorado when it still felt like hot air. Recreating his sweet behavior through these stories was a very specific sort of psychological torture, the last thing I wanted to do—especially so raw.

Justin didn't like to see me drunk beyond coherence, he said it "dims your light," and I considered that my stopping might make him happy. Experiencing more, I also remembered how I missed him, the pain of his loss throbbing as I typed.

Reaching a section of our story that felt uncomfortable—our first intimacy—I unconsciously drifted over to Facebook. Justin's page had no new posts, none since he left. My newsfeed was filled with engagement announcements and infants, couples I knew elliptically beginning adventures of partnership, too often kissing.

Before I knew it, an hour had elapsed click-clicking half-strangers' photos, aimless. Exhaling, exasperated with myself, my lack of discipline, I closed an album of newborn twin boys lying on a blanket in the grass. Freed of alcohol, I was not making swifter progress but rather just unthinkingly embracing another distraction.

In the clarity of new sobriety, empowered to reclaim control of my days, to use my time with stern intention, I decided to deactivate my Facebook account. Locating the button, the site asked me to confirm my action; and I clicked Yes.

The next screen that appeared was one I hadn't seen in months: the pale blue and white sign-in page—there was still an account listed. But it wasn't mine; it was "Justin Matis."

In the open space of Password there was a row of little black dots. It seemed his log-in information was still saved in my computer. My chest fluttered—I pressed Return.

To my joy, my *amazement*, my computer logged me in to my husband's profile.

I clicked through his private messages, excited—until I realized he hadn't sent or even responded to one of them in several months. A month ago, he had received a sweet message from his older brother, concerned about him. I half-considered writing Jeffrey back to alleviate his worry.

But I didn't. I logged out of Justin's account, overwhelmed.

My soul humming with hyperactive longing, I ordered another coffee, my fourth already. Hands unsteady, cupping the ceramic mug, I shivered; then in a wicked surge of curiosity, I wondered—*is his email password saved on my laptop also?*

I logged myself out of Gmail.

A fresh sign-in page appeared—his name and face were there, his passcode again showing up as simple small black spots like a line of ants; I hit Enter—and it worked! Our cyber-lives remained interlocked.

I quickly found his recent emails. I scanned everything my husband had sent and received since the day he vanished, reading with vibrant hunger. I couldn't discover a physical location, but deduced from purchase receipts that he was someplace in frigid Ouray, Colorado—the same small town where we'd attended an ice-climbing festival together in the initial winter of our love. I remembered the man-made waterfall, a spectacular natural gorge that was sprayed each November with fire hoses so it would freeze over. With ice picks and ropes, we ascended the falls, hearts pounding with endorphins.

Sitting in the dry heat of this late-night Manhattan café, upright in yellow candlelight, I scrolled down to our old emails together, sweet nothings—the forgotten love notes we'd exchanged.

After I reached our beginning, I kept going. Seeking an answer, hints; a hidden meaning I'd missed. I ventured deeper into my husband's past, tracking him backward, further and further, voyeuristic. In red-gold light I felt wicked, exploring a history that was not mine to see, and yet here I was. The place dim, couples huddled around french fries and bottles of wine, my laptop screen glowed like a stranger's lit window.

Looking at his life before me, I unearthed a secret. I found an intimate exchange with a woman, revealing something unbelievable—I was not the first person Justin abandoned.

My husband had been with a girl named Allie for six years, and she had wanted to marry him; but he vanished, into the wilderness—where he met me.

19

HIDDEN CRACKS

Striding back home, reeling, all the ambiguous signs from Justin's whole family reverberating—not seeming alarmed at first, requesting that I not call the police—their strange calmness finally made some sense: They had known about Allie.

Arriving at the apartment, I immediately sprawled out on the floor with my computer. Valuing my clarity over my husband's privacy, desperate to find real answers, I scoured his ancient private emails, hunting.

I looked for hidden cracks I'd missed—who was *Allie*?

Reading their exchange of echoes, Justin's omitted history, I discovered they had met at their Ivy League college, fallen hard. They'd adopted two cats together, Elton and Giuseppe—back in his parents' house, these had been *our* cats.

Struck by a message two years into their relationship, I learned she'd been upset that he'd had no friends of his own, that all his friends were also—in fact—hers. She wanted him to make a life for himself, not just to "appropriate" her world.

Absorbing his past girlfriend's words, I felt strange comfort. I could relate to her frustration.

I thought again about our aisle-less wedding. Forty of my closest relatives and friends flew to Washington to witness our vows. Our families had been integrated—Justin had been adamant that he did not want to separate our sides of the aisle, and I'd thought it was romantic.

I suddenly realized—only his parents, brother, a distant cousin, and two former colleagues had come for him. Had we separated our sides, his would have had only six people.

Secretly I still wore the bra I'd married him in, holding my breasts every day, now gray and threadbare.

Looking at our whole relationship through a darker lens—of *omission*, Allie's existence—I felt energetic, like I was on a treasure hunt. Every discovery was a gemstone I'd unearthed, the brilliance of clarity. The moon a sliver, a pearl and silver glint of brightness in the dim blue haze of clear dawn skies, I skimmed through time.

In one message thread that began in the days after Justin had stopped working on Wall Street, Allie was angry. She expressed disapproval of his decision to abruptly leave a "very good job" in finance, accusing him of "thoughtlessly" quitting.

Justin defended himself, declaring that he was "finished with pointless jobs."

Staring at the origin of my husband's call to altruism, *beyond* money, was surreal—a glimpse into the history of his fundamental values. His tireless desire to have a higher purpose in our society, while threatening to Allie's need for security, was an aspect of his essence I adored.

The final message in the career email back-and-forth was articulated in the direct and confident tone of someone who was *fed up*. Pleading with him, Allie expressed that she wanted him to find a new job, "and soon." Still hoping he would change, she signed the email "Love."

Toward the end of our time in Manhattan, I had shared with Justin a similar hope. If he were to get a job that was not volunteer, we could start a family. Although I loved his yearning to contribute to the world in a significant way, I also was beginning to want the wellbeing and protection that would enable us to responsibly have kids.

I flashed to one night, long ago, toward the end of our first hike together. We got hamburgers and shakes at a sleepy diner in Washington State, and the waiter asked us what we did "in the real world" that allowed us to take six months "off" to walk the trail.

"We're in the real world," Justin responded. He seemed annoyed. "I did finance stuff, and I'm retired." He was "retired" at only twenty-nine; while I was nineteen, just beginning.

Throughout our relationship, Justin had called me his "investment." The term had not been flippant—he had seen me as an asset from the start. Ever-consistent, that first night in Manhattan he had told me that he would be happy as a stay-at-home dad while I wrote books, supporting us.

In New York, I wasn't ever allowed to take a cab—the expense was forbidden, and I had hidden my occasional rides from him, with fear. Remembering the extreme frugality of our shared life, Justin bringing home food from the city sidewalks, I reevaluated his scavenging—a practice I had always viewed as *resourceful*—as him just trying to squeeze out time until his investment paid off. That "industrious" behavior was actually him saving every penny because he would never work again.

Seeing his association with work and money unfolding across the course of a decade and through two different long-term romances, I had a revelation: Watching my *Girl in the Woods* deal come to fruition—precisely what he'd wished for—he discovered the unglamorous reality of an author's life. Many nights of silent writing for unremarkable money; little of the abundant fruit he had expected, the book advance not paid out all up front but in three modest installments, spaced by years.

He helped make a miracle happen, and what I reaped was invaluable to me, a budding career—everything I'd dreamed. But the return for him was meager—I could not support us for even one year. Now I wondered if his decision to leave for Colorado was a product of him not wanting to pay New York City rent and feed another mouth for the foreseeable future, indefinite time.

And it was possible he'd been running out of money.

The day broke through a gap in black shadows to the east, a white and yellow trace of warmth; and this manic quest for insight into my husband's past no longer felt exciting. Rather, it was starting to depress me. I rested my head on Justin's old pillow, silent and sad.

~

In glaring morning, the sun hiding behind the back of a brick building, I wandered the sleepy Village, noticing the deadness of the trees. Pausing under a window-box of sky-blue plastic flowers, an idea bloomed in me like a hope—

At a little florist, I created a gigantic bouquet of pink roses and baby's breath, a countless bundle of white tiny upturned faces, delicate as lace. All told, the whole arrangement came to forty dollars—putting my bank account under a thousand; but this purchase was too important. Leaning on the plum-blush marble countertop, I handwrote a message of deep regret, still feeling horrid as rotten milk for neglecting my friend.

Nervous, I dropped off the card and flowers at Val's apartment, hoping she'd accept my apology. I knew this small gesture wouldn't erase the suffering I'd caused in these past months, but it felt like a beginning.

Home, I instinctively returned to Justin's email, settling into his old favorite spot, the futon's sunken left side. I wasn't sure this peeping was beneficial—yet incontrollable curiosity drew me back again, caught in this web. I wasn't strong enough to extricate myself from Allie's story.

After Justin left his finance job, he began a reckless trajectory. The emails with Allie revealed he had bought a motorcycle, and that she was anxious about safety, begging him not to ride. She didn't want a boyfriend who was having an "identity crisis," feeling unsatisfied and insufficient; Justin's shift toward dangerous adventure scared her.

I smiled; I loved his wild nature. But then I remembered the dark incident, that moonless midnight in Vieques. Kayaking in the bioluminescent bay, he had jumped from his boat—into treacherous water, swimming with glowing sharks.

Like Allie, I'd been terrified, wanting a future with this man who didn't even seem to want his own. Learning that his reckless behavior had predated me, other instances where my heart sped in fear for him returned. Once, Justin had climbed a tree with a machete in his mouth—his ascent had frightened me. Sometimes when we were hiking, he would free-climb a rock-face cliff without the protection of any ropes or safety gear, messing around. One misstep and he could have fallen to his death.

Now I felt something new—*relief*. As turbulent as this time without him had been for me, I hadn't once experienced the sensation of pure terror: the prospect of senselessly losing my love.

Reaching their final page of messages, I saw that after six years, Allie gave him an ultimatum: Propose by her set date, "or I am finished." But he missed the day. And soon after, he got on his motorcycle she hated and rode westward—to hike through the wilderness, alone.

I saw with clarity that Allie's marital requirement had led to Justin's ultimate disappearance from her world. Yet what I couldn't understand was why, after so many years, he wouldn't marry her—marrying me so quickly.

Then I thought more about the inconceivable way we'd come to be married, our engagement almost by inertia:

Wandering the Garden of the Gods in Colorado, I'd wondered aloud if he thought we'd ever get married, and he'd asked, "Do you *want* to get married?" I had interpreted his question as a proposal—even though I could see now that it wasn't. Later that day when I'd asked if we were engaged, at first he hadn't known what I was talking about. And once he connected the dots, understanding, he had said yes because of how he had lost Allie—he didn't want to lose me.

On our wedding day, the videographer asked me how Justin had proposed. But I refused to answer the question. I told him, "That's our secret," wanting him (and most of all, my family) to believe it had been special—not wanting them to know what I now understood: that it had been a mistake.

Face hot, I thought of the first email exchange I'd had with Justin, breaking his silence forty-three days after he left. Worked up, he had asked me, "Do you know the pain of realizing that your problems are cyclic?" Remembering the odd question, now I wondered if his cryptic inquiry had been referring to Allie.

And I sensed the intense reactivity of our reality—that our shared life was all a consequence of the loss of his past love.

20

Without Glass and Wire

39 Days until Deadline

Hunkered down at the bar of a candlelit French restaurant, ordering only a coffee, I write, sentences flowering in the dark space—overstaying my welcome.

The masochistic practice of reading Justin's old email exchanges is actually helping my writing—uncovering bits of his psyche I've never before accessed, I am getting to know this man more deeply than I did when we were sleeping beside each other every night.

A woman who seems tipsy sits down on the stool beside mine. She leans toward me—I notice her breath. "Are you an actress or are you part of the crew?" she asks.

I look up to see her tanned face and auburn curly hair. I squint at her, amused. "Neither?"

She says she is Betti Bilson, a name I don't know, unsure if I should, and it is apparent that she is quite drunk. We begin to talk, and she wonders what I am writing about, who I am; I answer every question, not thinking. She can't get enough of my adventure, trying to comprehend how a teenage girl could hike from Mexico to Canada, alone in wilderness. "You're a badass! And, like the youngest divorcée in history," she says when I get to the end of the story. "Very cool."

Hearing *divorcée* shocks me. It's been nearly three months since I've seen my husband, and I suppose it's absolutely natural for people to make this assumption—yet the strange word stings. I hadn't once thought about legally ending our union, even though it seemed already over. Adjusting my body into a more comfortable position, legs uncrossed, I tell her, "I'm not actually divorced."

Throwing her arm around my shoulder, she declares that she wants to make a movie of my "life story," adapting my unfinished memoir. Now I'm certain she is wasted.

38 Days until Deadline

Awake at dawn inside my empty turquoise walls, the void of Justin occupies my mind; and I can conjure resentment, but only for a moment. The shapes of clouds outside are changing, dissolving. Secure in bed, my fifth-floor bedroom drifts through pale hazes of mist with grace and intention, like a wild bird or a needle through the white fabric of a wedding gown. I want anger to take over, to possess me—but I hear the song of love's nostalgia, the whisper of our joyful memories an interminable movie.

True fury fails to grip me.

Teary, crying without gasping, soundless, I am soaring to another home in my mind, New York empty without my husband. Our patchwork bed makes me feel his absence, and I miss Justin like I missed July when the August leaves rusted in the summers of my childhood, school beginning. My love for him is the color of remembered vacations: rosebud pink and silver, inexplicable in their wonder and their glory.

What attracted me so much to Justin was our mutual desire for adventure—for escape. We were aligned, bonded in shared recklessness. But of course, what drew me to my husband was the precise thing that compelled him to leave. The selfsame impulse that made him walk the trail made him disappear.

In spite of what I've learned, the truth is I still wish for him. My life with him possessed more magic, higher flight.

But he isn't coming back. And this morning in our blue apartment is lonely, his ghost silent.

37 Days until Deadline

By the light of a vanilla candle, I tell Corrina about Allie. Sitting cross-legged in bed, facing each other, I describe the parallel between this unknowable girl's experience loving Justin, and my own.

The Ballerina listens with pure attention, her strong eyes locked in mine. She takes my hand in her pale dainty palms. "Allie is evidence that this is about him," she tells me. "Running away is Justin's pattern, his *struggle*."

Her steady words uplift my heart, the firm tug of a hundred colorful balloons. "I feel like it's my fault."

"Course not, baby bird. You shared beautiful love for as long as you could sustain it with the nourished soil of your soul." She speaks into the vanilla-scented air, the flame a copper flicker. The heat is high in the nest, and the windows are all opened to the wild New York draft and harsh exhaust, a cold current. "He needed to go learn how to enrich his own soil so he didn't continue to steal nourishment from yours," she tells me. "You are about to blossom, free of Justin's heaviness."

I smile a fraction. "I like that." Inspired by her loving confidence, I am energized.

"And little love, believe me," the Ballerina says, "the best is yet to come. This is our time."

"Our time?" I can't imagine a future without Justin. Yet the status quo of our shared life is no longer an option. That path has disappeared, with him. Now tomorrow is unknown; without him, the future is again a mystery—

We light sandalwood incense and play Lana Del Rey in the dark, huddled on the dusty hardwood floor. Though I have three chairs, two of them cushioned, the ground is our space—down beneath the old white linen curtains billowing and twisting in the breeze like dancers, animated.

For the rest of the night, we do not speak of Justin.

35 Days until Deadline

Lying beside Corrina's sleeping profile, her breath steady but silent, I savor her good words. I didn't cause this, my husband's retreat from the world wasn't personal. His disappearance was not about me, it was pathological—the persistent need to escape, to run away.

I jot the Ballerina an upbeat note and walk out to get coffee, inspired by the thought of untapped power Corrina conjures in me. As I wander west, I consider with numb objectivity the seduction of vanishing: *Why might someone choose to disappear? Why might a person leave their life, traceless?*

Many valid and powerful reasons to feel dissatisfied with our present culture flock to my awareness. As philosopher Jiddu Krishnamurti observed, "It is no measure of health to be well adjusted to a profoundly sick society."

People spend their whole careers working in offices, executing tasks that they don't honestly care about—just to survive and fit in and be seen as successful, in the eyes of our society. Justin refused to do that.

When a person becomes discontent with his or her world, three options surface: attempt to transform the problematic aspect of the status quo; or accept it; or leave it.

Justin left it. I only wish he had taken me with him.

The idea of simply and completely vanishing from one's life—leaving behind all responsibilities, debts, and troubles—is a little exciting. I intimately know the intrigue of this urge. Of course, I left mine, too—a choice that led me to meeting Justin in the mountains.

Focused on my stepping feet, I am surprised to see the High Line's concrete walkway, the skyline over the Hudson River now edged with a dead garden, withered blooms. I stand stunned amid the skeletons of dry peach roses, tiny blossoms brittle in the February sunlight; as if my consciousness had left the brick-and-mortar world, I have no recollection of the terrain along my long walk westward. I have been wholly occupied by missing Justin.

32 Days until Deadline

At Joe Coffee, I type with vigor and intention. Just over a month remains until my final deadline, and my blood tingles with commitment. Yesterday, I worked for nine hours, and today I will devote twelve or fourteen, until dreams. Two weeks sober, intently focused, I've developed an empowering routine. I believe I've turned a corner, out of the blackness and into clear skies of lucidity and action, a precise strategy:

The nature of insight is mysterious, but the formula of creativity isn't; it is simple, a clean function of time. Writing spawns writing, ideas trigger ideas. One day off—removed from the interactive thought-dance called *writing*—is really two days lost.

I want to preach this methodology, as it's been working—and today I do so, to a sweet old man at Joe. The poor guy is clearly bored, not a writer himself, and he invents an "emergency" to flee me.

31 Days until Deadline

Valentine's Day arrives like a pink and crimson glow over the city, the window-shops and restaurants all decked with red balloons and paper hearts.

I avoid the world today, leaving Joe at noon, not wanting the romantic energy to make me remember.

Returning to the apartment a little sadder, I check my phone—sometimes I leave it home, to aid my focus. I see an email from Aaron Philip, whom I haven't once spoken with since Justin left, no longer present for him.

He tells me that he misses Justin and me, and he shares a poetic fantasy about "a lady with wings" collapsing his bedroom window into crystals. "It's not just a lady," he writes. "It's my mother."

The innocence of Aaron's words pulls me back to memories of our last winter, Justin bringing him a book about the universe and inquiring into what most activated his spirit.

Aaron hasn't seen his mother in person since he was five, and yet she remains the angelic subject of his imagination. Ever since the Lockwood concert, I have been picking up my own mother's calls again—but the depth of our pooled connection remains shallow. Aaron's persistent, pervasive love touches me.

Unfocusing my eyes on the blue afternoon, the air outside my window glittering with windblown specks of yesterday's fluff-snow, I know what I should do—

Answering my call, my mother's voice sounds upbeat. "Hello?"

"Hi Mom," I say. "Happy Valentine's Day."

"Sweetheart, thank you." She pauses. "How are you? How's the weather in New York?"

"Probably the same as Boston," I say. Below, silver frost sparkles on the black street. "It snowed the other day." For a few moments, my mom remains silent, and I add nothing more. It is as if we have both forgotten how to small talk with the common vigor, to speak happily of the inconsequential. Then I blurt, "Justin's in Colorado."

"You talked to him?" she asks.

Consciously, I haven't told anyone but Corrina about my secret window into Justin's life, worrying my discovery might be condemned as an invasion of privacy. "No, Mom, I really don't want to talk about this right now," I say sharply, though *I* had brought him up. "I should get back to work."

30 Days until Deadline

I wake up tired at dawn—I've slept only two hours. Lately, I feel constant grogginess, exhausted so often. I've long had a reckless sleep schedule, not prioritizing resting; but when neglecting bedtime in the past, acute focus would become a challenge, while nowadays my wakefulness feels like a blessing, a gift—I possess stolen hours for writing, which I view as only good.

Rising for the day, I log into my husband's email, just to check if there's anything new. Today, it's only spam.

Writing in bed for hours, I witness the eastern sky fade and new sun break. Eventually surrendering to my need for caffeine, I stumble west, to Joe.

28 Days until Deadline

Ordering my coffee at McNally Jackson, I realize it's my first time returning to this big-windowed café-bookstore since I met the Parisian man who lost his belt. Disturbed by this thought, the intruding echo of that night, I'm grateful I've gone eighteen days without a drink.

I settle in at a small table—and see I have an email from my agent saying that Betti Bilson, the inebriated lady who declared that she was going to make my movie, actually *has* reached out. She is interested in making my love story with Justin into a feature film, requesting something called an exclusive shopping agreement in which she would pay nothing up front. "The only chance of compensation would be after your manuscript gets accepted by your publisher," my agent explains. "Betti has already sent over a contract for us to review."

Immediately, I google "Betti Bilson"—finding that her award-winning clientele includes Britney Spears, Snoop Dogg, the Red Hot Chili Peppers, Bruno Mars, Willie Nelson, and Miley Cyrus. She is an accomplished music video producer, though she has never produced a feature film.

This seems a rare opportunity, yet it's difficult to gauge if it's legitimate.

~

Wandering the cobblestone grid of SoHo, my phone rings—a private number. Passing a boutique wherein the mannequins are big stuffed teddy bears in pink and yellow skirts, I answer, a little excited, "Hello?"

"Aspen! This is Betti Bilson. How have you been, girl?" After a minute of friendly chatting, she tells me, "I want to fly you out to Los Angeles for our movie meetings!" She says her industry connections are excited to meet me and I'd stay the week in her spacious home's extra bedroom, "just a block away from the Pacific Ocean."

Having only visited Los Angeles once, I am growing excited, feeling lucky. I tell her, "That sounds pretty amazing."

After we hang up, I feel the terrible pressure; this deal would add stakes to the book's completion. Although I've been writing freely, swiftly creating, I have over a hundred pages left to compose in order to complete the entire draft.

I realize there are only two outcomes: Either I miss the deadline, have to pay back the first part of my advance, and lose the book and movie deal; or I meet the deadline, receive the next payment, and possibly have a film about my life.

Back home, I respond to my agent's email: "I want to do this." I sign the contract—agreeing to let Betti put my not-yet-existent book onto the silver screen.

27 Days until Deadline

In the hostile cold of night, I take a walk with Nic, our first outing together since I marched away from her in drunken fury. A huge rat darts across the sidewalk before us, into the gap between the blackness of the park's gate; I tell her, "Everything Justin did to me, he did to Allie." In detail I explain the new discovery. "I'm grateful to know that I didn't cause this," I announce, a little defiant. I grin at her. "Because clearly Justin's soil hadn't been nurtured as well as mine." I echo Corrina's exonerating words.

But my mentor doesn't smile back. We turn a corner of the park's boundary, our pace quickening. "Truthfully Aspen," she says, "you gave him no choice but to leave. The same as Allie did."

Her sharp words hurt. "I don't think so," I mumble. But I don't want to fight with Nic; I am too tired. Trying to redirect the conversation, I share something I know that she'll be happy about: "I quit drinking." Nic is also sober, and she has penned two renowned books about addiction and the quiet beauty of sobriety. "Writing's been much easier, ever since."

"I think that's excellent," Nic says. She smiles big. "How long's it been?"

I shiver in the wind. "Almost three weeks," I say. Then I tell her about the movie deal, excited.

She warns me to be wary—her first book, *Five Men Who Broke My Heart*, was optioned for film *three* times. "And nothing real ever came of it." But her dark eyes shine golden with love, not disapproval. "Basically, that's great you're focusing better on your book and fantastic you're sober."

Feeling heartened, so lucky she is still in my corner, I kiss her on the cheek, surprising us both.

22 Days until Deadline

One starless night, still sipping coffee ten minutes before Joe closes, I get a text from a number I don't recognize. The message compliments my "wildly engaging" Modern Love story and my "vivid" writing style. Another message appears, this one from a different number, also flattering. I study the nameless admirations, wishing to make sense.

"I would love to meet with you. A producer could pick you up and bring you to the set in Greenpoint where we'll be shooting GIRLS," the first stranger writes.

Then a third unknown phone number adds, "Tomorrow. How's that sound?"

My mind smiling with curiosity, I look through the many messages, excitedly grasping for a fuller picture of what's happening—*Who is this? Who would love to meet with me?*

Face glowing with wonder, I study my phone—until I get another message from the initial number: "By the way, this is Lena Dunham!"

My chest is beating, an energetic bird. I whisper, "Holy fucking shit," feeling at the verge of giggling, my head a spill of technicolor glee—and I wonder if it was Betti Bilson who mentioned me to Lena.

Once home, I slip out my fifth-story window, into the fresh black air. On the frosty rooftop, I twirl as if wearing an invisible ball gown, excited as a new butterfly discovering itself.

Flapping my arms in the half-dark, the neon lights of MacDougal Street color the ground beneath my building red and pinkish in the cold dimness of late winter. The air smells of Indian spices from a restaurant below me, that old pavement an alternate universe of normalcy.

Elated, forcing my tone to be casual, I text back Lena Dunham and her *Girls* team: "I'm available tomorrow! Anytime :)."

21 Days until Deadline

The sky vibrant as tropic water, I wait inside a Starbucks in the West Village to be picked up by someone from *Girls*—I can't sit still, too giddy.

Through the glass, I see an elegant man, thirty-something and handsome in a tan suit, standing as if waiting. I step out into the cool sunshine and boldly say, "I'm Aspen. Are you—?"

"Yes!" He introduces himself as Jordan, an associate producer with the show. "You ready to head over to set?"

Jordan and I take the subway to Brooklyn together, and we make polite conversation, but I feel my words are awkward. I shift my weight from one foot to the other, back again, very conscious of my body as the train sways. Under my jacket, I am wearing Justin's old Pink Floyd T-shirt with a rainbow through a crystal, and I wish I had dressed up more.

When we emerge from underground, after just a minute in the light, he brings me into a nondescript corner bar: an on-location shoot at Bar Matchless. The space is dimly lit and crowded with walkie-talkies and dark jeans.

It is the actors' lunch break, and Jordan leads me through the crew, to a packed table. Lena Dunham and her collaborator, Jenni Konner, are sitting with a few others at a booth, the big curved wooden bench worn smooth from years.

Over salads, Lena asks me a long string of earnest questions about survival on the trail, curious and excited. "You are so brave, mosquitos for five months would be my hell," she jokes. "What did you eat? Did you have Gatorade or drink the wild water?"

I giggle. "I drank from streams and springs," I say, a little proud. "All the food I had was packaged, lots of granola bars and chocolate. I was ultra-light, I didn't carry a stove, so everything I ate in the four months before I met Justin was cold." She is leaning toward me, transfixed by the experience I shared. "Each night, I slept in my little tent I pitched, and sometimes I cowboy-camped, which means sleeping directly on the ground, under the stars."

"I can't *imagine* sleeping on the ground for so many months without showers, you're amazing." She asks about what foods I craved most in the woods, and about my life now. From her fascination, it's apparent that she has read my essay with care, hungry for more insight. Lena explains, "I am interested in playing you in a movie."

When she asks when the book will be out, I tell her I'm submitting my manuscript in less than a month, and the memoir will be published "soon."

After lunch ends, she invites me to stay. During filming, I run to the bathroom, shutting the creaky door with a loud bang—actually disrupting the production. I didn't know that you have to be silent on set while they're shooting. "Oh my God, I am so sorry," I say, embarrassed.

But Jenni Konner smiles and waves her hand, unfazed. "Don't worry about it," she tells me. "It happens all the time, for much stupider reasons." Her kind response makes me feel at ease.

Later, I sit in a tall black folding chair in video village, the little closed-off area where the producers pace, a makeshift "backstage" office. "You can watch the shoot on these monitors," a young production assistant shows me, pointing to the different little screens that softly broadcast in real-time the scene that is being filmed just twenty feet away. The crew stares at the monitors with interest, the scene reshot again and again, and again.

Watching Lena's face on the screen, I imagine how cool it would be to see her as *me* in a film. Fantasizing about Hollywood, I anticipate my post-submission visit, already suspecting that my host, Betti, is today's unseen puppet master.

Feeling inspired, I grab my laptop from my bag, start writing, typing as quietly as I can, desperate to not waste this miraculous opportunity.

19 Days until Deadline

Dressing in the dazzling sunshine of my bedroom, I am dizzy—a little sad, and I don't know why. I should be blissed out, given my sweet luck—Betti Bilson and Lena Dunham—and the miracle milestone of today: one month sober. Yet, in the mirror, I see my profound aloneness. In stillness, I am terribly aware that none of this grand magic would be happening, if not for Justin.

He worked so hard to save so much, so we could live and I could write. He'd led me to The New School, to Nic Solomon—created this *all*. I consider how, in ways, he was more like a guardian angel than simply a husband. And still, I miss coming home to him.

Descending flights of stairs, I realize that the first of March is just three days away—rent will be due, but for the first time, I won't have it. Justin and I were never once late to pay.

Wanting to communicate the situation before it's an issue, I knock on the third-floor door of my building's superintendent, Tomas. A good-natured older man from Mexico, he answers the door in stained beige work coveralls. "Yes?" Already he seems annoyed, and for a moment I fear that I have woken him.

"Hi Tomas," I say, bracing myself for possible eviction. I ask him, "Would it be possible to pay March and April together, in a couple weeks?" I tell him that I'll be getting paid soon.

He scrunches up his face, slowly nods. "Sooner is better."

14 Days until Deadline

I write at Joe as hours pass, oblivious to sundown, typing a memoir passage in which I met a black bear on the trail at yellow dusk. When I look up, the ground outside is black, a streetlamp casting twin golden rings of light, like orbs—I've been working for six hours, without standing. My final deadline for submission is in just two weeks—I'm overwhelmed, genuinely uncertain if I'll be able to deliver.

In line to get a fourth coffee at 7:00 p.m., I feel a hand on my shoulder; I turn to see the man I woke beside the morning after the last time I was drunk, the night I forgot Val. He smiles at me, and my stomach tightens with guilt. He speaks words I barely hear. His tone jolly, he has no idea about the impact of our night together—and I realize that he marks an ending, new freedom from an era of self-obliteration.

I smile back at this man I barely know, relieved he'll never drink with me again.

I've been sober for nearly forty days now—I *can* do this. I will meet my looming deadline *because* I am not drinking.

Sitting down with my hot coffee, I face a gap of time that's been absent from my memoir, too sad to remember, the day I met Justin:

I first saw him in the river-cut woodland city of Bend, Oregon. He squinted at me, said hi. I said hi back. We were both in town to get hot food and a bed, rest our legs and shower, as hikers did about once a week or so. You can always spot a thru-hiker by their filthy clothes. Even after they've been washed and no longer smell pungent, gray dirt darkens the armpits. His were nearly black.

He told me his trail name, "Dash," but I forgot it right away. I'm pretty bad with names. I did remember that he was handsome, remembered his slick muscles, his suntan, his big lips, ice blue eyes bright under thick, dark lashes. He had big hands and muscular arms strung with veins. He was tall. I was blinded by him, as if I'd looked at fire and then away, into the dark. Then he left. I stared at the blue door to the stairwell, wishing I knew his real name.

Later I noticed a torn shred of paper tucked under my black journal: his number. I called, and he invited me to join him "on the ball field across the street."

Showing up to meet him, I sat next to him cross-legged in the outfield of a baseball diamond at dusk, and his knee brushed mine. He smiled. I smiled, too. "What's your name?" I asked him.

He stared right at my eyes, squinted, his eyes were so bright, pool blue. He told me, "You asked me that fifteen minutes ago."

I didn't look away. I could hardly breathe. I felt like my face was on fire, I was burning up. He was so damn hot. "Sorry, I don't remember."

The sky was cooled-coal gray, we talked for hours, night erasing the trees around us. He was almost 30, he told me. I was 19 with that narrow sense of what I wanted. I didn't know quite how to talk to him. He was an adult. I had no allure. I had no style. My secret fear was that he'd be able to sense that I had never been loved romantically by a boy ever, and find that there was a detectable reason for it.

I do my best to recreate the thrilling time we were first falling. Writing, I am wistful, my heart with my lost groom—I have returned to the strange beauty of the trail, our origins there, trading histories and flirting in the outfield.

Rereading the brief page, I see with pride that the bliss of new love's western pinewood mountain summer is not impossible for me to capture.

9 Days until Deadline

Corrina texts to ask if she can sleep over tonight, her words seeming urgent. My stomach churns with nerves—I know I should be writing, but she has been present for me every hour of my need, reliable as the sun. Book submission pressure swelling, my stress ballooning, at dusk she steps inside my turquoise walls.

Arriving, her eyes are etched with veins, cheeks streak-bleached with past tears. I immediately hug her—arms wrapped firm around her long strawberry-blonde hair, which smells of coconut. "Is everything okay?" I whisper, letting go.

She sits down in the big soft white chair, trying to smile, her slim frame folding, graceful as a fawn. Her elegant cheekbones still pink from winter's wind, freckles radiant. "It is." Her eyes fall shut. "I just sometimes don't know what I'm doing here."

I sit down on the floor, listening. Looking up to her, I ask, "Here in New York?" Her arms are crossed in a loose pretzel across her stomach, and she subtly hugs herself with open hands.

"I overslept this morning," she eventually says. The Ballerina explains how she showed up to her shift at the vegan restaurant an hour late. She tells me, her hushed voice wavering, "I still haven't found my place in this city."

I stare at her in wonder, astonished to know that she'd been feeling lost. Then I tell her, "Me either." Sad to see her so vulnerable, wanting to help her as much as she's helped me, I stumble over my words. "What makes you feel that way?"

Her eyes sparkle with water; she doesn't answer. And wishing to transmute this space into a soft oasis, to brighten things somehow, I light every candle I can find—a scented circle of little flames around us. We sit together on the cold wood floor, and without planning to, feeling safe in her gaze, I tell her, "I never deserved Justin." The whole room flickers, white and golden.

"Aw little bird," the Ballerina says. "Why would you think that?"

I know the answer, but I'm ashamed. "Because he took care of me," I confess. "I've never put my contact lenses in my eyes, myself. It was always Justin. That's why I've only worn glasses since he left." The words humiliate me as soon as I speak them, but they are honest.

"I'm certain that if you tried, you'd be able to," she says. She plays with my hair, her posture upright.

"I just can't. I cannot touch my eyes."

Corrina finishes a tiny braid in my messy curls. "Now it's time to learn."

"I've tried for years." I blink at her, thinking how I have failed and failed.

For the rest of the evening, we type by candlelight. Close to her, I can sense my angelic friend's soft sadness, her blues a kindred song—a young artist who crossed her own forest, as I have, to New York. I think how, long ago, I stopped the Ballerina from vacating her mission in Manhattan; now, she is making this island sweeter for me, rescuing me from wintery isolation.

8 Days until Deadline

At dawn, the Ballerina and I climb the rickety fire escape, and on my rooftop, we have a silly little ceremony: shouting out our wishes to the pearly sun hovering just above the horizon, faint beyond clouds. We are holding hands, noses pink in frigid air. "This place is becoming a Ballerina Nest," I tell her, "your namesake," and she smiles.

1 Day until Deadline

The night of March 16, the last hours before submission, I construct my book's final scenes, painting the world of my wedding, unstoppable.

This is the first time I've thought of that occasion without pain, and flooded with confidence, my heart directs my hands, my mind freer.

For days, I haven't left the turquoise walls, except to pick up nuts and deli cheese—sprinting through my home-stretch, inspired by wild promise as I type.

There's no chance of sleep tonight, working with my whole heart, believing that *this is it*—it's all going to happen: the movie deal, every blessing.

0 Days until Deadline

At 4:00 a.m., washing my hands, I am powerful with adrenaline, bolder. At the mirror over my bed, I feel possessed as if a switch has flipped, and I open a new box of contact lenses. Squatting on my mattress—after my whole life of trying and missing, in about two minutes total—I put my contacts in, myself, for the first time.

As I blink in the second lens, my room and my story come into clear focus. Looking at my face without glass and wire adorning it, I beam with joy.

Then, jittery and proud, I reread my final chapter, the sun in my eastward window flashing, resting in the center of the glass. Light kisses my cheeks and fills my tall mirror with bright silver. Dawn rising blue, I skim my book; staring at the end—

I submit.

21

CITY OF ANGELS

In the clear and early sky, blue as soft hydrangea petals, I boarded a big gray plane with red wingtips. And just like that, only six days after the submission of my book, Betti Bilson pulled me out of the East Coast cold, and toward the honeyed endless spring of California.

Threading dense clouds, I listened to playful music, the soundtrack of my daydreams. White sunlight on my face, enraptured in skyway hypnosis, smiling, I held within me a wildness, an invisible zest as strong as desire itself—a latent braveness beneath my girlish skin.

Looking out the airplane window, I caught a faint reflection of my naked eyes; wearing contacts that I'd put in myself, I felt liberated from codependence—freed of long helplessness. In my confident image in the sky, I saw a serendipitous symmetry with my other bold flight to Los Angeles, five springs prior—to begin the Pacific Crest Trail.

A cheerful flight attendant gave me a plastic cup of sparkling water, the bubbles hopping on the surface in a fine, cool mist. "Would you like to purchase anything to eat?" she asked me.

My stomach felt cramped, too empty—but I still hadn't paid my March rent, though the month was nearly over. "No thanks," I told her. Yet I wasn't worried. The second part of my book advance would be arriving any day. Hopefully, I would eat tonight with Betti.

We floated above an ocean of luminescent silver clouds, lit from within by a low sun—and I realized we were in the skies of Colorado.

In a still moment in the air over a mountainous world hidden by shining haze, I imagined what Justin might be doing—where he was, down there. Drifting over the Rockies, content, I hoped that he was feeling as whole as I was. For the first time, I wondered how these months had changed him. Looking down at my notebook, I was shocked to see that I had doodled his name.

Returning to earth, grounded, the California air was warm and dry, the hot winds sweet, like unseen lilac blossoms. Above me, great palms decorated the perfect cobalt sky, their sprawling leaves as flat as huge green feathers.

Betti Bilson picked me up at the airport, herself. I loaded my luggage in her trunk, just a single bag: one tiny dark green suitcase. "Very minimalist," Betti said. "*Love* it." Hugging me, she smelled of cinnamon and rose.

In a shiny SUV, we glided into cloudless dusk, windows down, pop music soft under an overpass—and onto the widest highway of my memory.

I didn't know much about this City of Angels, and some of my friends had said bad things about it. I'd heard the city was a place of vanity and "bad values." In *The Brass Verdict*, Michael Connelly wrote Los Angeles "was a transient place. People drawn by the dream, people running from the nightmare. Twelve million people and all of them ready to make a break for it if necessary." I was nervous, braced to confront the hostility of anonymity, an uncaring metropolis that was alienating and vast.

Yet this world appeared pastel, all fresh. Strange trees we passed seemed tropical, exotic.

Bubbly and attentive, Betti spoke with enthusiasm. "I devoured your book," she told me, her tenor warm. Along with my editor, I had sent her a copy of the manuscript on March 17. "It's *so* good. Wonderful writing, lady." I was encouraged, a promising sign. Then she asked me, "Everything's still on to publish in late summer?"

"Yes!" I answered quickly. "Definitely."

"So exciting!" She reached over and double squeezed my shoulder. "Thank you for surviving everything you've been through. I can't wait to move forward with the movie."

We parked outside a slate-gray home with modern metal stairs. Betti's place, where she lived with her fiancé she jokingly called "Mr. Big," was a mansion overlooking a glittering waterway. Out western-facing windows the sun was a blond globe in hazy ether, the canal golden. "Make yourself totally at home," she told me. "The fridge is always way too full, eat anything."

Opening the refrigerator, I felt tremendous relief: Not only did I have a place to stay, but it was fortuitously filled with milk and eggs, fresh vegetables, and cartons of leftovers—I wouldn't have to spend a dime on food.

Betti showed me to the lower level. On the wall hung a huge painting of a young woman's stoic face—she looked a lot like me. I was stunned by the resemblance, almost scared.

My room, a stunning white alcove, was suspended like a floating bubble over the water. I had my own private deck, a low balcony above the shimmering brook. Stepping out into the hallway, giving me space to rest and unpack, Betti called back, "Get settled! Then come join me for a drink." Sliding my compact baggage under the bed, I thought about how fun it might be to have one cocktail with this interesting woman.

When I returned to the main living room, Betti was sprawled on the couch, smoking a joint, a bottle of Riesling on the blue-glass coffee table beside her. She outstretched her arm, extending the weed to me by way of invitation.

"Can I run and grab some food real quick, first?" I asked her. "I pretty much forgot to eat today."

After a moment of squinting at my face, as if trying to remember something, she told me, "Go for it."

In the kitchen, I loaded a plate up with leftover Mediterranean food and roasted chicken, famished. I poured myself a glass of milk, to the brim, then settled in on the couch beside her, chewing.

"I'm feeling amazing about you," Betti announced, kicking her feet up on the delicate table. Pouring herself a glass of wine, she began to tell me about her vision for the movie—shot on film, *not* digital, a retro, hazy look. She raved about all the "totally brilliant" people we'd meet in the coming week; grabbing a second long-stemmed glass—for me—she filled it halfway. "More?" she asked. When I didn't say anything, she winked. "Don't worry, we've got another bottle."

After so much restraint and focused work, having a little fun tonight—even though it would break my personal promise—felt justifiable. And I wasn't feeling sad, so if I drank tonight it wouldn't be in pursuit of numbing my heart. I stared at the half-full glass she was offering, the palest canary yellow, glinting in the ceiling's pendant lights like a cat's eye.

As if seduced by a sweet memory of oblivion, I lifted the pretty cut-glass stem, cradling the smooth bowl of its round flute in my hot palm like a friendly crystal ball, my comfort. But tired from the flight, I knew that if I took a sip, I'd probably fall asleep within the hour. "Thanks," I told her. Then I added, my conviction growing, "But I want to be fresh for our meetings tomorrow." Without having a single swallow, I placed the glass back down.

Betti slapped a hand on her thigh and smiled, as if I'd said something comical. "They're on *Monday*," she told me, catching her balance. "Tomorrow's all yours, babe."

In my room that night, the water and wild heavens through my window blacked-out for the evening, I was proud of myself for resisting, besting the stabs of nostalgic desire. Feeling capable of anything, excited for the coming week's boundless unknown, I removed my contact lenses.

At peace, I fell fast into dreams.

~

The peach sun on the canal awakened me early. My glass room was a greenhouse, heating with the day, the water a silver branch of light. I checked the time, astonished to find that it was only 6:57. Rising early was a new experience, altering how I knew myself to act—the early light spotty and fresh for me to witness, formerly only observed on rare mornings that marked the endings of all-nighters. I put my contacts in; today it took me half an hour, struggling with missing.

Upstairs in the sunny kitchen I drank a gigantic glass of milk; and another. My stomach vibrated with a soft groan of ongoing hunger. Betti was awake also—she had already taken a jog along the ocean. Making us scrambled eggs and peppers, she called me a go-getter. "A morning person, after my own heart," she declared, showing me how easily I could redefine myself, here.

After breakfast I walked from Betti's house, along the morning water, buoyant. The young sky was effervescent blue, friendly, not a lone white wisp. Each beachfront home seemed to have different exotic flowering trees and cacti, the air salty and sweet, a clean sea breeze. The sun high, my swinging arms were warm and copper. I felt calm and strong—what was this strange feeling? Not recognizing it, I paused, stopped walking. It struck me: happiness. It had been so long—I was *happy*. I took a photo of a purple jacaranda tree, a thousand tiny blossoms shaped like bells.

Passing a house the color and texture of sandstone, I noticed a golden rain tree, like a willow made of vibrant yellow blooms, long hanging bunches shaped like lilac clusters of little gold-white petals, pointing earthward. Beside it grew a smaller mimosa tree with its fluffy pom-pom fans of beige and pink, whimsical blossoms. I could not get over the wild and eclectic beauty of this Los Angeles morning, stopping to take a picture every few steps—walking nearly two miles to get a coffee at cheerful Intelligentsia Coffee in central Venice, an industrial warehouse transformed into a "caffeine laboratory" and brew bar. The space was huge and chic, a system of glass tubes and a hanging bicycle high above my head.

But too excited to sit still, I just kept walking, warm coffee in my hand. Wandering without thought, I emerged into a completely *other* world, beautiful beyond reference. The sidewalk-lined street became a pathway along a ribbon of water, iridescent blue.

A few boats passed in a row, and next a beaming man paddleboarding down the water. I had happened upon a sunlit network of sapphire canals with white arched bridges, a sanctuary—led here by effortless chance.

Quirky houses lined the pathway, quaint against bright water. An imaginative Victorian was sunset-colored, candy pink and clementine. A great treehouse had a rope-swing sized for a giant, the odd structure overlooking the walkway like a lanky lighthouse of the jungle. The air smelled of wild rosemary, and the curious homes seemed surreal in their bewildering emergence.

Colorful kayaks were hitched to wooden docks. A shadowed stretch of the water's edge was lined with violet and blue canoes. Walking, I felt I was intruding, entering private backyards of homes with large doors open, the people inside sprawled on their sofas and cooking in the kitchens. Yet no one seemed to mind my presence here. A couple out power-walking passed me swiftly. Then a petite young woman on a jog slipped by.

I didn't feel like I was in LA—or any city, at all—but rather, this grid of brooks and bridges felt like somewhere completely different, an elsewhere of fantasy. I wondered if I'd discovered an obscure treasure, or if this web of waterways was well known; I couldn't understand how

I had never heard of such a place. I imagined moving to Los Angeles, right here. Living serene off the beaten path, the scenery of goodwill.

Stepping across a bridge, I stood above flowers of every color, all hugging the calm water. The day was not too hot and the beach breeze felt loving, like kisses in the quiet—I was emotional, as if I'd won something. And in a blissful little area of my chest, the heavy atmosphere of my heart was lightening.

Across the water's border, a divide, a mom and father ambled along the path with two little kids, the smaller one gripping her mother's hand. In a warm pang, I felt grateful for my parents. Though they didn't even know that I was on the West Coast now, I longed for a future time akin to childhood—a bygone world when I could tell them anything.

I passed a yellowed home with a crepe myrtle tree, exotic ruffled orangey-red blossoms native to Southeast Asia. A few doors down, an evergreen pear tree stood with its tiny white lacy petals, delicate and pure as summer frost, impossibly graceful. In forgiving sun, I strolled and said good morning to an old man with a pink shirt walking his golden retriever; to a gay couple in broad sun-hats, their tiny baby in a big-wheeled stroller, greeting the faces of this otherworld.

Back at Betti's, fascinated by the complex of bud-lined canals I'd stumbled upon so auspiciously, I curled up with my laptop, researching. I learned that Abbot Kinney, the developer of Venice, had sought to evoke the appearance and essence of Venice, Italy—and exploring his creation, I'd truly felt transported.

I wanted to share this vision with the world. I'd deactivated my Facebook in New York, needing to preserve time; but now, that reasoning felt moot, obsolete—I was done with the draft, free! And I missed how posting photos made a scrapbook of my life, capturing my favorite moments and granting me an access back to them. So I reactivated my account and uploaded a picture, my very favorite: a red rowboat with big black polka dots, like a ladybug resting on soft-blue water, its interior shining snowy white. A tall palm tree in the background reflected in the channel's calm surface, straight and softened.

I fell asleep at 8:00 p.m. that evening, serene yet still dead-depleted from last week's mad rush to completion, my computer resting on the pillow beside my cheek.

~

For our first meeting, Betti drove us to a "mystery place," as she called it, a parking lot outside a huge white tower. Cylindrical, the space was grand—Capitol Records.

On a high floor with a panoramic view of hills and sunlit buildings, we gave our names to a pretty receptionist in a leather jacket who recognized Betti. "Hello beautiful!" the lady said, "Alex is expecting you two." She ushered us down a pearly hall to a closed door, knocked, entered alone; in less than half a minute, she came back out. "He's ready for you," she said. It all felt so important and official.

Inside, a slight man, thirty-five or so, sat in an ivory swivel chair behind a big wood desk with his legs crossed. He was casual, wearing jeans and a faded gray T-shirt. The walls around him were decorated with gold and platinum records in clear frames.

Listening in on their industry talk, I was excited in this room, sitting between the woman who would make my movie and a successful music producer. When I finally got a word in, I asked, "Alex, I'm so curious. What's your vision for the adaptation of my book?"

He smiled, his eyes vacant. Then his countenance became interested, lively. "You wrote a *book*?" He told me he was working on one, himself.

"This is Aspen, she's amazing," Betti cut in. She winked at me. "I knew you two should know each other."

By the time we said goodbye to Alex, an hour or so later, it seemed that this meetup with Betti's "film-industry connection" was really a hangout with a friend of hers. A cool glimpse into the world of music, but it wasn't really about our movie, at all.

On the drive to our next "big meeting," I was starting to feel a little skeptical. I asked her what the objective of that hour with Alex had been.

"Alex will do the music for the movie, he's brilliant. Sound mixing in film is more important than anyone realizes," she said. "One of his guys won the Oscar for it."

I remembered my dad had told me that the soundtrack was the factor that made Hitchcock's classic *Psycho* terrifying—that the sly way the great director got the movie approved under the strict production code of the time was by screening it without sound, thereby muting the resonance of the frightening images.

As we pulled up to a boxy beige building in a strip mall, I grew excited, hungry to know who we'd team up with next.

Inside, we walked through a long room of cubicles where she tried to introduce me to a young man with a beard, but he said, "Betti, I'm a little busy." Loudly, Betti introduced me to a blonde woman who was seated at her desk, and she nodded, polite—said a breathless "Nice to meet you"—but answered her phone mid-Betti-sentence, when it rang.

"Welcome to my office!" Betti told me. I felt confused—these people didn't seem to work for her.

Upstairs, in a mirror-walled dance studio, we watched young woman after young woman pivot and bounce, their agile bodies graceful and athletic. After each, I said to Betti, "She is so good!" But, a former dancer herself, Betti squinted at their forms, unimpressed. Her eye must have been more discerning than my own. Confident, she shared her feedback on the auditions with the director.

I wasn't certain what I was doing in this building, Betti's workplace—this felt like take your daughter to work day. After the casting, Betti needed "a minute" to do some administrative stuff. "Go find a snack down in the kitchen," she told me.

Chewing a free granola bar, grateful to momentarily escape this day's strangeness, I emailed Nic: "You might be right about LA. Unfortunately :)." Nic's cynical outlook on potential "movie deals" felt warranted. Still, no true harm was done; at worst, Betti was my access to this sunny state of dazzling canals, the architecture of a daydreamed playground. My kind host who housed and fed me. And when this lovely free vacation concluded, I still had my New York—and my memoir, which *was* real.

Gliding down Wilshire Boulevard, I glimpsed the Hollywood sign in chalk blue hills. Speaking about the upcoming appointment, our final one today, Betti told me, "It's someone you'll probably recognize, someone *big*." I giggled, Betti's relentless hype endearing.

We arrived a full hour early at the waterfront bar where we'd be sitting down with this mystery celebrity. Betti needed a drink, so we separated, and I got some air.

Outside I followed a paved path along the beach, snaking through the buttercream sands, the palms dim poised figures in new purple nightfall.

As if floating in a dream, I passed royal blues and warm orange-ambers, and dark greens—*Starry Night* by Vincent van Gogh, the famous painting recreated on a massive scale, covering a building. Beyond, the dark water glinted, catching the butter moon. Music played from a taco shop and a loud dive bar, clashing tones, and the ocean's rustle smoothed the circus, waves ever-breaking. The salt air smelled of candied nuts and summer. It was as if I'd cheated winter.

Turning eastward along the pedestrian promenade, I passed a boardwalk mystic and a white-faced clown. A crystal ball vendor, her red wagon cart as ridiculous as it was charming.

Removing my shoes and stepping off the path, onto the soft sand of the beach, I walked along the Pacific's breathing edge. The ocean's glassy lip submerged the pallid shore, the violet-ebony atmosphere reflected on the soaked sands like an obsidian mirror. Time amorphous as in a trance, water lapping in an endless dance of crashing, spreading, and vanishing, I forgot why I was here.

My phone lit up, and I feared I'd wandered for too long. But checking, I had nothing from Betti. Instead, I saw an email from my publisher.

From the first line, I knew something was wrong. My editor called my imagery "quite striking," but ultimately, he did not feel my draft was a complete book, as of yet. I reread the message. Slowly, I understood the meaning: my manuscript had not been approved.

He requested that I take three more months to "get this right." For now, though, no more money was coming. And none would—for at least a hundred days.

Despondent, I put my sandy shoes back on and reversed my tracks on the chaotic boardwalk.

22

$EEKING

Staring out the bedroom window, back at Betti's after another hollow meeting, despair was blooming in my soul like terrible ink in water, everything drabber, the color of the ground and heavens darker. Vitality and joy recoiled from me, my future bleaker. I couldn't for one minute switch *off* my rambling brain, my thoughts distressing.

I fought to find the hidden silver lining, reminding myself that while the timetable was delayed, the book deal wasn't dead. But still the bottom line was that I didn't know how I was going to eat in the next months; pay rent; survive. At 5:00 a.m., overwrought, the sky sinister velvet, I lay on my stomach and checked my bank account balance online—I had just $527 to my name.

Propped up on bent elbows in the shadowed bubble bedroom, desperate, I googled "how to make money fast," scrolling through the search results. I needed an honest miracle. Before my face, my laptop became an optimistic list of "opportunities" and advice.

I clicked a link, an article titled "Best Ways to Earn Cash Now."

The piece suggested thirty distinct "quick and easy" strategies. I could take paid surveys; get a $300 bonus as a new Uber driver (I didn't have a car); download the Nielsen app (and collect $30); walk dogs in my neighborhood (for $18 an hour). Digging through blog posts and how-to articles, it became clear that there were many viable and legitimate jobs for someone without a college degree and limited professional experience—yet that none of them would address my urgent need for thousands of dollars.

April just days away, I called my building's superintendent. Pre-sunrise skies flat-white as bone, he answered on the first ring, "Yes?"

"Hi Tomas, it's Aspen." Through the line, I heard faint honking. "I was wondering if it's okay if my rent's a little late?" Immediately I realized how ridiculous the question sounded—it was already *very* late.

Tomas cleared his throat, breathing heavy. "You haven't paid March."

"I know," I told him. "I'm sorry." I squeezed my phone, shaky. The connection was quiet for a few nerve-racking moments. "Tomas?"

"I need you to pay," he said slowly. Though he was very kind, I knew he answered to the landlord, and collecting rent was fundamental to his job. When he abruptly hung up, I felt for the first time the fear that I could lose my turquoise walls.

I finally considered calling my parents, asking for help. But I couldn't touch the buttons. Justin had awakened in me a desire for radical self-reliance, taught me to crave the completeness of that freedom. *We can take care of ourselves,* I had grown to understand. And I wasn't going to tell my mom and dad "I need you."

The weak sky bluer in the east, I returned to my digital search—I *had to* find a solution.

~

Reading through an article about the "booming do-it-yourself economy," I found a mention of a site called Seeking Millionaire—I clicked the link.

A purple home page appeared, the white words "Seek a *richer* love life" written in a rounded serif font above an image of a well-dressed young woman with red lipstick and red nails, wearing diamonds, her elegant fingers touching a man's stern cheekbone. The couple's eyes were above the frame, cut off. I read that "Seeking Millionaire is a website where successful men and aspiring women find their soulmates and lead a finer life."

I tried to figure out how much I'd get paid, and what I'd have to do. But nothing specific was stated directly, as far as I noticed. The real question I was trying to find the answer to was: What would be expected of me? Kissing? Or simply holding hands as I escorted a man in a suit to his glamorous affair? Googling, I found real user reviews:

"SeekingMillionaire.com is the more conventional wealthy dating site, only accepting the most refined, noteworthy singles," a young woman in a pink tank top wrote on her personal blog. "It targets confident, charismatic, intelligent women who are seeking rich, successful, sophisticated gentlemen—men who, in turn, are looking for young feminine charm."

Another blogger assured interested participants that the website was legitimate and simple to navigate. She wrote, "Finding a match on this site and making 5K a month shouldn't be a laborious task." These women seemed knowledgeable, trustworthy.

Then I found a section of the Seeking Millionaire site itself, written for men who were interested in joining, that directly stated "women set their own terms and nothing is assumed. Don't expect sex," soothing my psyche. This made good sense to me, as prostitution is known to be illegal. And in this instant, the option emerged as a *real possibility*.

Once I believed that intimacy wasn't promised, I had a clearer picture of the situation: I imagined a lavish sushi date at a five-star restaurant with a wealthy entrepreneur. I'd join him out to dinner or a fancy red-carpet event, his decorative companion for the evening.

For a split second, I imagined Justin finding out. I felt the heat of defensive self-righteousness. *There is nothing wrong with this—my true friends will understand,* I thought; *they will not judge me.* And it wasn't as if I'd be selling sex—there would not be much to even denounce.

Growing confident that the pros outweighed the cons, I hit Apply.

A detailed form appeared. The registration was a little complex, yet—to my relief—for women, membership was free.

Filling out my profile, I answered personal questions. What was my age? *24.* My body type? *Athletic.* My race? *Caucasian.* My height? *5'4".* Did I smoke or drink? *Neither.* I was proud to check all of the "sober" boxes. What is your marital status?

Justin and I were still legally married—the truth was not an option. I chose, simply, *Single.*

Finished signing up, I uploaded a sole photograph: myself smiling, only my face visible in the frame.

Immediately, I received a deluge of messages. In half an hour, I had more than twenty. I opened each as they came in, interested to read them. But most were comments on my physical appearance—even on parts of me they hadn't seen, couldn't possibly know. I ignored this kind of contact, waiting for someone who seemed sincere. A black-blue raven perched on the deck's railing, eerie as a ghost.

Seven months earlier, I'd been happily in Vieques with my husband, and now I was alone, desperate for money—sifting through digital catcalls I'd invited with a numb heart.

Then I saw a message from the screen name Producer1966: "You're very lovely. I am a 48-year-old movie producer. May I take you out to dinner tonight?" His note was my only direct invitation that did not involve getting drinks or, worse, a "sleepover."

My fingers trembled. "I've never done this before," I admitted.

He replied instantly. After a brief and exhilarating exchange of banalities, we agreed to a first "date"—at 7:00 p.m., just a half-day away.

"And where shall we go?" I wrote, unsure what I was hoping he would answer.

"You can come to me in Beverly Hills or we can meet somewhere."

I thought about it for a minute, responded: "Somewhere in public, please. Can I let you know?"

After half an hour of back-and-forth, he was silent. I lay in bed exhausted, rereading our strange correspondence. Then, twenty minutes later, he wrote me back, "Sure no prob." I felt bizarre relief that he'd responded, as if he were my boyfriend and I wasn't sure if we were fighting. Then he sent, "My name's Jonathan, by the way."

I wrote back, "I'm Aspen Matis," unthinkingly forthright. "Nice to meet you, Jonathan."

~

Still awake at 8:00 a.m., my phone lit up—a Facebook comment on my Venice canal photo from my only friend who lived in Los Angeles, Suzanne. "You're here Aspen?! I'd love to see you! I'll be at Soho House in WeHo this afternoon if you want to come." Seeing her photo, I felt a moment of composure, calmer.

I dressed and went upstairs, finding Betti sipping her post-workout coffee. "Morning," I said. I asked her the best way to get to Soho House. My upbeat tone a little forced, what I couldn't tell Betti was my memoir's bad news—I truly needed her to let me stay a few more days while I figured out what I was going to do.

Her emerald eyes smiled at their edges. "Ooh, who are you meeting?" she asked me. "I'll take you, if you want."

"My one friend in LA," I joked, pouring almonds from her cupboard into a plastic baggie to take in case I got hungry later. "She's a British writer and actress, really inspiring."

Riding east that afternoon, I glanced at my phone in a discreet moment. Tilting the screen away from Betti, I saw that Jonathan had written me: "Have you decided where to meet?"

Still unsure, I didn't reply.

The ride with Betti was quiet, a little awkward, and it occurred to me that I could now find out what I'd been wondering for weeks. "Oh by the way, I wanted to ask," I began. "Were you the one who connected me with Lena Dunham?"

"The girl from *Girls*?"

I nodded. "She's interested in playing me in the movie if—"

"No, she's not right at all," Betti cut me off. "I don't know about her as you." She turned off the radio, glancing at my face. "We can do better." I was surprised by her rapid rejection of such an incredible actress, without a moment of consideration.

Twenty stilted minutes later, Betti dropped me off at Soho House. To my surprise, she insisted on waiting outside until I texted "In." Despite the hollowness of her "film producer" pretense, I appreciated her maternal hospitality.

I stepped through the looking glass, a translucent door in the garage, onto a red carpet slashing down the middle of a shiny ivory-tiled hallway, passing a metallic mosaic sculpture of a Gibson electric guitar that read "The Doors" and "Light My Fire," spotlit under blond wood walls—into a shadowy room with an unfinished concrete floor and an elegant pink and yellow leather sofa with dimpled backing and a gigantic black clock with chic Roman numerals and intricate ebony metal arms on the white-painted brick wall. The decor was eclectic and modern, a tall desk before me. Two stunning young women stood behind it, and one asked, "Who are you here to see?"

I was jittery, a little nervous. "Suzanne Heathcote, a friend," I said.

The other young lady scanned a list and told me, "Go right up, hon. Thirteenth floor." The upward ride was swift, and I felt heavy.

The elevator opened to a magnificent lobby enveloped in glass walls, a sparkling chandelier suspended above a pearly staircase, stone and crystal. Ascending, the California view boundless, I felt I was on the summit of a mountain, light-headed.

Turning slowly, searching, I spotted Suzanne, her blonde hair up in a messy little bun, intent blue eyes focused on her laptop screen. She was sitting at a small wood table that faced the clean sapphire sky, typing. This highest space was mostly hues of brown and endless air, and sunshine spilled across the expansive hardwood floor, the room intimate and warm, almost nostalgic. I touched Suzanne lightly on her shoulder.

We caught up, telling each other of our literary projects and adventures over the past months. "Nothing is going as planned," she joked of her career. An accomplished English playwright and a member of this exclusive creative club, she remained humble. Smiling, she looked pretty, like a girl with a fresh spirit, soulful and clear-eyed. I really looked up to her.

Then, as if confessing, I told Suzanne, "I did something kind of crazy today." She tilted her forehead back, not wholly convinced. "Tonight I'm going to meet up with someone—" I started, breaking into a nervous smile, feeling overheated. I regretted opening this door, already. "Have you ever heard of a site called—Seeking Millionaire?"

Suzanne's smile fell, her posture straightening taller. "What? My gosh, love. You're not doing that?"

I told her how I never had, but I was going to try for the first time, tonight. "He's a producer, and he seems really respectful," I told her. Seeing concern darkening her eyes, I assured her, "Don't worry. I'm not going to have sex with him or anything."

She took a sip of her tea, boldly holding my gaze with power. "Does *he* know that?" Not sure how to answer, I asked her how to find the bathroom.

Standing at the washroom mirror, the countertop milky granite with fine veins of soft beige and smoky gray, I considered Jonathan's intentions for the first time, what he might be expecting from our "date." The sun was caught in the vanity, reflecting relentless light, this space too bright for me to see clearly.

When I returned, Suzanne did not switch the subject, as I'd hoped. To the contrary, it seemed she'd made a plan. "If he's such a big producer, he'll be a member," she told me. "Alright, if you're going to meet him, meet him here."

Her concern seemed earnest and immovable. I messaged Producer1966, "Meet me at Soho House at 7. Are you a member?"

Right away he replied, "I'm there all the time." Then he asked, "Hey, what's your number so we can communicate without this clunky app crashing." Not consulting Suzanne, I gave it to him.

After that, the mood a little lighter, she and I decided to get some work done while we waited. For the first time since submission, I reopened *Girl in the Woods*, trying to tighten the scene where I met Justin, wishing to minimize him in my story.

At six forty-five my phone lit up: "Go and put my name down." So Jonathan was *not* a member, as he'd implied. Nervous, I asked Suzanne if she would put him on the list.

"I want to look him up," she said. "Ask his last name." Watching Suzanne's ocean eyes glint with determination, I felt the comfort of her fierce support.

After a few minutes of withholding, he texted his full name. We googled him to find out who he was. On LinkedIn, we saw the same photo that he'd used on Seeking Millionaire. He was who he said he was—a real man with a real job, who wanted to come upstairs.

Suzanne turned to face me fully. "Why would you do this?" In her stressed voice, I could tell that verifying his identity had not been the point of this search—she felt she was failing, needing to reach me. "You realize that his screen name means he was born in 1966, which means he's, what, like almost fifty? Literally twice your age."

Mortified, I told her I was sorry. "I really need—I just don't have money right now."

"I can appreciate that," she said to me. "Fine. So let's play this through." She sipped her water, her directness intensifying. "What do you really think will happen tonight?"

The sky around us was hazy grayish, indistinct. "Well tonight we're just going to have dinner," I told her. I hadn't imagined the reality of our time together with crisp detail. "I hope that he gives me some money, but I'm not really sure how that works."

As she made a scrunched-up face of disbelief, my stomach dove with shame. "Well I think how it *works* is he pays you money," she said, "and you would have to do something for that money."

"The site said that men shouldn't expect sex," I said softly.

She put her palms down on the table, closing her eyes. "There's a zero percent chance that he doesn't expect sex."

Thinking logically, I suddenly heard her. "I'm not going to have sex with him."

"But he doesn't know that," Suzanne said. She still hadn't put his name on the list.

At seven o'clock on the dot, I texted Jonathan. "I'm so sorry," I wrote, feeling a little guilty I'd misled him, wasting his time, "but I don't think I can do this tonight."

"Just put my name on the list," he responded. "And we'll hang out for a few minutes. Just to get to know each other."

Showing Suzanne his reply, she texted him as me: "I'm with a friend right now. I simply can't." I stared far out the glass, the high air now rosebud pink, day fading, and I realized that he wasn't coming up. And I was not going down. It was not worth it.

Then came something new: Jonathan's resistance. "I drove all the way from Beverly Hills," he wrote me. "Half an hour, just to come see you where YOU said you wanted to meet ME." I could hear his fledgling anger.

This time, I didn't write back, and Suzanne's expression brightened. "Join me for supper?" she invited. I shifted in my seat—of course, I could not afford a meal here. But before I could protest, she added, "Order, Aspen. It's on me."

Jonathan texted again, but I didn't even read his words, silencing my phone.

Studying the menu, I chose miso-glazed salmon, a twenty-nine-dollar entrée. When the food arrived, my friend was chatty, her respite palpable.

During dinner, my cell brightened with text after text, Jonathan madder. Seeing his swift rage, I understood that I had dodged a gunshot. I dropped my phone into my backpack—relieved and frightened by what I'd almost done.

The fish was moist and buttery, invigorated by lime and fresh cilantro, delicious.

When we finally rode the elevator down two hours later, a little after nine, Suzanne grasped my arm, hard. "Oh my God. Aspen!" Glancing where she motioned, I saw a heavy man in jeans and a blue baseball cap, a button-down and a big blazer, though he was wearing sneakers. He was sitting on the pink and golden sofa—it was Jonathan.

"Aspen!" he said, as I squinted at him, disoriented. His pudgy face was an orangey-tan that looked sprayed-on. "You *know* me."

Stuck in the moment's shock, I froze as Jonathan rose up and came closer. "Get away from her," Suzanne said, taking my shoulder.

"Should we get security?" one of the young women behind the check-in called out. "He's been waiting here for hours." He'd never made it past the old black clock.

Suzanne and I rushed along the ivory hall's red carpet, out the glass door of this bizarre rabbit hole. Entering the garage I looked back; Jonathan strode, *following* us, his refusal to hear my rejection becoming extreme. He was not running but striding briskly, his face reddening.

Locking her car doors, Suzanne sped us through the shadowy parking structure, tires screeching, as if inside a movie—outside, into sudden tranquil night.

Shaking in the passenger seat, rolling down Sunset Boulevard in silence, billboards and nail salons receding in the rearview, I felt homesick. Staring out the window at navy darkness, red and silver car lights forming blurry strings of brightness on the flowing streets of this strange city, I didn't know how I would have told my parents if I *had* left with him.

In a long moment of quiet, I finally looked down at my phone, the device now feeling sinister, like a portal. I saw Jonathan's stream of relentless texts, ranging in tone from rational to furious. I realized the extent to which I really hadn't known this man. How he could have been anyone, and I had nearly made myself completely vulnerable to him, carelessly assuming he was level-headed, good-hearted, trustworthy—all just for money.

The City of Angels held out her hand with so much beauty and so much sin. I whispered, "Thank you so much." My friend rubbed the back of my head with her careful fingertips, her eyes fixed on the road.

We passed under rows of dark palm trees, escaping the worst cross-roads of my adulthood.

23

OUTLAWS

All my "big meetings" with Betti wrapped, I couldn't stay at her house any longer; yet I couldn't return to New York—I still didn't have rent for Tomas or money for food. And I didn't want to lapse back into shoplifting, regressing. The day was boiling, though it was only 8:00 a.m., and I was pacing on Betti's porch, my bag inside all packed, not knowing where I would take it.

Impulsively, I called my in-laws' house, despite the strange context. Months had passed since Justin left, since I'd *heard from* Justin. Listening to the *ring-ring*, the dead space painful, I felt dormant resentment blooming—Walter and Lucy had concealed Allie. Withholding from me the source of their calmness, they had left me in blind darkness.

I had the urge to click End, pretend I'd never had the thought to reach them—but I was desperate.

Then Lucy answered, "Aspen!" Her tone was warm, not wary. "Hello dear." I was relieved she sounded happy to hear from me.

I greeted her, then blurted, "I have some information about your son." The words sounded more ominous than I'd intended.

"You've heard from you-know-who?" she asked, excited. I gathered from her question that she and Walter still had not. And in her eager softness, I could hear her sadness. "You two spoke?"

I told Lucy that we hadn't been in touch, "unfortunately." But I wanted to comfort her with something tangible. "Last I heard," I said, "he was renting a place in a little climbing town called Ouray, but I couldn't find an address."

"Ouray," Lucy said, "I'm writing that down."

Then Walter's voice came through—so he was also on the line—and he asked me how I knew that.

I considered sharing the truth, but the admission would be risky. Instead I lied and told him, "Trail-friends. The trail-vine."

"Thank you," Walter spoke, his voice solemn; and I heard a click but no dial tone, the line still connected.

Then I said that I was down in LA "for work"—and I missed them. "I totally understand if this isn't possible," I said, "but I'd love to come and visit you guys." The air shimmered with heat, the blue of the canals almost electric.

"I'm going to ask Justin's dad," Lucy told me, but the sentence felt dismissive. I realized that he had hung up his receiver. "If it's okay with him, it's okay with me, but we'll see," she added quickly. When we said goodbye, I feared I wasn't welcome, suspecting Walter would be too uncomfortable with me staying in the house without his son.

Checking my room at Betti's for any forgotten belongings, a lost sock or misplaced box of contacts, I could understand why Justin's parents might not want to host me. I was a symbol of their son's abandonment.

Leaving Betti a note of thanks on the kitchen counter, I zipped up my suitcase, and left.

Drifting farther from the beach, I saw white wings across a black brick building; next, a mural of a giant shirtless boy, four stories tall. And in spite of the unknown map of my tomorrow-home, not certain where I was going to sleep tonight, I felt a penetrating serenity—after surviving Soho House with Jonathan, unscathed.

When my phone rang, "Justin's Parents" showing on the screen, I answered on the first ring. "Come visit!" Lucy said. "Just tell us when."

Smiling for the first time since the news of my manuscript's rejection, I asked if I could come tonight—and she said yes. Now I needed to find my way four hundred miles to the north—

With just a few hundred dollars remaining, I bought an eleven-dollar bus ticket to Oakland.

~

Standing in fierce sun, waiting for the bus, the great blue sky looked crisper, the colors of the air itself more vivid; and my forehead baked in bone-dry heat. Like standing under a violent waterfall, sprayed with wild mist and iridescence, or wandering the waterways and flower trees of Venice, the act of returning to my husband's family without him stirred my soul, my heart enlivened and awake—I felt the thrill of unknown days ahead.

Boarding in blasting air-conditioning, less than half the seats occupied, I noticed how almost no one shared a row—it seemed that here in the city of stardust, every eye was wary.

Facing tonight's new ground, I paid more attention to everything on the road, riding in an alert mode of hyper-presence, the shades of the roadside world and my future intensifying.

Until, roaring north, dead-quiet as I passed farmland, my mind left me—drifting off, to the utilitarian phenomenon of prostitution and the startling ease with which a young woman can become compensated for the presence of her body.

Staring into my reflection in the tinted window glass, face tensed, it occurred to me how girls today exist in a tricky situation, automatically positioned atop a perilous tightrope our culture has unconsciously designed. One on which we need to be really strong and quite watchful in order to *not* monetize our youth and beauty. How easy and tempting the possibility to do so *always* was, the option undeniably lucrative and perpetually available.

Men have been willing to pay for sex since the origins of civilization—thus birthing the oldest profession—yet only very recently has this option become available to every person with an internet connection.

I had *endangered* myself—for easy money, like the black hole of a drug. Pieces of paper allowing certain men to control and access young women's bodies, *lives*. The ease and stunning accessibility of this serious brand of transaction astonished me. I was struck by the precarious nature of being a girl in this world, seductive.

Men aren't dangerous or bad, in general, I still believed—but the demographic on Seeking Millionaire is not men-in-general; rather, it's a self-selecting group, one that is signing up to purchase women. Putting myself in Jonathan's position, I understood why he was upset—he'd likely used the site before and succeeded in meeting someone; his reaction to me changing my mind was a product of the dynamic he bought into. His anger was a symptom of his expectation that I was already his.

In the clarity of a new day, distancing myself from the City of Angels, I realized I had been just a click away from a different life.

The freeway shot like an arrow through electric green fields of alfalfa sprouts, faint silhouettes of mountains receding.

Dusk was a thick blue when I knocked against my in-laws' tall wood door. Lucy and I hugged close. For dinner we ate roasted lamb chops with colorful sugar-peppers and three bittersweet salads.

After, sitting around the table, Walter showed me pictures he'd taken on their recent trip to visit family in Ireland; and my mother-in-law made the bed for me in the extra bedroom where Justin and I used to snuggle all night. Door shut, I held the blanket we'd once shared to my face and inhaled, hoping to smell him in this soft plaid so worn that the red appeared dusty pink.

Drifting off that night, I smiled at a thought: If my husband were ever officially my *ex*, then my in-laws would be my ex-in-laws—my *outlaws*.

In the morning Lucy drove me to the Elmwood Café in Berkeley, the same marble tables and countertops where Justin used to bring me.

She bought me a mug of coffee and joined me at a little table of white stone. We sat together with few words, emotional to be reunited, until finally she said she'd written something. "It's a short story about a child who's addicted to computers," she told me. Her eyes were fixed downward, on the floorboards. I instantly thought of Justin. "The child is antisocial, and the mother became concerned early. But a development specialist determined that the child had no abnormalities."

I wondered if Lucy was trying to communicate something to me about her son. "Is this fiction?" I asked.

"It is," Lucy said, lowering her voice. "The child's a girl."

When she left me to get back to work on my memoir, I typed with new freedom, revising with unfiltered sensation, raw. Nothing felt so serious or dire after the seediness and deception of Los Angeles.

Pausing to finish my coffee, I watched two cute little kids having brownies with their young parents. The boy's name my husband and I had chosen returned to me, *Winter*: the coldest season. The young father's arm draped around his wife. I had sadness—for the children we were supposed to have. For a moment I imagined Justin looking through the window, finding me under the same yellow and white striped awning lit by sun.

That evening, my sweet in-laws picked me up together, and we wandered the counterculture streets, flower-power grandmas selling knit peace symbols, a painted rainbow arching through the black sky over one of Telegraph Avenue's iconic bookstores. We strolled in the warm night's breeze together past vibrant storefronts, and Walter asked how I felt about dessert.

At Ici, an ice cream shop known for its strange flavors, I ordered Open Sesame, black-sesame lavender ribboned with golden honey cream. Savoring the cone, I felt safe.

And on a whim, I asked to stay—my husband's parents said yes. It was incredible, empowering. I discovered that unlike him, they *wanted* me.

~

Now *I* was the missing person, dropping out of my New York life, not telling anyone why. The antiquated Elmwood Café became my new office. My absolute *final* draft was due in a few months, and I was committed to rendering the essence of my long walk with integrity and truth. Living in the city where we had been newlyweds helped me to revive our brightest love, on the page. Each evening, Lucy picked me up from a day of difficult writing. She chauffeured and fed me, like a loving mother.

I felt taken care of, living in my husband's childhood house.

Over the next few weeks, Walter, Lucy, and I attended classic movies at the Berkeley Art Museum and local live theater. We took sunny day-hikes together as a unit, striding close—exploring the mountains and coastlines of Bay Area parks, apparently a family.

At home with my kind in-laws, we three were peaceful, breezy. I cooked with Lucy's tastes in mind; she did the dishes. We found a sweet routine.

And in the empty hours when my own writing was stuck, I helped Lucy revise and reimagine her sensitive short story. In her piece, the young protagonist becomes an unlikely hero. In the "fiction" my mom-in-law had written, I could see how, as flawed as one's child can appear in their mother's eyes, parents still wish to see their offspring as capable of greatness.

On a clear morning in early May, the city washed with copper light, we drove to a waterfront park, San Francisco a pale sparkle across the Bay—the first leg of an itinerary arranged for Lucy's joy. We were celebrating Mother's Day.

Eating dinner that night, Lucy inquired between bites of sautéed eggplant how things were going with my parents. She looked concerned. "Have you visited them lately?"

"I saw them a few months back," I said. I took a sip of iced tea, didn't elaborate. "Things are okay." I thought how I should call my mom tonight, but it was probably too late.

Walter glanced at Lucy. They knew about our lack of communication. His pork chop was half-consumed, the bone weak translucent yellow in the low light. "My sister went a long time without speaking to the family," he told me. "Things clear up with time."

I turned my cheeks into a smile, wanting to believe him.

After dinner, I helped my mother-in-law finish editing her short story; and she brewed flushed amber cups of English breakfast tea. "I'm writing because of you, Aspen," Lucy said softly. "Thank you for empowering me."

Late that night, I couldn't sleep; moonlight shining silver through the window, I wandered out to the main atrium and sat down into a soft lounge chair, feeling peaceful. The safety of Walter and Lucy's house was almost meditative, their transcendent kindness fueling a mysterious energy in my heart. My sense of home here opened in my mind an inquiry into the boundaries of "normal" family relationships and love, beyond the institution of marriage. I realized that both my arrival here and my in-laws' acceptance of me—independent of my husband—were unusual.

Fascinated, I began to wonder, *what is family*? And if I were to one day divorce Justin, would they still be mine?

Relationships are fluid, the state of bonds like water—I knew this from personal experience with my own. And every family is like a culture, or a country. Some are democracies; others are dictatorships, a dominant parent imposing all the rules and consequences, defining the parameters of its members—its subjects' personal freedoms. Some are peaceful; others are at war with themselves, literally violent, kid-subjects hit for breaking rules, or for no reason. Some are manipulative, fronting love but feeding their members disempowering beliefs, lies.

And the mystifying, most intriguing reality was that, from the outside, it was impossible to know what kind of culture a given family actually enacted, within it. How it operated was always largely a mystery unless it was your life.

The middle ground I stood on here was dubious; there was no seeing in without altering it—I didn't know if Walter and Lucy behaved the same with me as they did with their two sons. All I knew was that, to me, they were lovely. Together, we were peaceful yet subdued, unified in a world of a single shared heartbreak that underlay our every conversation.

The shadow of this bright connection occurred to me, shameful: here I was, living with someone else's parents, when I'd barely had a relationship with my own in so long.

~

The next evening, Walter and I took an unclouded walk together in young sunset, like I used to with my parents back in Massachusetts. Mist hung over the cerulean hills below us and, unprompted, my father-in-law told me stories about Justin as a little kid, how self-sufficient and easy he had been. "I never had to remind him to do his homework, he just did it," Walter told me. "Different than Jeffrey."

Slipping through tree-shadowed foothills in Berkeley's leafy park, we emerged from woods to a new view: sprawled out beneath us appeared the astonishing sparkling city of San Francisco, frost-pale under the redness of the last dusk of America; I asked, "Were the boys very close, growing up?"

Walter's eyes looked duller, distant. "Well," he said, staring at the fields of wild grass, "Justin was born on Jeffrey's second birthday." I remembered how at my wedding, Jeffrey joked to me that my groom had stolen his birthday, usurping him. "Justin was very independent, and his big brother wanted his approval." I learned that while Justin was an Eagle Scout, it was actually Jeffrey who had wanted to become one.

"Justin showed me his Eagle Scout project when we stayed here," I said. I smiled, recalling that era. "The set of stairs he built in the middle of the woods."

Walter nodded, his hiking posture straight and proud. He told me how Justin had been a stellar student, advanced beyond his age in mathematics, earning a full scholarship to any state school in California. "Instead, he went to Cornell." He chuckled. "One of my sons was trying to get away. And the other moved back in."

Strolling in gold dusk, I learned that something "terrible" had occurred with Jeffrey; he'd had "a kind of break," difficult to comprehend. They'd tracked him down last fall somewhere in Eastern Europe, having dropped out of his PhD program in Maryland. And since then, until recently, he had been staying in his childhood room, apparently doing little more than playing computer games, consuming an endless stream of Diet Pepsi.

What struck me was the undeniable parallel—Justin's older brother had also dropped out of his world without a word, suddenly and in his thirties, now addicted to a screen. "That must be so hard," I said. Without thinking, I added, "Justin loves computer games, too."

My father-in-law brought me deeper in the hills, up to a ridge-line trail through oaks and wildflowers, wide views of the far-off fields sprawling at our feet.

Ascending, he shared a memory from the fire, his version of the horrific story I'd only heard from Justin. While the house was being rebuilt on the ashes of the singed lot, the family endured twelve hard months of relocation. "In the makeshift housing, things changed," he said. "It used to be that Justin and Jeffrey would climb into the bed with Lucy and me each night for story time," he recalled, face downturned. "But after the fire, family story time ended."

I couldn't imagine—how could a family ever possibly be prepared for such a senseless and sudden catastrophe. "No one expects their home to burn down, it's unthinkable," I told him, hoping to provide comfort.

He told me how, in the new house, the boys had isolated themselves in the basement. "We gave them a set of video games, a brand-new Nintendo," Walter said, his voice tighter. "We just wanted to see them happy again." I thought about all the times Justin had gone into the other room with his computer and shut the door. "But it became their pacifier."

I told him he'd protected his kids and taken care of everyone as best he could. "You kept everyone alive, got your family out safely."

Walter led us higher still, through an exposed field of wild orange poppies, blue views of the distant hills rolling like waves beneath us. Pale Mount Diablo stood ominous in the distance. At the high point atop the crest, he told me, "You never know what Justin is thinking. He doesn't show many emotions. He doesn't complain, but—" He stopped his words midbreath. "It's important to my life to have my son back." Striding through the chilled, immaculate winds of the state I'd once dreamed of living in forever, wedded, my dad-in-law was too expressive to speak.

The sky was a pale pink slipper of God, and I remembered the high of my first stay in these hills, how I'd imagined the people here must be happy all the time. Of course I was nineteen, then—I didn't yet understand that the longer you look at something beautiful, the less you see it. "I miss him too," I said, seeing the pain in Walter's turbulent face.

"When Justin comes back," he told me at last, "I hope you'll forgive him."

~

The golden hour dying back home, Lucy and I moved through the shining kitchen in the orange glow of burning dusk. I turned the stovetop on, the cobalt flame appearing like a dangerous bloom, and together we cooked two separate meals—hers for Walter, who preferred meat and potatoes, and mine a more vegetable-centric meal, for us.

As I stirred a cool paprika cream yogurt and minced mint for a chutney, I felt uneasy. Walter's hope disturbed the waters of my heart, bringing to the surface the unresolved grit of everything withheld. Swallowing air, watching Lucy cook with efficiency and composure, a rehearsed dancer, I thought back to when she told me not to call the police, Walter too. They knew of their son's pattern. "Has Justin ever—" I started. "Did he ever disappear, before me?" I was not testing her, but rather wanting to confess that I was aware of Allie.

Lucy was searing lamb steaks beside the hot pot of boiling rice; she appeared to be thinking. I was seasoning eggplant and zucchini with garlic salt for oven-roasting, and we cooked in dissonant quiet. She was pensive for an awkward moment before saying only, "No. Not like this."

I was hurt, needing her to tell me the truth. Uncomfortable—I wanted to press her, but I feared this line of questions would feel to her like an interrogation.

Unaware of my turmoil, Lucy smiled broadly. Then she told me, "Having you, we've lost a son and gained a daughter."

That sharp-starred evening after tea, I sat outside amid the backyard trees, the flowers ghostly stains against the weak light of falling day— Lucy's affection inexplicably unnerving. As close as we'd become, the idea of her seeing me as one of her own shocked me. This home that had felt like an oasis, my salvation, felt different tonight, unstable at its base—*were* they my family?

Back inside, the house was entirely dark—I flipped a light, a little spooked. Tense, I climbed the wide slab-concrete stairs, compelled to go see Justin's childhood room. Model airplanes he'd assembled hung from the ceiling on clear cords. His bed was up high, on a loft; I climbed the ladder. Years earlier, engaged, Justin and I had ascended these rungs together, gleeful—his lofted bed had been sweet and whimsical in my eyes, a hideaway.

Now I replayed Walter's plea in my mind like a warped proposal. *Would* I forgive Justin if he came back? Overwhelmed, I was uncertain, not grasping the truest origin of our disintegration.

Yet I no longer felt a warmth, the relaxed pool of deep trust missing from my heart here. I felt betrayed, his parents *still* concealing, not open with me—not my own.

Back in the room where Justin and I had slept together in our new beginning, I hugged the blue pillow, lying beside a framed picture of my husband in his wedding suit the color of dry sand. His blue eyes were warmly lit, frozen on me.

Checking my Chase account online, $288.23 remained; and scouring Skyscanner, I found the soonest ticket to New York City I could afford. It was for the day after tomorrow, a $204 graveyard flight.

24

CITY THAT NEVER SLEEPS

New York's late spring was dreary as a storm-cloud. I listened to the rain as the middle-night darkness became redness, morning breaking, though I could see no sun.

I had not slept at all, and I craved the peace of rest. In day's gray light, my soul exhausted, getting up in this daze felt truly futile. The sky outside my window a brown field of haze, I lay in bed, having dreamed no dreams, wishing for a glimmer of new promise.

Downstairs, finally digging through my overfull metal mailbox, I saw a final turn-off notice from Con Edison. I hadn't paid for the gas that heated and cooled my apartment in four months, and this was my last warning before they clipped the line, leaving my home sweltering and muggy.

Hungry, I wandered in the frigid drizzle from café counter to grocery store to bodega, seeking out free samples of house-made peanut butter cookies, fresh goat-cheese brie, toasted sugar-snap-pea cracker snacks. I meandered through my city, sad and isolated; home again, my stomach content, I finally replied to Nic's sweet string of emails, all variations of the question: When are you coming back?

That night, the periphery of Washington Square Park was wistful, a shadowed path of concrete and longing. Walking with Nic, both of us talking rapidly, I told her about Los Angeles and Betti Bilson. "I was basically flown out to LA for meetings that didn't exist."

My mentor looked serene, as if she were amused.

Needing guidance, I finally broke my actual bad news, telling her of my manuscript's rejection—"I think I'm going to lose my book deal."

Nic pulled her hood up, unfazed by my frustration. "You won't," she told me flatly, stepping fast. "Needing to do multiple drafts is very common and not the end of the world. This just means it's time to get to work."

I didn't know how to explain that this delay was much more serious than she understood. "I am literally broke," I confessed.

Even this new information did not seem to alarm her. "Be someone's assistant, babysit," she told me. "There are about a thousand good ways to make quick money."

We continued in the damp darkness past the northwest corner of the park, walking away from the inky trees and turning right on East Eighth Street, approaching her building in silence.

In the calming warmth of her lamp-lit apartment, Nic gave me a platter of leftover food from a colleague's book-release party she'd hosted the night before. In my arms, the tray was heavy, laden with deli meats and soft cheeses, pink boiled jumbo shrimp and red pepper slices beside a thick white dip—enough nourishment for me for several days.

"I've thought about putting my apartment on Airbnb," I told her as she showed me out, "but I'm not sure where I would stay, if I did that."

Nic squinted at me, considering. "Your parents are up in Massachusetts, right? Go home?"

Ambling toward MacDougal around midnight, the Village busy and drunk, I thought about Nic's question of home, and my reservations. Could I go? What was stopping me?

That night came and passed without good sleep.

The next afternoon, I didn't want to be alone. Wishing to revive the Ballerina Nest, that sweet and dreamy nexus of February's joy, I asked Corrina if she could sleep over.

Then I walked to Joe Coffee, blocking off my next eight hours for revision. My editor had given me dozens of notes and suggestions; I was unsure of the best method of applying them. Since Berkeley, the manuscript had ballooned into a 570-page mess, more than double the expected final length. In some ways, I still felt as lost as I'd been the morning after that long-ago Valentine's Day, pacing our apartment's sudden cage—

Committing to writing my book that foggy bygone winter morning, I had not known that the story still wasn't over—my heartbreak had blindsided me, changing my view of the world I was writing into existence. And now the ending felt impossible to grasp.

Sitting in our old favorite café, I struggled to revive my husband's skin, that musk scent I'd once craved. I realized how foreign my love with Justin felt now, like a wooden life dreamed up in figurines. In order to write about an experience vividly and with power, I would have to return to the aromas and music of that time—and that lost state of devotion felt even harder to access now.

In remembrance of the sweetest fruit of our united power—the night on the trail I told him about what had happened at Colorado College—I typed:

I didn't want Justin to see me as damaged, and yet I wanted him to see me. In darkness, still awake, I took a huge breath in. I slowly breathed it out. My lips were against his neck. I told him softly that at college, I'd been raped.

He didn't flinch. He didn't ask me "Why?" He didn't ask me how I was alone with a guy, or how it had happened. He didn't ask me any question at all. All he did was almost nothing but exactly everything I'd needed everyone I'd told before him to do: he shifted his body to open his arms. He reacted with absolutely untainted compassion. I slipped in.

He held me. I leaned into him deeply. When the weight of my head was on his chest and I was sure he couldn't see my face, my cheek melting into his warm breathing chest, I silently said: I love you.

~

At dusk, the sky flat blue, I walked home to meet Corrina at the apartment. She was wearing rich cherry lipstick and black high-heeled boots with elegant laces that crisscrossed around her ankles and a flowing black halter-dress with green and turquoise blossoms, stunning. "Wow, where *were* you?"

"A silly party," she told me, untying her pretty shoes. Smiling, she curled up under blankets on the bed in the buttercream room. I finally felt ready to share my jarring Soho House experience with my closest friend. I told Corrina about Jonathan—

The sky above the city dim gray and candy peach in my windows, white cotton curtains open, the Ballerina hugged me.

I noticed a fallen eyelash, a smooth mark of dark C on the tip of my finger, but I made no wish, the sky becoming blacker. To my dismay, a belated tear dropped onto the beige blanket, its dark water stain like a coin. "I just have no money left," I told her, "and I can't go home."

Corrina drew a spiral on my palm. "Of course you can."

Jewels of tears fell in fat raindrops. "I don't . . . ," I said, "don't really think so." I sought out better words, my breath erratic with quiet pent-up sadness.

Corrina's mint-green eyes became huge. "I'm sure your parents would love to see you," she promised me.

The sheet beneath me was damp in my clenched hand.

~

Less and less rest came to me, sleep evasive as a butterfly. All day I drank dark coffees, in order to focus. All night, I'd stay awake, writing or trying to. Or curled up with my pillow, watching the air around me become transparent pink and silver.

On the late May morning when I finally got up the courage to check, I found that I had forty-five dollars in my Chase account. I felt desperate, living on free samples and leftover party platters from events at The New School that Nic would email me about, vigilantly helping me survive. It had been nearly four months since I'd drank or shoplifted, but I feared I was on the verge of stealing.

That evening, my building's cast-iron steps were black and sad. Exiting into starless neon night, I combed my brain for options, stepping through cool velvet wind like a sleepwalker, the Village deadened.

Reaching a late-night diner, I opened my laptop with conviction, my fingers poised on the black keys. I wished with all my heart and hands to write the story I needed to tell, with speed.

Yet the fog in my mind stopped me from restarting. The fear that—after all this struggle—I would not survive long enough to even finish this book. Before I could face this higher, cerebral task, I needed to solve my financial issue, right now. Money was essential, and I *did* know a way that I could get it—

In spite of what I'd gone through in Los Angeles, which had frightened me, I still found myself drawn to the idea of a mutually beneficial relationship. I opened Seeking Millionaire.

Reactivating my account would be easy, a single click. I sat in a cold pool of thoughts for a long time—picturing a quick stream of messages from strangers who wanted to pay me for sex. Surprising me, the sweet server refilled my coffee; I jumped in my seat, chest knocking—I hoped he hadn't seen my screen.

But sipping my hot coffee, feverish, I found myself visualizing the destabilizing night in my Colorado College dorm room, and all I had lost there. Then weeks later, filled with lead, heavy and hardened, I finally

told my mom, and her reaction had seemed wooden and emotionless—
still hard to forgive.

My mouse hovering over the red button, I realized the absurdity
of my thought process: not wanting to revisit the past, I was doing *all*
of this in order to avoid going home. Not brave enough. Was I actually
considering selling my body over seeing my mom and dad? Ashamed,
I ached with melancholy weight.

Staring into my reflection in the laptop's darkened resting screen,
my face alert, my breath caught in my mouth. With three quick clicks
of the mouse, I deleted my Seeking Millionaire account.

Opening a new window, I signed up for Airbnb. I touched a green
button and made my apartment listing active.

By midnight, a couple from Madrid had booked it—for tomorrow.

At four o'clock in the morning, unable to fall asleep for the third
consecutive night—I'd been awake for sixty-three straight hours—I felt
almost dysfunctional, faint purple puffs like shadows under my eyes,
brain foggy. Smelling the warm caramel aroma of fresh coffee, a phantom scent, I searched for affordable transportation out of the city.

Hands unsteady on the keyboard, I used fifteen of my last twenty-
one dollars to buy a bus ticket to Massachusetts, to my childhood home,
packing before daybreak.

As I stepped onto a blue bus, to leave New York in the same way I'd
arrived, minus Justin, warm déjà vu overwhelmed my body, that ephemeral phenomena of alignment so perfect it is eerie. The strong sensation
that this real-time departure had happened before, precisely this way.

But it hadn't. I hadn't gone home in ages, and after all I had done,
I wasn't sure if my parents would receive me with love or with distrust.

PART III

AWAKENING

The true paradises are the paradises that we have lost.

—Marcel Proust

25

Impossible Prescription

77 Hours Awake

Watching the golden sky above smudged evergreens, trees flying by outside the big bus window, I am so terribly tired. It has now been more than three days since I've slept—but wired, I still can't.

80 Hours Awake

Passing through Rhode Island, I hold my breath and touch Home on my phone screen to tell my parents I am coming, less than an hour away.

My mother answers, "Sweetheart?" Her voice jumps up in a jaunty turn, excited. "I'll come and pick you up!" I haven't seen her since the David Lockwood concert of blue longings and a copious flow of wine.

81 Hours Awake

At the bus station my mother holds me and kisses me with a firm mouth on the cheek. She tells me how much she's missed me—how relieved she is to get to see me, "looking healthy." She drives me straight from Boston to my childhood home in verdant suburbia.

Passing tall offices like shadows in the sky, then narrow feather-gray and seashell-cream townhomes half-illuminated by a loose and drifting headlight-river, Dunkin' Donuts and the recognizable rundown strip mall of highway-side Brighton, she asks me, "How's the book coming along, Debby?" Her upbeat demeanor is breezy, like a child on her birthday—she is happy. Yet I feel stiff, standoffish.

"My name is *Aspen*."

"Oh sorry sorry!" she says. She glances in my direction. "*Aspen*. It's hard to remember."

Staring away from her, at the tree-edged highway and the green white-lettered signs leading us home, I point my toes under the dash. Flex my heels, wishing to disappear. A heaven-blue convertible blinks by us, far faster. "Writing's going well, thanks," I tell her, revealing nothing.

The roads become familiar, the proverbial turns and dead-ends of my youth. Passing a russet brick church gripped in the elegant leafy fingers of Dutch ivy, down the night-grayed and winding street that drifts through maples, we snake through Waban, an affluent village of Newton—

My mom is still talking, yet I've tuned her out and don't know what she's just said. "Oh, also if you need any writing supplies," she continues, "I have lots and lots of notebooks and pens you can have, in the basement."

"What are you talking about?" I ask, condescending. "I use a laptop."

She stares wide-eyed at the road ahead, pausing to let a pedestrian cross. "We were excited to get your news about the movie deal," she tells me, struggling to salvage our burned-out interaction.

"I actually just came back from LA, for meetings," I mumble, sharing only the nice headline. Embarrassed, I don't mention that it was all an enormous waste of time.

We turn onto Cypress Street, my elementary school a long dark blur. "You look trim," my mom says, "really good."

The field is black-green out my window and I roll it down to feel the outside air. "I'm exhausted," I tell her, over-enunciating, defiant. "I haven't had an appetite, so it's not a good thing."

"Well you'll get some sleep tonight."

I do not say anything back, and for the next minutes, coasting, we sit in heavy silence.

82 Hours Awake

As we pull into the old driveway, the energy feels cold and rigid. I stride alongside the dandelion-sprinkled lawn, to the door, ahead of her.

Entering the old colonial, a traditional white house, there is too-bright light inside, the plain beige vinyl blinds all drawn—claustrophobic. I feel suffocated by sudden smallness, the familiar smell of the basil plants and cherry-stained wood.

My dad is reading the newspaper at the straw-blond kitchen table. I look away, out the bay window, as we hug.

"Good to see you," he tells me in a soft voice. He is typically a low-talker, causing people to lean close when he is speaking, pay attention.

"Thanks for letting me come, last minute," I say, taking a seat.

"I hope you know you're welcome anytime." He sits back down at the kitchen table, looking ahead and not at me; he readjusts. These niceties are shadowed by a palpable discomfort. The rich scent of garlic and baking breadcrumbs warms the kitchen, something savory in the oven.

"What can I get you to eat?" my mom asks, standing over us, ready to serve. "Scrod will be ready in fifteen minutes, and in the meantime I have orange Vermont cheddar and the green garlic olives you like, as an appetizer."

Inexplicable bitterness rises in my mouth. "I'm honestly too tired to eat," I tell them. "I haven't slept the past few nights, at all."

My mom places a bowl of colorful salad in front of me. "Well," she says, her brow scrunched with concern, "you have to eat *something*."

My father is finely grating parmesan cheese onto his salad like snow, focusing on his food. Staring at my lettuce, I push my plate forward.

My mom makes a strange noise, a low-pitched huff like a hard sigh; and my dad looks over at her, empathetic. "How's the writing going?" he asks me.

For a moment I don't answer. I'm imagining that in my parents' shared glance they are exchanging condemnations of my lifestyle, and of me. "I'm writing every day," I finally tell him, defensive—not wanting to reveal that I am struggling. Already, I regret telling them about the sleeplessness. "I'll see you guys tomorrow," I say, standing.

Climbing the stairs to my old room, I am numb. I am home, but it doesn't feel like home anymore.

83 Hours Awake

I undress in the bedroom of my teen years; without brushing my teeth or washing my face, I collapse into bed, wrapped in my soft-blue walls. My hanging paintings are blurry like strange ships, the white picture frames glowing soft indigo in the darkness. My biggest ski trophy remains perched atop the highest bookshelf, I remember without seeing. Delirious, I stare blankly at the pale ceiling—

For an instant, I feel the exhilaration of flying through boundless whiteness, skiing.

I shut my eyes and try to escape consciousness.

84 Hours Awake

My charged mind chatters on, relentless as a fly, buzz-buzzing—

I think how there is so much food here, a huge relief from scrounging for free samples. Yet I feel no peace. My head rushing in the direction of the pressure of the book—

Distressed—I fear I can't write, my deadline approaching like the dark shadow of a henchman. I imagine my editor sending a faithful follower, a kind-seeming stranger prepared to engage in dishonest practices by way of service: the publisher's request to terminate this dead-end book deal with me.

Looking at the fresh pillow beside me, the blackness of Justin's hair absent, I remember the last time I was in this bed: I was here with my husband the Thanksgiving I refused to submit to my mother's will to keep my assault private, when he helped me see that I'd never needed her permission.

The harmony of that joyful dinner, our two families inexorably intertwined, was really the peace before an inevitable storm.

85 Hours Awake

Rising from bed, I switch the light back on. It's 2:00 a.m., and I am a lightning bug, jittery. I figure, *I cannot rest, so I will try to write.*

I walk downstairs with my laptop and make a pot of coffee, gulp a mug like home-brewed medicine. Down another big one, fast—desperate for rejuvenation, true *awakeness*. And caught in the small hours, sky blackish purple, I polish off the entire pot, typing with persistence, living in the past.

88 Hours Awake

When the sky transmutes to yellow, I climb back into bed, hyper. I've been writing all night, a wakeful bird. A symphony of sparrows outside whistling with desperate intensity, I notice something strange on my Nordic poster. Studying the girl skiing toward the front of the composition, I see her face has become obscured by geometric diamonds.

Scared, I close my eyes tight, and wait; reopen—hoping for the illusion to disappear.

Looking once again, the phantom shapes are gone.

89 Hours Awake

Oddly energetic, I dress again in the clothes on the floor, the jeans and sweater I'd worn on the bus ride up. My parents still asleep, I sneak through the house, lights off—

Outside, I wander. Back when I was very close with my mother, people who lived on these streets around our house would recognize me as the little girl who was always walking with her mom. The suburban nights were quiet and very dark. Tranquil Crystal Lake gleaming in streetlamps, we strolled side-by-side over roots pushing through the cracking concrete sidewalk, decaying leaves slippery on the ground snaking the pond's rim. The silent homes all glowed the same soft yellow. Our evening route was three to seven miles, when we crossed the main streets, we held hands; I loved it.

Gazing through today's new sun, I walk alone, lost in memory of family. The street of my native soil forks, and I stall, disoriented as a fallen feather—for a moment disembodied.

Through my tired eyes, my hometown glares. Sunshine backlights the still leaves of the hydrangea bushes and the maples, making iridescent petals of green radiance, hyperreal. Every branch and twig seems endlessly intricate, unfathomable.

At the corner of Centre Street and Cypress, breathless and slick with a skin of sweat, I see intelligence in a leaf, its vein pattern the same as rivers and my lungs. In the face of great beauty, breathing, melancholia strikes me.

93 Hours Awake

In the Newton Centre Starbucks, I order yet another giant coffee—the barista's hands appear as faint as fog, translucent. I am frightened by this soft ethereal vision.

103 Hours Awake

Home after a hypnotic stint of wild productivity, I find a heaping plate of stuffed cabbage and parmesan roasted broccoli my mother has made me. I eat alone, my appetite ferocious, devouring everything.

My dad steps into the kitchen and fills his mug with decaf. "How was Starbucks?" he asks me, taking a seat. "Get a lot done?"

I blink at him, eyes glazed. "The barista invited me to come listen to him *jam*," I say. My flat stare breaks into a grin. "When I basically ignored him, he gave me a free latte."

"Stealing from Starbucks," my dad says, only half-joking. "As if their coffee were his to give away."

My smile dissolves. "It's hardly theft. It's called being *nice*."

"Whatever," he says, unfazed by my sharp tone. "Do you want to take 'the walk' with us tonight?" My parents do the same 5.2-mile loop every evening, sun or snow, similar to the one I sometimes did with my mom when I was little.

"I can't," I say, turning him down too fast. "I am on deadline."

104 Hours Awake

Up in the desperate milky stillness of my room, I crave warm presence. Watching a video on Facebook, a half-friend dancing in a strapless dress in the leafless winter woods, my eyes stray to a framed photograph of me as a toddler. I see a strange color-flare of soft orange and flecks of electric blue, as if a flame has replaced the yellow-brown teddy bear I clutched. Then a faint diamond pattern appears over the whole image: A fishing net or a chain-link fence, it extends beyond the edges of the picture—like a cage.

Scared, I shut my eyes.

109 Hours Awake

Strung out on adrenaline, I again do not fall into the respite of my dreams. I shiver, *tired*, my fatigue extreme and unrelenting.

I carefully walk downstairs, stepping slowly through thick darkness like black water. Not wanting to wake my parents, I don't turn on any lights, drifting through the shadowed house like an apparition.

My eyes adjust, but halfly, beige walls ashy. The living room is stark, its decor spare—almost exclusively paintings and glazed pottery I'd made as a kid: jade and turquoise ceramic vases and cookie jars, conspicuously displayed. Remembering the soothing ritual of Saturday morning pottery classes, I smile at my artwork's ubiquity here, its presence seeming greater than before. It's as if their home has become a shrine for what was missing.

Walking to the kitchen, I notice something strange on the hallway wall. Between two of my old watercolors of honey-and-rust fall foliage, a newspaper clipping is framed, out of place. In a slow moment, I realize with confusion: *It is mine.* My *New York Times* piece, the Modern Love essay.

My arms and hands tingle, as if made animate by a feeble electric static, my shoulders pins and needles, stiff and heavy. I don't know how to feel—

Indignation erupts in my body, contacting my heart. My mother must not understand. This article exposes something *bad* about her—why would she be displaying this? She was so oblivious that she had framed my public condemnation of her action and put it on the wall of her own home—evidence that my mom still didn't grasp the severity of all that had transpired.

The sky blushes ruddy crimson through the mint plant filling the bay window, and I flit from dim space to dim space, kitchen to dining room, a nomad in predawn.

112 Hours Awake

Typing in my bedroom, my mind treks to darker coves. This era of extreme stress is a black hole I am trapped in, seeming total. Detached and apathetic, I sense I am irreparably burned out. Blinking at my laptop, all I care about is finishing this book, which I will never do if I can't ever sleep—

Lying on my stomach on the hardwood floorboards, I google "Insomnia" and find that it is very common, more than three million cases in the United States per year. Most are related to depression, anxiety, or lack of exercise. Then I search, "How long can a person go without sleep?" I learn that the longest recorded time awake is approximately 264 hours, eleven consecutive days, but that the effects of sleep deprivation start to show quickly. After only three or four nights without rest, people can begin to hallucinate.

I think of Mystic, how—five days and five nights awake—he cut his life short. Doing the math, I realize with unease: I've been up for over four and a half days.

114 Hours Awake

Typing, anxious, I am uncertain if my wakefulness is ephemeral, rootless—or if it is the pressure of the memoir that keeps me a prisoner blocked from rest. The sun is glaring on my laptop screen, and I hear a *knock knock knock*, resounding. I am disoriented as a blind child in a new place until I hear my father's voice: "Can I come in?"

I trip over my own foot, open my door to tell him, "I'm still writing."

Scanning my tired eyes, he tells me that he thinks I should take the day off. "You can't go one hundred percent a hundred percent of the time," he says. In malaise, I feel impressionable and weak. He asks if I'd like to go up to Salisbury Beach—a sandy belt of Massachusetts coastline, to the north. A place I'd loved. "It might be good to get fresh air," he says.

115 Hours Awake

Riding northward with my father, my window open a sliver, the air is a sad turquoise and soft with sun and pollen, alive. My sensitive ears *riiing*, the car like the echo chamber of a cave, every exhale audible and grotesque.

Through the glass eastern white pines form a long jade strip like a watercolor river that seems endless. Half-seeing, my dead eyes registering less, I am inexplicably angry at nothing I can pinpoint.

"How's the book going?" my dad asks me, ending long quiet.

I am thinking about how I build walls with omissions, protections from all judgment. "Excellent."

A few towns farther north, he is telling me about his grandson, my cute little nephew, Tom, playing Little League. He speaks with excitement—but gliding down the off-ramp, though I've been saying "oh" and "wow," I realize that I haven't truly heard a single sentence of his story, a failure of my listening.

Then I do hear, distinctly, "How long are you planning on staying?" My dad is looking at the road, his hazel eyes focused.

I don't want to be stuck living back in Newton, with my parents. "I'm not really sure," I say, looking to the emerald stream of trees out the bug-splatted windshield.

He clears his throat with two soft coughs and tells me it is good to have me home, that I am always welcome, here. "Stay as long as you need."

116 Hours Awake

The baked skin of the sand breaks like dense old snow under our feet, the thin crust shattering and coarse grains beneath squishing between our toes like the wet grout of fresh concrete. My father and I walk the yellow beach, scarcely inhabited, past a white-wood lifeguard structure, which is vacant.

I am thinking about how the ocean contains every color on the spectrum of human emotion. Gold at birth, green at noon, navy in the depths of volatile night. Sometimes, it appears akin to blood. Or it will turn the crystal color of blue eyes. Right now the shadows of kites are flitting across it, and fields of sun-sky are painting azure everywhere. Black threads of distant birds drag over it like microscopic angels, barely perceivable.

Reaching the rundown boardwalk, a rusty pastel carousel glinting in sun, I stare; the ride is not turned on, but a small girl with loose curls of chestnut hair sits up razor-straight on a pink horse. She looks like me, just younger, years ago.

I run to her, entering Joe's Playland, a gritty golden field of cotton candy and fried bites, overlooking the shimmering sea. From this spot, the beach itself is pale expansive sand, a strip of shining silver, and I have a wave of disarming sensation: that the entire ocean is contained within my body. That I am maddeningly infinite.

My dad asks me if I want something—he has caught up with me. "Are you hungry? Frozen yogurt?"

I am leaning onto the carousel fence—literally looking into the dark eyes of my gone-self, a ripple of the past. "No," I tell him. But then the little girl disappears; my hallucinations are getting worse.

118 Hours Awake

I am in Newton Centre—the car ride back a cold blur, I can't remember exactly why I am sitting on this outdoor bench in my hometown, apparently waiting. The sun is lower, now, winking from out behind distant gnarled branches. I feel far away from myself, universally lost.

"Here you go," my dad says, handing me a chilled bottle of water. He has appeared from somewhere, breathless and sweating. "Can you get in the car?" I'm seeing the vivid diamond pattern with which I am now familiar, it jumps with the scared movement of my eyes—

In the car again, sipping, the water tastes like a mountain river. These streets familiar, my hands are tingling and my arms are tingling and the right side of my face hurts from my exhaustion.

A spark of fear catches my heart: the panicked thought that I will have a stroke.

Speaking strangely, as if underwater, my father tells me, "We are going to pick up Mom, and head to the hospital."

119 Hours Awake

The emergency room walls are toothpaste white with framed floral illustrations the size of index cards, an admirable attempt at humanizing adornment. Low waiting tables have magazines and children's bead-toys, green-painted wooden ovals to slide along a wire roller coaster; I give my name to the woman under bright lights as my parents find us seats beside the window.

At the moment, I am not having any hallucinations, and I pray that my false visions will not have any permanent or lasting effects on my mental health.

I sit down with my mom and dad on cloth-cushioned metal benches approximating comfort. Hoping to prove my sanity to myself, to *create* lucidity and order, determined, I stare out the window, tasking myself to identify the visible trees, recall these names I've known since childhood.

A jewel-green plant I see outside is short, its bark rich reddish brown, fibrous and peeling off in narrow strips. "Eastern juniper," I whisper, very proud.

Watching my self-test, a calm energy lights my father's face, visible in his eyes.

After answering simple questions, I am given medicine to take back home in bed, right away. I'm not to wait 'til nighttime. The ER doctor's additional prescription—what she actually writes on my discharge form—is "STOP writing the book." Because it is clearly hurting me.

I tell her that isn't possible for me. Abandoning *Girl in the Woods* is the one thing I cannot do.

121 Hours Awake

Back in my childhood room, awake in bed, I fear the magic pill won't work. A faint rainbow in the air by my wall is glistening, unreal. As I've been instructed, I allow the tiny white tablet to dissolve under my tongue.

26

A TEAM OF OUR OWN

I awakened to the scent of sweet ginger, my mom's salmon. Bob Dylan was playing faintly, a familiar ballad, and downstairs my dad was strumming a guitar, sing-talking rhymes. Looking at my phone's white glow, my heart skipped—time showed that I had slept for nearly thirty hours, rising in the red sundown of tomorrow.

Feeling for a light, unsettled, I recalled the nightmare of my extended sleep:

Holding a gold baton like a speaking conch, I found a classroom with my old name marked on the door. Though the entry was as small as a standard doorway, inside a great arena unfolded, a blue blanket becoming the horizon—there, a fierce gust like the air current of a hurricane blew, and to my horror, the room's walls fell over like a cardboard box opened by a great cold hand, as if this expansive amphitheater had only been a set.

Out of the corner of my eye, I saw the source of what I'd first believed to be a natural disaster: just an orange-faced man with beady eyes and a blond beard, his thick sun-darkened fingers careless, putting his lips to a little ring-shaped hole in my gold baton I'd put down, blowing hard—creating a terrible unstoppable wind.

Getting back on my feet, dressing, I realized that this bad dream was about my old ski coach, a man with auburn hair. Emmett Davis.

Wobbly, I carefully peered downstairs, hand steadied against the wall. My mind was dizzy as a twister, mouth dry and rough. I grasped the railing, descending to find my mom and dad.

In the hallway to the kitchen, glimpsing the framed article—ready to be incensed by my mother again—I lingered. But this time I didn't feel that hot rush of righteous anger. My strange bout of sleeplessness over, I didn't know *how* to feel. Standing straighter, I only felt weak.

Stumbling in slow motion as if wading through molasses, I found my parents in the kitchen. My mother was pivoting, lifting a frying pan of asparagus spears from the blue flame of the stove, noticing me. "You're up!" she said.

This visit—born of purest desperation—was already my longest stay in my parents' house since high school. Gazing at her, my distance seemed a little foolish.

Every bite of food was *rich*—red salmon with ginger and tangy soy sauce; a glass of cold milk; bright green asparagus and silky golden butter—each taste reached beyond itself, charged with vibrant good-ness, *flavor*.

My dad suggested we all take a stroll together, after dinner. "Walking will be good," he said, "and the June lake."

I was holding my milk, disoriented in a daydream of reunion. "Sounds good," I answered, swallowing. Present to the kindness of my parents through my faintness, I couldn't clearly see the root source of my long and painful absence.

In evening's navy chill, I walked between my mother and father, tracing the edge of Newton's central lake, the leaves dark and blotched as night itself, melting with sky. I stepped with quiet tenderness—feeling vulnerable in their presence on this old, familiar path.

By his natural fast rhythm, my dad often walked ahead, my mother trailing. Consciously, I slowed to fall behind and match her pace.

The way of this walk felt familiar as a friend, benevolent Crystal Lake cradling the moon, obsidian water black like God's twinkling eye, shimmering in the streetlamps as if perpetually winking. I swam here every summer of my childhood, splashing in the shallows with my mom. Noticing a shadow above the reeds edging the pond, I spotted someone fishing, casting his line precisely as my dad used to in mountain lakes when we'd go backpacking as a family, a little wilderness tribe I'd cherished, half-forgotten.

Beside me, my mother was smiling, a glowing grin. "So the pill worked," she said. "You finally got good sleep."

"I slept so long," I said. All the disappeared hours were still unbelievable to me. "I had a dream last night," I told her. I paused to see her profile, her green eyes gazing at dark water. "Mom, do you remember Nordic ski team?"

Sharply, we turned the corner, onto well-lit Beacon Street with its elegant Victorians, porch lights shining through the charcoal trees. "Yes, I remember." Her warm smile had disappeared.

~

When I was a junior, I had been determined to create a cross-country ski team at my high school. I loved ski racing. Emboldened by this vision—*a team of our own*—I set up a meeting with Newton South's athletic director.

His office was small, his wood desk cluttered and worn. The brick walls had no windows to the outside, only to the noisy hallway in front of the indoor track. "To make it happen, what would we need?" I asked him. I felt confident and excited.

Adjusting in his rolling chair, he ran a hand through his spiky gray hair; he grinned. "You need thirty athletes," he told me. "I commend your enthusiasm. But you're not going to be able to do that. Recruit so many students to a basically unknown sport."

"But if I sign up thirty racers, we get our own team?" I confirmed, standing to leave.

He laughed. "If somehow you get thirty, it's a deal."

I thanked him, beaming. And for the first time in my young life, I had a singular mission.

∽

"It was incredible, what you did," my mom said. We stopped to let a car pass.

My cheeks opened into a bright smile. "What do you mean?"

"The flyers you designed, the way you called everyone in the phone-book to invite them to your informational meeting." My mom seemed proud. "You were determined."

∽

The night before the big day, hoping to recruit thirty student-skiers, I baked five dozen chocolate chip oatmeal cookies. Up until sunrise, I prepared a speech, expecting a large crowd.

My mom phoned at lunch to say that she would pick up three boxes of donut holes, in case the cookies went too quickly, and soon as the last bell rang, school over for the day, I jogged to the wellness classroom, hurrying, my heart electric.

When I arrived, it was near-empty, just three kids looking lost, and my mother waved at me, ready with the sugar-frosted treats I now feared no one would consume.

But within minutes, the room began to fill—twelve; twenty; forty—more teens than I could count! At the front of the class, I turned on my handheld mic. "Please take a seat," I spoke, the volume too high.

Then I nodded at my mom, who blinked the lights, the space a twilight zone. A hush fell, the mass of students settling into stillness.

A bold confidence of spirit overtaking me, I began to deliver my speech, evoking the beauty and exhilaration of ski racing, its sensation akin to flying. The camaraderie of training for competition. Attempting to paint the adventurous nature of this sport I loved so deeply, I described the ice-glittering destinations we would travel to as a team: the snow-coated fields and mountains of Vermont and New Hampshire, Maine and western Massachusetts.

When the informational meeting was all over, I sat beside my mother at the table with the sign-up clipboard, bracing myself for blank lines. To my elation, the first three pages were covered with scrawled names. And every last cookie was gone.

The next day during lunch, I skipped to the athletic director's office, euphoric. "We have thirty-five yeses, committed," I told him, placing a photocopy of the sign-up sheets down onto his messy desk.

His smile grew, a toothy curve lifting his cheeks, and he told me that he would find us a coach. "Congratulations. You've got a team."

This miraculous fact felt like the greatest accomplishment of my life.

~

My dad stopped at a green bench along the lakeside, stretching his muscles by sitting straight and leaning forward, so his forehead neared his knees; straightening again. He did this ritual in reps to ease the shooting pain he sometimes felt in his lower back.

"What a terrible man," my mom said, her head moving side-to-side in a rapid subtle shake as we caught up with my father.

"Who's that?" he asked.

"Nobody," I mumbled. Through the years, my mother had occasionally tried to bring up what had happened—and each time I'd shut this conversation down. *Angry* with her, as if my mother were prodding a wound. "Somehow, we're talking about Nordic ski team," I told him.

Sensing my discomfort, my father gave a nod. "He was a maniac."

We all began walking again. "He *was*," I told them. I emphasized my syllables with the precision of sharp anger, my throat tightening. "I still can't understand."

~

The new Nordic ski coach was Mr. Emmett Davis, a middle-aged tenth-grade algebra teacher with thinning red-blond hair.

One evening in mid-February, the ski track dark and windy, he told a group of freshmen that waxing your skis with yellow was best for the coldest snow—which was incorrect.

In front of a handful of kids, I asserted myself: "*Blue* wax is fastest on cold icy snow. Red for medium powder. Yellow is for spring snow that's slush, the worst for tomorrow's race. The forecast is like twelve degrees, very cold." This was an important distinction to understand. Had I not overheard, my teammates might have taken his advice, senselessly ruining their races.

We soon discovered that Mr. Davis actually didn't know how to ski.

Yet our team captains that year, Tamar and Paul, never corrected him—they respected his authority, which was intense. Through his praise and temper, our coach rewarded conformity and cut down skiers who asked questions.

As the season progressed, I scored better and better in races. Stretching for my final league competition of the season, warming and focused, a wish sprouted in me, playing in my heart's projector like a golden movie—a vision of my senior year: being *captain*. This desire certainly wasn't a stretch—I was knowledgeable and hardworking, with perfect attendance. And yet it thrilled me, as if astounding: the thought of officially leading this team I had worked so passionately to create. Skiing to the start line, beaming with fresh ambition, the old snow appeared silver, dappled with light.

～

My dad strode ahead, continuing; and falling back with me again, my mother said, "The whole experience changed you."

I looked into her bright eyes, wide open emerald worlds. "No it didn't," I insisted. I was sure she was attributing too much consequence to one incident.

"It seemed to affect you," she said more quietly.

～

In early March of my junior year, my mom dropped me off at an end-of-season ski party at a teammate's purple house. She told me to call her when I wanted to come home. "Have fun!" she called out. And then she drove away, gone in thick Newton night.

Inside, the house was dimly lit, already teeming with kids holding red Solo cups. I passed an elegant spiral staircase strung with little paper snowflakes, metal trays of cupcakes and potato chips on a countertop, mostly untouched. Popping from room to room, Coach Davis announced the plan: the team would meet in the living room to vote on next year's captains. He seemed excited, buoyant and proud of our team's success, even of me.

We gathered in a sitting room filled with bean bags and plush couches, and in a high-pitched call, Captain Tamar announced: "Take a seat everyyyyone."

A warm hush spread through the room like a gold orb as Captain Paul explained the rules: "You'll have about ten minutes to write down your picks on these scraps," he called, holding up a stack of gum-pack-sized paper rectangles and a handful of Bic pens. "When the hat comes around," he said, and Tamar held up a velvet top-hat, waving it like a stiff flag, "drop your names inside, and that's your vote."

"This is a democracy," Coach Davis spoke into the quiet. "So the guy and gal with the most votes will be our captains."

When the hat came to me, I said a silent prayer as I cradled it, dropping my two slips in. I had voted for Sam, a skinny junior with a spray of freckles who strived his very hardest in races. For the girls team, I wrote down my own name, Deborah Parker. A blissed wave of pride filled me, my *excitement*.

The voting over, low whispers raised to a loud din, and Coach Davis announced that he, Tamar, and Paul would be back with the results.

Olia, our team's best racer, touched my arm and told me, "I voted for you." Her blue-gray eyes smiled. "You are already like the captain."

By the time Tamar and Paul came back, Coach Davis tailing them, I was overwhelmed by jittery joy. "The new captain of the Newton South High School boys Nordic ski team," Paul announced—he double-cleared his throat—"is Tyler Fisher!"

We all applauded, cheering. A girl called out, "Go Tyler!" and someone *woot*ed. The current captains motioned for Tyler to come to the front of the room, and he did. He was grinning as they placed a paper Burger King crown atop his head.

Coach Davis took a half-step forward, toward us. "And the girls' vote was *unanimous*." He paused, dramatic. "Next year's captain is . . . Courtney Chaloff!"

The room remained silent for a moment, then confused clapping started. Perplexed, a few people started talking, Sam saying something into Olia's ear.

Unable to restrain myself, I spoke up, "Unanimous? That isn't possible, I voted for myself."

Coach Davis responded to me—and everyone, the whole room was listening—that Courtney had won unanimously "once all the bad votes were taken out."

My tears fell into mounting silence, moistening my eyelashes and cheeks. "The votes for me were *bad*?"

Smirking, he didn't respond. And then, as if an awful dream, the strange ceremony resumed. Both Tyler and Courtney were called up to make acceptance speeches. Tamar placed a plastic gold tiara onto Courtney's dirty-blonde hair.

As she spoke about how much fun she'd had this season, my whole body tingling, bracing—I walked right up to Paul. I whispered in his ear, "Did you see the votes counted?"

Looking me right in my wet eyes, Paul said, "I saw." Then he added in a soft voice, as if an afterthought, "You actually won. He just wanted Courtney."

Music grew louder—time for the party—and I was in shock, betrayed and targeted by an adult. How could a coach, a teacher, so bogusly lie? And *why*? Most of all, I wondered what it meant that the votes for me were "bad" ones. I fixated on what that would imply.

Back home, I couldn't regain control of my breath, my air shallow. Sitting in the kitchen, both my parents with me, I struggled to tell them what had happened. But I was devastated, speaking unclearly. *It's okay, you're okay,* I told myself—but I wasn't. Finally, in broken sentences, I expressed the bullet points of the night.

Appalled, my father called my coach's actions "egregious." His face became red with anger, empathy.

My mom told me, "We're going to explain this to the athletic director. We'll go in tomorrow." They both comforted me, promising that what had happened was wrong, and it was not my fault, and they would fix it.

And I truly felt much better. My parents would make this right.

The next morning, outraged, my mother met with the athletic director while I was in Chemistry. Then I got called in from class to join them.

Trembling, I told the AD what had happened. How it was unjust—I needed him to rectify it.

He hadn't said much, listening and thinking. "I'm going to look into it and speak with the coach, and we'll correct this," he finally decided.

Three days later, my parents came back from a second meeting with the athletic director. The three of us sat down at the kitchen table together, my heart and hands quivering.

Over a cup of decaf, my dad told me the outcome. That, ultimately, the coach chooses the captains, "so nothing can be done." He was looking at his mug. "I'm sorry, Debby."

The next season I would quit the Newton South team I'd worked so hard to start, abandoning the sport I'd loved.

~

I stopped walking. "If it changed me, then how?" I asked my mother, feeling cornered.

She tried to touch my arm—I pulled away. My father was well ahead now, only a shadow against an endless chain-link fence. "If you look at your class photo from the beginning of your junior year, you're smiling," my mom told me. "And then look at your class photo from your senior year. You're miserable."

I squinted at her dramatically, infuriated. "Oh my God, Mom, it's a *photo*. It's one moment," I told her. "I was just done with Newton, it's not the place for me."

What I couldn't articulate was the overwhelming feeling that something precious had been stolen. After that ski season, it was true that I had faded like a cloud, dissipating into myself.

My mom was still speaking, but I was only partly listening. "I wish we could have done more," she told me.

"Yeah," I said. I sped my pace. "Me too."

27

VANISHING ACTS

In my room I reread the first poem I had written when I left home for college two thousand miles away. The words had been scrawled in red rage, ink in my notebook smudged by fallen tears:

> My parents, both lawyers,
> hadn't the conviction
> to convict Mr. Emmett Davis,
> my Nordic ski coach
> who didn't know how to ski.

The temperature of anger rose up in my body, still potent half a decade later. Before the winter of my junior year of high school, I had believed that my parents had my hand, my back. They were on my team, and we were a strong team, in my mind. They could make things right. They had the authority and the will.

Maybe I had never forgiven them. And seeing this poem, I still wasn't sure I should.

I felt the sobering truth of my mom's words—*It had changed me.*

The next morning, I returned to work on *Girl in the Woods*, clear-headed and rested. Sitting at Starbucks, I thought about how, to little kids, one's parents are like demigods, infallible. And when our heroes are exposed as merely human, they don't diminish just a little in our vision; they dissolve like statues of sand, touched by a gentle wave.

Sipping milky coffee, I saw I had an email from Lena Dunham. She was working on her own memoir, *Not That Kind of Girl*; and in the message, she told me she'd been writing about her long-ago college date rape. She wrote that my Modern Love was what empowered her to finally share her story: "Thank you for emboldening me to reexamine what happened to me in college and making me brave. For being who you are."

I admired Lena Dunham and was stunned by this surreal message—to know that I had impacted *her*. That my uncomfortable honesty inspired her to tell the truth.

Feeling powerful, I began to write of my first solitary excursion into wilderness, thinking this story might belong in my memoir. Exploring, I typed freely:

> *Most people, when they leave home at seventeen, do so to elope and grow a new life. But in my case, the seed was different, because I planted it. There was no man. There was no terrible childhood to escape. There was only a calling I heard like playful music in my dreams when I went to bed, preventing me from feeling satisfied to stay home.*
>
> *So one night, awake in my dark room, I devised a plan to explore the wild of California that I thought my parents would approve of. I already had the maps and a crisp guidebook, I'd found them in the attic—everything I needed. I told my mom and dad that I was guiding a National Outdoor Leadership School alumni trip I'd put together through chat groups—I, at seventeen, was the self-appointed leader. Now I claimed online that I was*

leading a backpacking trip—through the organization. Though there was no such trip.

I logged into the fake account I had created, in which I claimed to be a nineteen-year-old undergraduate student at Harvard—I could pass for one. I had misrepresented myself to the prospective future attendees. Whoever signed up would meet me in Yosemite Valley at my set date and time.

My parents believed the entire story and they told me I could use their credit card for all of my expenses. I had never lied to them, as far as they knew.

With my sole follower (a Dartmouth-educated 39-year-old female doctor), I hiked into the most remote granite peaks of Yosemite and Sequoia. Yet she soon became ill, throwing up all her food. Though I was a minor, I took care of her, carrying her backpack as I led her through the mountains to a ranger station down at the edge of a meadow. There, I made sure she was evacuated safely; and I kept going—

Blissed out in the great wilderness, I backpacked for 220 miles. And so, the summer after my junior year of high school, I took a walk in the mountains. I was in California, on my own, and the silver granite peaks and cold wind seduced me. I was searching for the center of nothingness. It was beautiful, and I felt free amid the cold blue lakes and pines, stronger.

When I returned home, days before the beginning of my senior year, my father was fixing the dishwasher, fiddling with the alignment of the racks. The machine was open and smelled like soap. He told me that he knew: I had been hiking alone without telling them and had made up the whole "alumni trip" story.

"I just had to go," I mumbled. I didn't know what to say. "I didn't think you'd let me."

My dad jiggled the rack, glaring inside the washer, not looking up. Then he gave me the sentence, "I will never trust you again."

My coffee gone, I was now shocked by the audacity of my teenage self. And this great adventure was only my first vanishing act—of many.

For a few months following that initial escape, I was able to quiet the furious storm in me. But the second day of twelfth-grade Thanksgiving break, I left again. In the Green Mountains, I recklessly trudged into Vermont's snowy woods, backpacking alone in single-degree weather.

At eighteen, I became troublesome to all who loved me, not thinking of my parents. I had a war in my mind, ongoing. And in that primary year of adulthood, I solo-backpacked just shy of one thousand miles, often out of communication with the world beyond my nose—my family in darkness. The universe inside me was of silence.

On that hike, I wrote poems of stomped-on rose beds and a sapling uprooted by a thoughtless man, the abrupt loss of innocence.

And at nineteen, after being raped on my second night at college, I dropped out. My parents were mystified, heartbroken. Depressed and shocked, I sought solace in a remote wilderness, my place of childhood joy. I walked from Mexico all the way to Canada, through the deserts, mountains, and woodlands of the American West; my mom and dad lived in constant fear for my tenuous safety—their daughter's life.

I could think of the many times I left—and why? It was as if I had amnesia, now forgetting my years of ironclad reasoning. I ran away and ran away—from *what*?

After the faux ski captain election wasn't rectified and nothing happened to Emmett Davis, the injustice, I'd felt like my mother and father had been pretending to have power when, in reality, they had none—promising me unconditional protection with no backing of true action. It was all hollow—

My sense of support ruptured; and my faith in them collapsed with this crack.

All these times I'd vanished I had been trying to act like the vote didn't mean anything, but maybe it led to *all of this*.

My first solo hike had been the summer right after my junior racing season. Now with a pain in my head, a throbbing understanding, I saw that Coach Davis had led me to the woods at seventeen, that the timing of this "escape" was not a coincidence. I had never done anything like that, before him.

28

A MOTHER'S PERSPECTIVE

Walking with my parents again, the night-ground was dark with moisture, and the neighborhood smelled like wet grass and honeysuckle—inside all day, I'd missed hard rain.

We looped around the shimmering ink lake and through the villages of Newton, the trees in the streetlamps full and amber, all sparking water droplets in a puff of wind—and as usual, my father pulled ahead.

Widening my gait, I sped up to him, my mother trailing us, her elongated shadow still under my shoes. "Hi Dad." Beside him, I felt nervous, younger. "I hope you can trust me again," I said, assuming that he would recall the distant day I was referencing.

"I trust you—" my dad started, his words slow. "What do you mean?" I couldn't tell if he really had forgotten, or if he was pretending, becoming upset.

I was looking at his stepping feet. "After the John Muir Trail . . ."

"We all do dumb things when we're young," my father told me. He produced a napkin from his pocket and loudly blew his nose. "When I was sixteen, I hitchhiked from the Bronx to Montreal." He paused. "You could have just told me it was something you needed to do."

"And you would have let me go?" I couldn't quite believe it. Stopping at a wooden bench overlooking the colorless water, he didn't say anything; but as he sat I thought I saw a subtle flash of smile.

"Tell me about your book," he said, an abrupt switch in subject. "How—" he paused. "I know it's been a struggle. How can I help?"

Taking a seat on the cool wood planks beside him, I finally admitted that the draft I'd submitted a few months back had been rejected. "I've missed every deadline and I'm afraid if I miss another, I'll lose the deal."

He was looking directly at me, now. "Nothing here is life and death," my dad told me. "The good news is you finally got some rest." The five sleepless nights ending in the emergency room had clearly frightened my parents. My mother's silhouette was growing in the distance. Then my dad told me that he was very proud of me—"I cannot say that enough"—for even *getting* a book deal with a real, respectable publishing house, "a dream of many."

"Thank you," I said softly.

My father stood to resume our walk, the three of us together, now. "Each of my children is different and none of you were ever conformists," he said. He told me that we always marched to our own beats. "That's how I know that I've done something right."

~

The windows of my father's office building, the World Trade Center Boston, glinted white above the steel-blue harbor flecked pale gold with sun. "It's so pretty," I told him. "I didn't remember." I hadn't come with him to work since I was eight or nine.

Inside, we rode an elevator skyward, and a grand gray marble lobby opened before us. Arriving on his floor, my dad introduced me to his secretary, a cheery middle-aged lady named Beatrix, telling her that I would be writing here for the next few weeks and we needed to book me a vacant conference room each day.

I dropped my bag in my father's airy office, his space overlooking the seaport. The room was small but grand; and spinning slowly, I noticed that the walls were all decorated with colorful enamels and framed paintings I'd made when I was little.

He set me up in the "bubble room," an open meeting area on the fourteenth floor, floor-to-ceiling windows creating the illusion of impossible suspension. I sat down in the solid structure of my father's long-time workplace, ready to face this task—reopening my unfinished manuscript.

After seven hours of seamless writing, finally reentering my marriage, I dragged my fingertips over the smooth sixteen-person table, my mind returning to where I was—in a beautiful conference room, alone. I felt supported, ready to find my father.

That evening I went to bed early, sleeping fully through the night. And awakening, I felt a warm breeze, a little more peace in the house. My window was open a crack, the scent of flowering crab apple wafting through.

The next weeks were a rising wave of momentum. My book's storyline became a clear line of thinking, creating a path through loss—an access. Following it, I was uplifted.

Each morning I rode into work with my dad, and in the car we'd listen to jazz and folk, and talk. I would work in whichever lovely space was available that day, usually one close to his office; all were sun-filled. As each sun set, the sky blushing a celestial pink and red, I shut my laptop, feeling accomplished, closer.

One exceptional day, I woke at sunrise and immediately typed a sentence I had thought of in my dreams—a sudden line of my subconscious that evolved into an energetic page. I kept going, my fingers leading my words before my thoughts, true heart spilling. It was as if I were possessed. I wrote from waking until dusk—twelve fresh pages, nearly four thousand new words.

On a Tuesday in the middle of the week, in a bright blue flash of *seeing*, I knew that I was going to hit my deadline; there was no longer any question. And I exhaled a deep breath of long-held tension, great relief warming my limbs. It was a cool clear day, three weeks into my Newton return, and the sun was low over the city and would be setting soon.

Back home from work that night, I sat down on my bed, nostalgic. A picture from my wedding day still sat on my bedside table—me smiling nervously, trying to look pretty in a car with silver balloons—and I studied my younger face. I thought about the defiant state of my mind when I'd met Justin. I was dissatisfied with my role in the world—and with *the world*. Like him.

We were aligned: "Forget our so-called obligations. *Screw* this society that doesn't understand us, that tries to use us for its gray and unsustainable, meaningless and greedy purposes—wants us to be what we are *not*." We were bonded in our shared abandonment, deleting worlds.

Downstairs with my mom, we got ready for the walk. I tied my sneakers, and she handed me a sweatshirt, perhaps overkill on this pleasant summer evening; but extending a hand, I accepted.

Waiting for my father to come join us, I looked at the framed article, still in disbelief that she displayed such damning words by her daughter—about her.

Walking with my parents that evening, the ebony sky scattered with bone-gray stars, I tried to grasp my love for disappearing.

Of course, the idea of simply and completely vacating a life—leaving behind all responsibilities, debts, and troubles—is a little exciting. And there *is* real benefit to new adventure and to fresh space, solo. Time and tangible distance can give a person the opportunity to think with sharper lucidity—unfiltered and undirected by the thoughts of everybody else.

But "escaping" via complete and total bailing to "find" oneself can also be a mode of withdrawing from the world—seductive, but ultimately cyclic.

Skirting the lake, I glimpsed my dad squeeze my mom's behind and mumble something to her, playful; I was impressed by their easy comfort with each other, the longevity of their intimacy—nearly a fifty-year marriage, healthy and ever-tender. I'd lost Justin—but in their quiet kindness, my parents made it clear that I would never lose them. That I had their unconditional support. I was running away to get away from this persistent love. Now, it didn't make sense.

Crossing Cypress Street, then old tulip-edged Bow Road, I said to my mom and dad, together, "I've been thinking more about the end of ski team." I could see that what had happened with Emmett Davis and the subsequent lack of fairness was not the fault of my parents—it had never been their failing, as I had believed. "I know you guys did everything you could."

Glancing over to my father, my mother responded, "I wish we could have done more," her smooth alto vigorous with the heat of deep caring. My parents had wanted the same thing I'd wanted, a sense of justice. And when they had not gotten any, they'd felt devastated, too—distraught to witness their only daughter's rising sadness. But their only true inadequacy was that of *reality*—of not being omnipowerful, as I'd believed they must be, still a child.

Home for the first time in well over a year, I had been a missing person in my family. Like Justin.

In their hopeful green eyes, I understood that I had put my parents through the pain of a thousand battles. I had not been compassionate, blaming them for angst and the natural pain of growing. During this prolonged stay, they hadn't once mentioned my mute distance from their lives. In a calm clarity, I understood the reason: they were afraid that if they did, I would respond by disappearing, again. In this way, my own mom and dad were afraid of me.

I did not want them to fear me, to tiptoe and navigate around my reactive mind, my *immaturity*.

Walking with my parents in maturing evening, I was grateful. I hadn't lost them.

Under the glistening red maples, I told them, "I am sorry for everything. I love you."

~

Home after the walk, I felt pulled to look again at the ink text and fine glass of my *New York Times* essay. It occurred to me now that I'd been pretending my mom had reacted without compassion to learning that I, her teenage daughter, had been raped. When in fact, she was trying to shield me from the rape-shaming of her generation. Her hesitancy to speak of my assault was not born out of disapproval, but of protectiveness.

I finally considered my mother's perspective: loving her daughter *so much* that she would frame an article that expressed unkind things about herself because—more than she cared about the contents of the article, my condemnation of her—she thought displaying it might mean something, to me.

Rather than burying it, she had showcased it. And re-seeing the article tonight, I understood that it was actually evidence of how much my mom loved me.

29

THE NATURE OF HAPPINESS

The budding colors of New York summer intensified, splashing the windowsills and flower-potted streets with pops of apricot and ruby blossoms. A warmer season blooming fully, the air possessed a rose-bud tinge, spirit awakened, as if the wind itself had become pink-hued, idealistic. The four-hour bus ride had been peaceful, a smooth trip of endless green; and I was giddy, typing my entire way back home.

Returning to the Ballerina Nest, the turquoise walls seemed cheerful, their tone now effervescent. My Airbnb guests had been tidy, it was as if they were never here—except for the $2,300 in my account that would allow me to partially catch up on long-due rent.

Before I even unpacked, I took a long walk, slipping in and out of neighborhoods: the concrete parks and red flags of Chinatown; the Lower East Side with its newly built upscale oyster bars, intricate cream-and-black tile designed to appear retro, and music clubs like caves with their neon spray-paint mouths, gaping; Little Italy, that dark red and emerald hamlet with her golden painted shoes, a hundred storefronts selling hand-cut homemade pastas and thick, traditional ragùs; SoHo's expensive dresses displayed like fine ornaments in heaven-white windows—each neighborhood distinct, its own small world. The patchwork nature of the city felt to me like an aromatic collage of little postage-stamp-sized villages, each of unique, fresh texture, seductive and complex as an impressionistic painting, a masterwork.

In a sidewalk café, I savored a poached egg sprinkled with toasted pumpkin seeds and black sesame, my table overlooking the cobblestone street, the pale ground dappled with white sun. The breeze tasted like fresh basil in the face of July harvest.

Then I stopped at Joe, my old oasis, resting in a bleached pool of sunlight; my last task for the memoir was to decide whether to provide a glimpse of epilogue—to include the reality that Justin and I were no longer together, that he left.

Months ago, I had planned to end the memoir with a moment from where the trail ended, that unremarkable gap in dense northern forest, with the excited words "I kissed back the man who would become my husband." I'd also considered ending with our wedding, speaking our vows as the last sentence—quoting the cursive line that had been printed on our blue wedding invitations: "In every walk with nature one receives far more than he seeks."

But that conclusion—a resurrected ceremony, a joyful scene—no longer felt honest.

Instinctive, I wrote a cryptic, yet true sentiment: Justin "disappeared down some new side-path into his dark woods." Then I submitted, my last shot at acceptance. If I didn't want to be evicted from my adopted city, I needed my editor's yes.

Yet whether my book was published or not, I had my family—I was going to be okay—and this time I felt no clutch of desperation.

~

A week passed, its warmth eclipsed by waiting; and another began. Freed of the ardor of composing *Girl in the Woods*, I tried to find a smooth pathway back to normal living; but I had no routine existence. The last year had been a turbulent evolution, *change* the only constant.

Some evenings I saw Corrina; others, I took aimless walks, alone. I'd sit in Joe, trying to start a novel—really, I was reopening my email a dozen times a day, preoccupied. I so badly wanted to surrender with grace to the reality that this next step was beyond my control, that I could no longer impact my book's fate—to believe the outcome had no bearing on my writing's validity and power. Yet I was a human artist, and a hot blue flame in me still needed the validation that my days and months of painful writing had not all been for nothing.

But on the afternoon of the eleventh day, sunlight streaming through my window, I checked my email, naked and warm atop the worn sheet of the bed Justin had built us; my editor's name appeared—I opened up my message like a fortune, and the verdict was a gift: *Congratulations.* My manuscript had been accepted, and would be published! Purest euphoria struck my heart, an overcoming energy—

Outside, my city glittered like a prismatic field, shimmering in hot wind, a funhouse of ambition and wishes granted. I saw beauty in every concrete block and passing pair of eyes; in the elevated veins of strangers' relaxed hands. Drunk with happiness, I was witness to a thousand acts of grace: A young mother cradling her infant, rocking on an elegant white bench, a baby-blue painted stone walkway running beneath her shoes. The newborn's tiny fingers were wrapped around her mom's delicate pinkie. A gentle butterfly the color of milk; a brick townhouse with charming mint-green shutters; and a sidewalk-psychic with a lovely violet shawl, smiling slightly at my slow approach.

Giddy with the miracle in my pocket, I strolled, seeing New York through a sun-warmed lens—too energized for mere walking, I began skipping. Northward, cobblestone ground gave way to the dark asphalt madness of Times Square under my high-heeled boots—and I fantasized, imagining myself on a book tour, speaking across America. Inspiring women to see that a sexual assault need not be the end of their lives—rather, the beginning of something bigger. A tragedy such as a rape is a passageway to facing buried pain—and to finding a voice, a greater purpose.

I would speak about how the broken are thrust into a landscape of muted color, forced to discover the nature of their shadow—the part of oneself that is unknown.

In grief, we find a new view—a fresh perspective, which organically generates fresh expansion: personal revolution. Because in the wake of devastation, growth becomes the only survival option. In this way, loss is the shocking catalyst of transformation.

Trying to survive, confronted with the challenge of the wilderness, I discovered my power and my calling.

Now, I hoped to share this alchemy, helping other wounded souls to find their joy—perhaps under blazing stars; perhaps in bold acts of creation.

Again the ground transmuted, changing here into a narrow tan ribbon: a footpath through Central Park. Following the elevated rim of the calm blue lake, lily pads twinkled like emeralds in the sun.

Snaking trails were dotted by tree-sheltered benches engraved lovingly with names. Watching the bluegills and bass cut under the water, dull flashes, their amber faces frowning, I felt the peace of a splendor so close to home: the happy power of recognizing, *noticing*, the charm of hidden fish and silver clouds. Each stumble and every twinge of piercing heartbreak I'd endured had led me precisely *here*, to this perfection: an enchanting garden reverie, hyper-crisp and vivid, countless strains of roses smiling pink and scarlet and friendly orange. Noticing species of particular whimsy and quaintness, each bloom's wide petals ruffled at her edges, like torn lace, I wished this pace of appreciation, luxurious and slow, had discernable markers telling me its name.

And more concretely, I craved signposts offering the names of the different roses, but they had no identification. Fitting—New York City does not come with comprehensive instructions.

Everyone comes here without a map. Still, bohemians before me lived the creative history of my neighborhood, a particular nexus. Their brilliant creations were torches, guiding me—the works they'd left behind like gemstones embedded in these rough streets, bright vectors directing me.

Walking into copper skies, then glittering dusk, my home felt a part of a great tradition that arched back a hundred years, an heirloom.

Emerging through dark trees, the Shakespeare Garden appeared like the sudden colors of a rose-gold vision. The many blossoms of this botanical treasure teemed with squirrels and families in the gray city light. A quaint stone bridge crossed over a little brook, linking people from pale English roses to the Parisian blooms, fragrant and rich crimson. Hidden spotlights blinked on, illuminating the central fountain, new night's sky deepening violet.

I took a picture, longing to capture everything.

~

In tomorrow's blue morning, I called Nic. She disliked when students phoned her, preferring email correspondence, yet I couldn't wait.

She answered on the second ring, voice tender. "How are you doing?" she asked without greeting, as if worried. I realized she must be concerned about my health—I'd shared with her the details of my long sleeplessness, still in its throes.

"Really well!" I said. I'd planned to tell her the news in person, but I couldn't help myself. "The book was just accepted! I'm finally *done*."

To my surprise, she asked if I wanted to come over in an hour. I'd never walked with her during the daytime—I'd barely ever seen her in the light.

Sitting in the open atrium of Nic's apartment, I felt this space was a benevolent portal to a different existence, the big beautiful bookcases that lined the walls seeming to possess an animate quality, almost hugging us.

We emerged into a summer afternoon, my heart awake. The cloudless sky contained blue multitudes, the endless buildings sprawling faintly in strong sun. I told her, "None of this would have ever happened, without you."

Striding through crowds, energies manic, Nic talked about how fulfilling speaking about my book would be—how fun. Deep brown eyes smiling, sweet and kind, her mode had flipped from professorial and sage-like to girlish, filled with the warm wonder of a fresh dream.

She had a new novel forthcoming, *What's Never Said*, a semiautobiographical story about poets behaving badly. "Let's do a teacher-student book tour!" she declared. After New York appearances, we would jet-set across the country to Los Angeles.

"I can't believe this all started from your Instant Gratification class," I told her. Nic had truly created my career.

Loving and magnanimous, my mentor hugged me. "Three pages can change your life," she said.

Striding with her around the green periphery, tracing the east side of the park, I saw how Nic, my fellow Village night owl, was a living part of the sustained and rich literary tradition of New York City. Her infamous speed-walking office hours around Washington Square Park had become an eccentric treasure of her students' nights, stoking determination.

Jogging a half-step to keep up with her, turning a corner, I said without thinking, "Touring is going to be a little hard without Justin." I told her how, sometimes, I still missed him.

Nic stopped abruptly to stretch her calves on the black metal fence that edged the verdant square, pressing her heel downward toward the concrete. She squinted at me, as if incredulous. "Remember," she said. "This is what you wanted."

Trusting there must be something to glean from my mentor's confident decree, this time I didn't argue.

~

At ten o'clock that night, the Ballerina came over so we could celebrate. In the bruise of shadow the bedside table cast across our faces, she told me, "You're going to inspire so many people." Her jade eyes beamed, pearly with delight.

I imagined sharing my story, giving interviews at colleges and bookstores and even on television—answering whatever personal questions people had for me. "I hope so." I shut my eyes, trying to visualize these thrilling aspects of the future. Yet as I turned my mouth into a smile, mirroring hers, I noticed a tightening feeling behind my collarbones. My heart sped, dreading. I tried to match her enthusiasm, but the high of early morning—of acceptance—had faded. "It might be tough, reading excerpts of my first night with him."

Corrina drew the design of a tree on my back over my T-shirt, barren branches outstretched to the blank sky of my skull. "Baby bird, I know," she said. "But this is so exciting."

I thought how nothing was as it seemed; and this time I had assumed would be, in my fantasy of expectation, one of the most serene and joyful eras of existence—the actualization of becoming an author, long my wish—was composed of an entirely less stable material:

The progression of these bittersweet post-Justin months had become a return to my essence, in a way. An unfolding of wondrous happenings—I couldn't quite see each blessing until it was gone. And my world became a contextless newness, beautiful and raw.

I'll get a book deal, then I will be happy, I had long believed. Yet here I was, holding the self-proclaimed elixir of contentment—and I felt weak relief but no immersive bliss.

30

OAKLAND TO DENVER

The envelope from my publisher was slim in my fingers, the red and blue lettering smooth under my thumb—tearing it open, I found my second book-advance check, at last!

Stepping into the heavy humidity of New York in July, an abbreviated dash from air-conditioned apartment to air-conditioned bank, I wasted no time depositing my hard-won compensation.

Already accepted, my intention this afternoon was not to write, but to spend the day just enjoying the sunlight of this triumph, free. Reaching Joe, my old office—the coffee shop where I had written so much of my book—I sipped a latte with no laptop for the first time in over a year, empty of tasks.

Sweaty on the stroll back home, I reflected with gratitude on the many people who had helped me to survive these past months' hardships. Uncomfortable, I thought of Walter and Lucy.

For weeks I'd stayed upset that my in-laws had clearly known of Justin's history, keeping it from me after he left. But spoiled fish fumes enveloping the block, swallowed up in the harshness of this metropolis I loved, I could admit that they were not the ones who had left Allie; and they weren't the ones who left me, either. On the contrary—like my parents—they had remained present for me when I'd needed family most.

Back in May, I had fled Berkeley without explanation—leaving their house childless, once more. Yet punishing them in this way wasn't fair. They had truly been punished enough. Continuing to alienate Walter and Lucy would do no one any good. Calling Justin's parents in the heat, my breath caught in my chest—a sharp cocktail of excitement and dread.

Lucy answered, "Aspen!" and my heart pirouetted.

I updated her, "I'm all done with the book," and I thanked her. "You and Walter made it possible to finish."

"Oh Aspen, that's terrific," Lucy told me, her voice cracking. After a few minutes of niceties, she asked me if I was alright. "At the end of your visit, you left so abruptly."

I promised her I was okay, telling of my recent homecoming. "But I'm sorry I worried you."

When I asked her how *she* was, she instantly spoke of Justin. They had been reaching out, emailing and leaving the occasional voice message—but no answer. It had been eight silent months, now.

Having felt the crater of pain I'd formed in my own family, something outlying called me with power, pulling intimately at my spirit: I wanted to help Walter and Lucy cope with the terrible muteness of their son. To heal this most piercing cut—the scar on the hearts of Justin's mother and father.

Back home, the scent of Vietnamese broth from the restaurant downstairs wafted through my cracked open window. Desperately feeling Lucy's heartache, it occurred to me that it is easier to empathize with a person who has been through something undeniably difficult—a tragedy or disaster—than with someone whose pain is unknown to you, invisible. And the people we most connect with are so often those in whom we see ourselves—because we've had similar experiences. I knew from my own great mistakes how hard it was to repair passionate strains of love-rupture—how difficult it was for parents to connect with their children once the foundation of trust had cracked.

Through my parents, I felt the spring of fresh compassion for Justin's parents fast becoming a narrow river, flowing swifter. A warmth in my soul-heart. Instrumental folk music was playing faintly from a neighboring apartment, carried by a soundless unfelt wind.

Remembering Walter's voice cracking, telling me he wanted his son back, I couldn't fathom the extent of his suffering.

I had stopped reading Justin's email since before Newton because living in that cheapened world of digital correspondence felt too disturbing, a small and limited heart's home. And perhaps because it had all been for naught—beyond unearthing Allie, nothing real had come of my lonely seeking; vigilantly tracking him, I had found that sometimes he went weeks without sending a single message. Still more weeks passed without him receiving anything, his new world silent as I remained stuck in his past. This spying had been an unhealthy fixation, wrong.

But grasping how much reconciliation mattered to my outlaws, I realized that I *had* to find Justin for Walter and Lucy, to help this family—*my* family.

So for the first time in over two months, I reopened Justin's account, my abdomen tightening. Sitting upright on worn bedcovers, I scanned his recent messages. Yet all I found was junk mail and receipts.

I closed the window and searched his Facebook; still nothing of interest. I switched over to my own. Bold with determination, I sent detailed notes to old trail-friends, hikers we'd both known in the woods and the mountains of our former life. I asked each if they had seen or heard from Justin at all, or if they had any idea where he might be living.

One couple we'd met in Washington State responded immediately that they'd seen him on the Continental Divide Trail in New Mexico several months ago, but it was someplace in a stretch of desert red rock, no permanent address.

I googled "Justin Matis" and tried to dig. I was seeking any new information; a true address; a clue. Everything that appeared in my search results was related to the two of us, mostly wedding photos. Then I limited the filter to only the past month—finding videos of whitewater-kayaking maps he'd uploaded onto YouTube. I watched one, and though his voice and face were absent, the red arrows over the topographic lines were demarcated with his cheeky written commentary.

I got a message back from a hiker I barely knew, a man with the trail name Strider, who'd heard through the trail-vine that Justin had been living out of his car in a mountain town in western Colorado. "But that was four months ago. He was about to move in somewhere."

Quickly, I wrote Strider back, asking if he knew where Justin next landed.

Imagining my once-husband sleeping cold nights in a sedan, practically homeless, I wondered why he hadn't gotten an apartment right away. Then I thought of rent—

I went downstairs and knocked on Tomas's door. Opening up, he smiled; and I stared into his watery chocolate eyes, old and kind. I handed him an unsealed envelope containing two checks—one to pay late rent, precisely what I owed; the second one for August and September, ahead for the first time, ever.

But walking back to my unit, something stopped me: a cardboard box in the hallway outside a neighbor's door—a package from Amazon. I noticed the white sticker—an address.

I rushed upstairs. For the first time, I loaded Justin's *deleted* emails.

It was filled with receipts. The first few I opened were from coffee shops, pizza joints, and climbing gear stores around southern Colorado. This was confirmation that he remained someplace in that snowy state, yet it was insufficient, not news.

Then I saw it—an email from REI confirming a recent order. Scrolling through the small print of his purchase, there it was: his shipping address.

I'd found him.

I sensed meaning in his choice of location—he was now living in Buena Vista, a village filled with artists that we'd descended to from higher mountains on the last backpacking trip before our wedding.

That night I tossed and turned under my covers as if too alive to dream. I could barely sleep, feeling giddy—powerful. When the ruby light of sunrise painted the buttercream room luminous scarlet, I felt the warmth on my cheeks of morning alpenglow, imagining the Colorado mountains where Justin was tucked away—

The moment it was late enough to dial California, I called Walter and Lucy.

"I've got good news," I announced, blushing with nerves. "Justin's address."

Through the line, something clamored on the counter. "Thank you, Sherlock!" Walter said, elated. I read their son's location from my screen, repeating each number twice.

My mother-in-law was grateful to learn where her son was. He had locked them out, like he had me, missing for eight long harrowing months.

Walter told me that he was searching flights.

I listened with great excitement as they purchased two tickets for next weekend from Oakland to Denver.

31

VICTIM

Nic invited me to a panel she was moderating called "The Secrets of Book Publishing." The discussion would take place inside the Strand, an independent East Village gem known through the city for its "18 miles of books" and lively literary calendar.

I stepped through the heavy summer heat into a honeyed spill of light, the bone sky scattered with wild and tawny-orange clouds—to the corner of East Twelfth Street, two blocks south of Union Square, where I entered.

Early, I browsed the tables of new books. This shop had a rich and inspiring creative history. Many Lower East Side artists had worked at the ever-expanding Strand, including musicians Patti Smith and Tom Verlaine, the latter of whom had, according to bookshop lore, been fond of the discount book carts overtaking the sidewalk outside, towering like a miniature city.

Nic's event would be on the gigantic store's beautiful third floor, in the spacious Rare Book Room. Her invitation to this venue was an honor—and a testament to my mentor's luminary status.

Upstairs, the room was set up as if for a ceremony, two hundred or so chairs arranged in arching rows around a single twelve-foot table with eight outward-facing seats. The elevated walls that encased us were lined with rare and antique books, their maroon and mahogany spines shiny from age, protected in this space. The hardwood floor was like the faded boards of a well-worn ballet studio, polished smoother with time, edges softer. Passing two enormous white columns of astonishing height, I chose a seat in the front row.

When the panel began, lovely petite light bulbs that hung in strings across the distant ceiling blinked on, shining whitely. Dangling from delicate cords along the exposed pipes high above us, the tiny electric flickers created the illusion of sudden starlight. The two hundred chairs had all filled, only standing room remaining; and the eight seats of the front table were also occupied—Nic at the center, wielding a handheld microphone.

With quippy brief bios, she introduced the other seven, her panelists. Her magnetism transformed the Strand's grandness into the dim space of an intimate dialogue, like a living room talk. "Three pages can change your life," Nic told the room. "One great provocative personal piece can lure professionals to call *you*, saving you a frustrating and lengthy search."

Nic's guidance and dazzling candor captivated the newbies in the room—but I couldn't quite focus. My mind's eye was elsewhere.

I felt so good about my fruitful investigation, helping my kind in-laws—I pictured the excitement on the plane next weekend as Walter and Lucy soared to Colorado, how hopeful and eager they were, and all the possibility, the anticipation of reunion. That family had persisted through so much calamity and sorrow. Lost in the strung-lights above, I hoped that Justin would not be upset by the sudden, uninvited appearance of his parents.

I tuned back in to Nic proudly listing great successes. "I've had more than a dozen students get book deals from short pieces they've published in national news outlets like *Psychology Today*, *Newsweek*, the *Wall Street Journal*. Many agents and editors scour these publications and certain others, looking for prospective book projects," she told the enraptured room.

Having heard these triumphant stories many times, my mind again drifted. I thought about my own family's reunification—how, in desperation, my parents and I had bonded. How fulfilling, almost magical, that reconnection still felt, enhancing the present with greater peace and my unknowable future with heightened meaning—

But something still misplaced was palpable in my heart: an understanding of how my marriage had failed and why Justin had gone so far away from me. A sense of finality.

Bittersweetly, we were still husband and wife. I wondered what that meant, if anything.

I felt the eyes of everyone in the room on me—it wasn't my imagination. Nic was pointing at me. At her cue, I stood; twisting, I waved a little, awkward. When the clapping died away, I sat back down, listening better now, as she spoke my name again, "My star student, Aspen Matis."

~

When the audience question-and-answer was over, dozens from the crowd swarmed Nic, rushing to the head of the room to ask her advice on their specific projects—I remembered being one of them, manic with dreams of my first big publication.

Waiting for the crowd of Nic-fans to thin out, killing time, I skimmed the printed plays that sat in metal wagons along the back of the room. I noticed a first edition of *Buried Child*, the Pulitzer Prize–winning drama by lauded local playwright Sam Shepard, who had also been an employee of this bookstore. His desolate and poetic black comedies were surrealistic, depicting the fragmentation of the nuclear family—the breakdown of traditional household values, in a context of disillusionment with the American dream.

An endorsement on the back of Shepard's play described freewheeling characters who lived on the thrilling fringes of society, summoning in my heart the faintest ghost.

At last I saw an opening—a tall bald man was shaking Nic's hand, saying goodbye.

I slipped up to her, and her face brightened with excitement. "You made it!" she said, though of course she knew I was present from when she'd had me stand. She thanked me for coming, studied my eyes for a long moment as if concerned, scanning for a sign in my blank face. "Walk me home. You can tell me what's the matter." She told me to meet her in five minutes by the lollipops, downstairs.

When we entered starless night together, the spicy scent of black cumin and Indian curry flowing from someplace unseen, I told Nic, "I found Justin."

She stopped walking. "What do you mean?"

Tears welling, I explained how I'd found his address. "His parents are going to Colorado in five days." Speaking this, I was overpowered by a damp melancholy.

Nic didn't attempt to comfort me. "If you still wanted to be with him," she said flatly, "you could."

I stared at my mentor, dumbfounded. Utterly confounded by her strange conviction that Justin's absence was my wish, my creation. "No I couldn't," I told her. "He left." A yellow cab whizzed by, nearly clipping me, and I flinched.

"That email you sent him was an ultimatum," she said point-blank.

"That was *Allie*," I said loudly, and a passing couple turned to look.

"If you were okay with him just playing computer games all day," she told me, "he would still be here." We had already reached her building.

The subject was unfinished, but in darkness we said goodbye, Nic thanking me once again for coming out.

As I strode back to my apartment, the squid-ink air of the back alleys curled around me like sinister fingers. Supremely disoriented, I tripped on a crack in shadowed asphalt.

Back inside the empty nest I removed my sundress and my bra, still that same cursed mermaid. I made myself a cup of chamomile tea, though I was already clammy with a bright gloss of sweat, unsure if I was hot or cold—

The last flowers he had given me, bold sunflowers from my favorite Village florist, now slumped in their vase like forgotten stalks of wheat, stiff and abandoned, their once-vibrant yellow now a washed-out pallid brown.

Looking back at the final weeks of our marriage, fuzzy and vague as a weak dream, most of what I recalled now was homemade fun and deep conversations. We didn't have typical fights, hardly raised our voices at each other, speaking vicious words. But the one moment that crystalized through the faint haze of shapeless time was the night Justin confided he was addicted to computer games.

A hot midsummer wind breathing through my billowing curtain, that interaction no longer felt so innocuous. In the aftershock of Nic's assertion, I knew the email she was referencing—

I recalled the "solution" to his gaming compulsion that I'd suggested: out writing the morning after Justin's sudden confession, I couldn't focus; and wanting to aid my husband, to "fix" his problem, I wrote him an email.

Now in unnerving stillness, I found the message I'd sent Justin in our final October that, through the softened light of distance, now seemed harsh. Overbearing, I had insisted that he needed "to make friends; to get a job; and to be more affectionate and physical with me." Thinking it might sound playful, I'd reminded him to spend more time outside, something he "used to love."

My hidden intention in this communication, the subtext of my soul in the moment I'd clicked Send, had not been purely selfless. We'd been married three years, and I'd wanted him to be the father of my children. My private thinking had been that if we were going to start a family together, then Justin would need to work for us to survive, even if he didn't want to.

I never once saw these sentiments as an attack or even unkind. My brave savior in the mountains had withered in the urban jungle; and at the time, I had gladly shared the email with Nic, proud how I was trying to make my marriage stronger. In sending the message, I had only intended to help. I had believed that if he did these things, we would both be happier. But now I considered how these demands must have occurred to him—how *I* would feel if the one I loved sent me these disapproving words.

If these actions I "required" had been so easy, of course he would have taken them already. Creating and sustaining friendships wasn't effortless or very natural for him. I saw how my message must have made him feel that he needed saving; helping; changing; fixing. He might have seen this blunt litany of requests as my asking him *to be someone else*. To become someone he was not.

I thought about how we have to feel accepted in relationships *as we are*. How, spending so much time with one chosen person, we need to feel totally comfortable to be ourselves in their presence. Not picked apart. Not pressured.

Allie had done this, she'd tried to tell him what to want when she gave him an ultimatum: Propose by her chosen deadline, "or I am finished." Trying to make him marry her had led to Justin's subsequent absence from her life. And, studying my well-meaning response to his confession, I saw how he must have again felt cornered—I finally appreciated his perspective:

That rather than having a loving conversation with her husband about the aspects of his life—and our connection—that concerned her, his wife had sent a hostile note, insisting that he must commit to changing. And that if he didn't, perhaps she would prefer that he just left—

But really, I only wanted him to be the way he was in the beginning, because I'd just loved him so much.

A breeze swirled through the dim room, chilling my cool sweat, raising goosebumps over my entire body. Inexplicably spooked, I turned on every light, my heartrate speeding. I pulled on an oversized sweater, shivering, and curled up like a fetus on our old bed, frantic, worried—

Maybe the breakdown at our root had been *my* issue. I could have been more self-reliant, putting my contacts in my own damn eyes—not burdening my husband with helplessness, my maddening dependence. I wished that he would show me more affection when it was in fact my behavior, needy and childish, that was the most unattractive to him of all.

What if this all really was *my* fault?

Now, looking at some of the emails he'd written me a couple months after he'd gone away, I saw his vulnerable words: "my life has become terrible in the last two months." This line struck me—clearly, *he* felt like the victim.

Breathing more slowly, with intention, I opened my contracted body, straightening—and I knew this line of thinking was indulgent, not productive. For nine months I'd been casting *myself* as the victim, and that wasn't wholly right; but naming myself the plain villain didn't feel true to reality, either.

As I reflected on our time's end, what was missing was something more intimate. Our marriage lacked the fluidity of easy openness, that freedom. The hidden cracks ran not through us but through our bond.

We would have lasted as long as we understood and respected each other—which, in the end, we didn't. We were both looking for our needs to be met in the other.

Justin was looking to me to provide him with acceptance.

In that thread of distressed messages from my husband, I found: "Do you know the pain of realizing that your problems are cyclic? The same thing happened years before." This cryptic question had first reached me in the darkest heart of my month of blackout drinking—and, bitter, I'd disregarded it in rage.

Now I understood. He was referencing his gaming addiction, which he'd kept on beating. Still, it would return, gripping him, a consumptive cycle. Like a nightmare that didn't end with waking, the computer's hold on him was corrosive, occupying him again.

I realized now that the reason he hadn't come to me with this problem sooner was that he didn't trust me to be compassionate and understanding. He had been ashamed.

Yet I couldn't blame him for this secrecy—from eleven, after his house burned, video games had replaced hard communication.

While Justin was struggling unbeknownst to me, I couldn't help but assume that his detachment was personal and feel quietly rejected. Asking for my love's affection felt horrible—and it was ineffective. The unmovable fact is that demanding love is not the way to generate it.

Somewhere in our shared two years in New York City, Justin's heart had drifted to the forest or locked itself in a game's plot, someplace elsewhere. Not with me.

And when I told him this distance wasn't working, he withdrew further inward. Then I asked him be different, and he left.

Yes, I was a victim in the story of our little family's ending—but so was he.

We had been so young, dual unwitting casualties of our own forceful and short-sighted immaturity. We were unequipped to support each other through the mundanities and tribulations of daily married partnership. Because we didn't communicate with the easy comfort of *trust*.

All these factors had created our fate as a couple—not Mystic's death. Not anything I'd urged my husband to become. Not even his retreat to games. Fundamentally just a diminishing affinity for each other; fading connection, emotional and physical; an insidious *lack*.

The truth is that he didn't leave me and I didn't send him away. Really, we broke up without ever saying the words, he then disappeared;

the loss of my husband made me feel abandoned and alone—and I *played* victim, unaware that it was only a role, a choice. I wasn't innocent *or* guilty, but I'd identified myself as the passive casualty, the wounded one.

In reality, Justin and I both didn't want what we had with one another, in the end. And neither of us knew how to make it better—stuck in this hard dance of retreat.

Realizing all of this, I stepped down off the bed. I was ready to get divorced.

32

The Heart's Pistil

Sunrise cracked open like a rich yellow yolk, the soundless room awash in rose-hued light. Rising, I made an omelet in the still hush of pre-morning—and called my mom.

The line ringing, I feared I might be waking her. But she answered, her voice bright and alert, "Hi sweetheart!"

"Hi Mom," I said, my first words of the day coming out scratchy. A little chilled, I pulled a silk blouse on over my head, talking through the fabric. "To start the divorce process, do you know what I have to do?" My chest felt open, a beating tin drum.

I heard her exhale, as if she were relieved of something long-held. "I think that's the right thing to do," she said. "First you'll need to go down to the courthouse and file a divorce petition." She told me there were several steps, and I should write them down. "You'll need to bring your name-change documents, your New York address, Justin's current address and phone number, both of your social security numbers, and a copy of your marriage certificate."

Fully dressed now, I was searching for something to write with. "Hold on, slow down," I told her, finding a blue highlighter. "I didn't realize it was so complex." Overwhelm blooming its gray flower, I felt the resistance of uncertainty.

"Once you get to court with all the documents you need—"

"Actually," I cut her off, sitting down in the old periwinkle chair. "I don't really need to do this right now."

For a moment my mother was quiet. "Well, if you want, I can come down to New York this weekend and help," she offered. "I think this is important."

~

That Friday night, sitting across from my mother at a casual downtown spot called Quantum Leap, we giggled like little kids at the waitress's silly jokes. My mom was fun to be with—a loving and energetic presence, she could barely wait to tell me our game plan.

On the Amtrak down from Boston, coasting through the leafy green woodlands of southern New England, she'd sat at a little table in the café car, working the whole way down—studying the many directives and procedures of New York divorce law, organizing all the forms I would need in order to file. Her undeniable proficiency, deftly navigating this confounding bureaucracy, impressed me.

Savoring my Malaysian-spiced red snapper, I thought about how parents can have so many distinct ways of showing their children how they love them, unique signs and symbols that require interpretation. Though she also told me the words freely, I knew that my mom's tireless, meticulous research and fast travel through states, to help me—such selfless acts of service—were her truest code for "I love you."

Walking home to the apartment together, we passed a small troupe of twelve or fifteen masked people wearing neon-yellow bodysuits and flashing lime-green lights around their wrists and waistlines, strobing, dancing. Crossing the festive warmth of their wild brightness, our bodies appeared in flashes as if we were flipbook characters, animations.

Turning a corner together, my mother asked me, "Are you okay with money?" I nodded, and she smiled broadly. "Well if you ever need any help," she said, as we passed into the more subdued illumination of a dive-bar storefront, "just let us know."

Like a hot wave of tropic *knowing*, I was struck by the understanding that my Seeking Millionaire debacle had been absurdly unnecessary—my parents would have absolutely given me money, if I were only honest about having needed it.

Welcoming my mom into my turquoise walls, I saw how vulnerability, the heart's pistil, so often shunned as powdery and weak—frightening and uncomfortable to touch—is the source of regeneration, the productive part of the flower of the soul. The pistil, central and hidden, contains potential kernels of new life's creation, a fragile stalk arising from the swollen bulb of seeds to a pollen-receptive tip, the stigma, variously shaped as the human spirit itself.

An experience of discomfort by design, the act of vulnerability is an *access*, a portal to more-profound connection. And bold honesty, this terrifying method of self-exposure, is also the medium for enriched and strengthened bonds.

Recognizing this counterintuitive nature of vulnerability—speaking the hardest truths as a *gateway*—my core was unearthed; and I felt exposed: if I had been able to talk to the people I most loved—my parents and my husband—with the brave openness I possessed while writing my story, I might have spared us all expansive heartbreak.

Corrina joined us back at the apartment for a sleepover; she'd graciously offered to come along with us to the courthouse tomorrow.

"It feels surreal to be twenty-four and divorcing," I confessed to my sweet friend, tucked in blue darkness. My mother slept soundly in the other room.

The Ballerina laughed quietly. "I think it's kind of edgy." But I didn't say anything, still a little blue. "You couldn't have grown into the woman you're becoming if you had stayed dependent on Justin," she told me.

For a moment, I considered this—it was true, and yet it wasn't. "But look at what he *helped* me become," I said. I explained how nothing would've happened in my career had he not brought me to New York, had he not believed in my possibility and promise. "He did so much for me. I should have been a better wife."

In a wordless lull, Corrina drew a swirl on my back with her smooth fingernail, calming me. "Have you read Joseph Campbell?" she whispered. "In every hero's journey, there is something or someone who gets you from point A to point B, the place you didn't know you needed to go. A mule."

I smiled sadly at the shadowed wall, thinking of my soon-to-be ex-husband.

"Justin was the mule," she said. Then she insisted that I shouldn't blame myself for our marriage failing, "that isn't fair to yourself"—and I realized that I had set her up to say this. I had fed her a story that I was the victim and, an empathetic friend, she'd been spooning it back to me this whole time—I had insidiously, subtly compelled her to take *my* side.

We stayed up late, whisper-speaking about the mysterious future and the imperfect past.

As we drifted off to silent dreams, the finality of tomorrow nearing, I thought about the seductive appeal of playing the victim. How we are all always innocent in the stories that we tell about our lives—we first name ourselves as passive, helpless. Our default role in our own stories is of the *wronged*.

I saw in myself this strong temptation of victimhood, the siren's charm of casting oneself as "prey." But, becoming aware that I was *not*, I was awakening to the fact that I was responsible for the state of my marriage, and of my life.

~

When I woke at eight, Corrina and my mother still asleep, I felt a little uneasy.

I quietly put my contacts in, as I now did every morning, and went out to go get coffee, the sky shining clear pure blue—on impulse, I called my father.

"Do you have a minute?" I asked him.

"I'm just out in the backyard, working," he said. "What's going on?"

Thinking of my parents' relationship, sweet and enduring, I said, "I don't know. I'm getting divorced, today." Hearing myself, the word *divorce* sounded dismal, so serious, as if a curse. I felt a sudden fear that I would be alone, that no one whom I loved would ever love me back. Not planning to, I asked, "Dad? What if I never fall in love again?"

I heard him open the screen door, a whining *creak*, then the deep *scrape* of a chair's legs against the kitchen floor's ceramic tiles. "Some people are stingy with love," he told me, "but you're not like that. You have so much love to give. No matter what happens, you will love again."

His words were a comfort, the right person speaking. Although I struggled to accept their truth, I took them as a blessing. "Thank you," I whispered, remembering the sad day he'd come to be here for me when we'd shared twin salads, teardrops dripping in my lettuce.

"Yours will not be a tragic life," he said, "I guarantee it."

33

Water Under the Bridge

At Manhattan's southern tip, approaching the New York County Courthouse from the back, we passed two allegorical statutes, *Justice* and *Authority*, seated granite giants. The building had six edges, its great scale giving it the appearance of a temple. Staring at this structure where marriages officially end, I wondered if I was doing the right thing. Now that I understood more deeply the issues that underlay our crumbling and knew where Justin *lived*, I wondered if I should go there, to Colorado—rather than end us here, without him.

We crossed around to the front side, broad stone steps sweeping up from Foley Square, and we ascended, treading beneath three intricately carved pediment figures: *Law*, *Truth*, and *Equity*. Standing at the enormous entryway, I considered *my* truth: that I still missed my husband. Was it honest and right to divorce a man who had never cheated or misused me, whom I still loved?

My mom strode ahead, and the Ballerina held the door open for me. My step faltered—after a moment, I walked through.

Inside, we were ushered into a long and snaking line filled with men and women in neat business attire; my mom was wearing a navy dress-suit, but Corrina and I were in jeans, out of place here. At the front, we placed our handbags onto a thick conveyer belt as if entering an airport, preparing to fly, stepping under a pale gray arch of metal detectors.

Once through security, my mom took charge, asking two guards in tan uniforms behind an exposed desk for the room number where we'd file a "summons with notice" and pay the filing fee. The strange answer was, "Two different places, ma'am." Inconveniently, these two connected tasks were geographically separated, the first in the county clerk's office, and the other in a second room, in the basement. "Filing fee is $210, ma'am. Exact change only."

We entered a great rotunda, enormous and soaring. Rising to a point, the dome was pierced with ten sparkling stained-glass windows emitting fresh sky light. I looked up to see a striking circular mural, bold paint azure and golden, divided in six half-moons, the pattern reminding me of a blue doodle I'd once drawn on Justin's arm.

We waited for forty minutes in an excruciatingly slow-moving line in a wood-paneled fourth-floor room; but when at last we reached the front and my mother explained our needs, the stout woman behind the long bar of wooden desk said without apology, "This is my lunch break. Go to room 111 now."

"But we're here and you're here," I said. "Can you just stamp it?"

"I will not," she said. "Room 111, downstairs."

So Corrina and I followed my mom, who seemed unfazed by the woman's complete apathy, down through the central lobby, to the basement.

Scurrying through the grand courthouse from room to room, we waited in long lines only to find that a different form from a different office was needed "firstly," a complex counterintuitive order of operations. Go here; go there; you've been waiting in the wrong line, all along; fill it out *this* way, not *that* way; please check again, that room number doesn't exist, ma'am. Persistent, we amassed more and more paperwork to complete.

Through each roadblock my mother pressed on, furiously focused—immune to the staggering layers of bureaucracy. Yet my apprehension mounted with each obstacle. The hours passing with nothing resolved, I truly wasn't certain if—when we finally *did* get to where we were going—I would really sign my name.

Following my mother around these halls felt akin to accompanying her to court when I was little. In a courtroom at six years old, I had raised my hand during a custody battle, as if it were a classroom, not knowing such behavior was inappropriate. Kind, a parent herself, the judge called on me; and I stood and said, "I would want to live with someone nice to me."

As a teenager, I saw her stay up until the middle of the night, typing legal briefs with the intention of liberating children from unjust and dangerous homes, finding them loving adoptive parents—through her life, my mother has fought to have a positive impact on the world. She marched with Martin Luther King Jr. for human rights. She was an editor of the *Second Wave*, an early feminist magazine devoted to achieving equality and generating a new respect for women.

Waiting in another slow line in the basement, this one longer than the previous, the Ballerina rested her cheek down on my shoulder. "Baby bird, is there treasure at the end of this trail?" she whispered in my ear, making me smile.

After another fifteen minutes or so, we decided to divide and conquer. Corrina went to find the records office, my mom and I remaining in the line that seemed to move a yard every twelve minutes.

Alone with my mother, I thanked her. "You've been really amazing, Mom."

"The courts make it so complicated so that you have to get a lawyer and go to court, to keep the courts in business," my mom joked, talking a little too loudly.

Standing in silence, I looked at my ever-forgiving mother, who was again focused on a pale blue form. She jotted something down on her yellow legal pad. Her eyes safely distracted from my face, I told her, "I'm sorry I didn't call you for so long."

My mom nodded, looking up. Her expression was blank. "It was a hard time," she said. "I didn't know what I had done."

I glanced down at the checkered floor, wishing to reverse time. "I wanted to call you but—" I swallowed my words, realizing how I'd disconnected from her, with Justin. I now noticed a startling parallel: in the same years, Justin had distanced himself from his family, too. And, passively, he had encouraged me to follow his lead—cutting credit cards and ignoring teary voicemails. Our island drifted farther from homeland's shore.

I had robbed her of a daughter—and robbed myself of a mother.

"Mom," I said, shifting my body to directly face her. "I really regret writing those awful things about you." I was referring to the Modern Love essay, and other angry things I'd written—to *everything*. "They weren't right, and you didn't deserve it. I just wish—" My soft voice broke with the sensation of overwhelming *feeling*. "I am so sorry. For all the pain I caused you."

Her warm green eyes gazed deep into my own, reflective with silent mist. "It's all water under the bridge, now," she said. She hugged me close.

I held her tight.

I was happy—no longer weighed down by an unacknowledged past. My face buried in her arm, I told her I wanted to go back to college. I felt a smile in her strong embrace.

～

We arrived at the final window. A frail hunched-over man with dyed black hair, white at its roots, extended his unsteady hand for my packet of completed forms. "Which of you is divorcing?" he asked. Corrina back, she and my mom stood by my side.

"*I* am," I answered, nervous. Though doing so would be painful as severing my own trapped limb, I needed to cut this tie that kept me tethered to a phantom of myself, a shadow of lost love—to complete this marriage. I handed the clerk my driver's license and birth certificate.

He squinted at me through tiny circular glasses, which sat nearer to the tip of his arched nose than to his brow. "Do you solemnly swear that you are Aspen Matis; that your marriage has been over for at least six months and you have no children under the age of twenty-one?"

The Ballerina giggled. "She's barely over twenty-one."

The bespectacled man didn't smile. With a ruler, as if grading a test, he examined line by line down each page of the thick stack of white and blue forms, looking for the error.

Standing with my mom and my best friend, shifting our weight from one foot to the other, waiting, my mother whispered in my ear, "He looks like something out of Dickens."

Finally, he raised a perforated page and said, "Sign here." He struck the form with a date-stamp, *boom*. "Next!"

34

SEARCH AND RESCUE

Instinctually, Corrina and I returned to Reggio, that classic café where Bob Dylan drank cappuccino dry and Jack Kerouac wrote joyously, once upon a time—the same late-night espresso shop where she and I first met, long ago. My mother was coasting north to Massachusetts, riding the long train back to my father, her home.

Huddled at a beat-up table by the window to MacDougal, my best friend and I toasted my divorce with jasmine tea. The street outside was washed with storefront lights and neon pink show signs, the brick buildings of lower Manhattan inky indigo, dotted with glowing blocks of gold—the scattered lit-windows of the wakeful. We were two of many in this city, sleepless at 1:00 a.m.

I told Corrina that this is what I get, a bride so young. Marrying at twenty is somehow different than marrying at thirty or forty; it's an innocent leap, a lapse that is lifelong—vowing to give up everything you knew you never had, 'til death.

Promising my life to Justin while not yet legal to drink, I had believed that—once wedded—I would have a kind of guarantee that I would never be lonely again, insurance against isolation. I had rushed to the illusion of stability and eternity—unwittingly setting myself up for a harsh awakening. And I'd been unmoored by my own childishness, our mutual immaturity.

Because—as I'd discovered—loneliness is not a function of company, but rather it is a consequence: an unpleasant symptom of a needy state of mind that desperately seeks to extract happiness from a source *outside* itself.

Our teapot empty, I walked the Ballerina to the quiet subway.

Back inside the turquoise walls, the apartment smelled of vanilla and sage, new incense. My reflection in the window's black glass stood a fraction straighter.

That night I unclasped the mermaid bra, forever.

A few days later, I got a call from Walter and Lucy. They'd just returned back home from Colorado. Slowly, they told me the story of what had happened there:

They located Justin's rented apartment, an old blue building. When they arrived at the address, no one was home. His mother left a note on his front door:

> *In case you're interested, we'll be at the Evergreen at 7 o'clock, tomorrow. Come if you want. No pressure. —Mom and Dad.*

At dinnertime the next day, they went to the diner and waited, unsure if he would come. Sitting in the bustling restaurant, hopeful, they tried to stay realistic about the chances of actually seeing their son.

Each time a man walked in, Walter would stand; then he would sit back down. And then the door swung open, again—it was Justin, appearing in the dim pub like a wish.

He looked good, they said. He seemed happy and healthy. Though he revealed nothing of his private life (they asked him no questions that might be thought of as too personal), he was charming and funny, telling stories of fun mishaps in the woods.

Over burgers, Justin's parents learned how he'd been spending his days: working for search and rescue, saving people who were in dire situations in the mountains.

Outside the restaurant after dinner, they noticed that all the seats in Justin's car had been removed. The vehicle now had no capacity for anyone else, just him.

During the next few days, Justin led them on pretty alpine trails along the Continental Divide, through spectacular pink fireweed. Walter and Lucy enjoyed the fresh-air feeling, the three of them hiking together as a family.

When they all said goodbye on a windy morning, Justin told them, "Maybe we'll go skiing this winter, if you come back out." He wanted to show them the beauty he'd discovered.

~

I climbed the fire escape from my fifth-story window to the rooftop, ascending to watch the ruby-edged setting sun find the grand horizon of New York.

The high-up air was an opaque sea of unending purple-gray clouds over a single clear stripe of glowing blue: pure sky. Standing in the red sun over my city, I considered how significantly my understanding of paradise had shifted; throughout the summers of my adolescence—and my marriage—I would escape into the mountains, these excursions almost compulsive, "essential."

Yet now for the first time in my life, I didn't feel the need to leave. There was nothing to escape. Called to be a writer, my innate purpose had transported me to Manhattan.

And New York, this city of misfit kids and bohemian dreams, where a long legacy of counterculture creators had flocked seeking community and inspiration, was precisely where I was supposed to be right now.

Justin's home, too, was where *he* felt summoned—which for him was where he was most powerfully useful. For a few years of his life that place had been our marriage, helping me.

But now I smiled. I reveled in the knowing that his calling was what had guided him to save lives in cold mountains, risking his own safety to protect and assist strangers. I thought how, while still a child, Justin had survived a natural disaster; and now, what he was choosing to do with his life was to recover people from avalanches and the elements, peril in the unexpected form.

He was in the perfect place, exactly where his purpose was ignited.

Watching the fiery sun's arched top disappear behind the backlit cylinder of a water tower, the day fading, I blew a small kiss west, seeing my ex-husband with dusk's soft pride, surrendered to this end. He'd found another world where he was stronger and could be the hero, rescuing people who are not me.

ACKNOWLEDGMENTS

Mom and Dad, these past years have brought us closer than ever. I just want to express how tremendously grateful I am that I've gotten to spend more time with you both, and that you've been so loving and supportive—since Justin left, and throughout my life. Thank you.

I love you both, so much.

Dad, you are a wonderful father and an extraordinary writer and thinker. I feel so lucky to have grown in a home that treasured literature and imagination, and widened my eyes to the thrill of inquiry, the power of discourse, and the beauty of the unknown. The openness of my mind is a gift I got from you.

I am a writer because you are a writer. Thank you for calling me a writer when I was only a kid. You are the best storyteller I know.

And above all, I am grateful for your ever-loving presence—how when things fell apart, you rushed right to New York. "Yours will not be a tragic life," you promised me, and I believed you—and now I cannot allow it to be.

Mom, thank you for your kindness, your stunning generosity, and your unwavering tenderness. And thank you *so much* for always encouraging my writing and my artworks, taking me to a million lessons and affirming the "great" value of my creations. Your faith in me—your love—has always been the fuel propelling the trajectory of my dreams. You are a tremendous mother, and I am lucky beyond measure.

Your marriage with Dad is fiery still, what I aspire to find. Thank you for teaching me how to be a partner, for showing me that it's possible to build a life around love.

Michael David Smith, Mystic, lost boy. My friend Mystic passed away at only thirty-three. He was the sweetest. I met Justin through him. I'll never forget his stories of footpaths through forests that led above stuck towns to ancient mountains the soft-blue color of ice. "It's a fairy tale," he said to me of the place where the Appalachian Trail ends, the summit of Mount Katahdin. "You get higher and higher. Everything gets beautiful."

I am forever indebted to beautiful and gifted **Tory DeOrian**, the sunshine girl. Tory was an artist, the creator of her dreams. From the moment we met at a San Francisco Sephora, she enchanted me and inspired me. We quickly bonded in a rare friendship of giggly lightness and deep and personal confession, simultaneous. On both coasts, we witnessed sunsets and shared stories of the sunsets and sunrises of our lives so far—and of our wild ambitions. Tory was a talented and devoted illustrator and designer with a style so whimsical and bright that her compassion for humanity was palpable in it, unmistakable as sunshine. She was a true, unique light in the universe—a brilliant torch lit by her passion. A warm fire fueled by an ever-glowing love.

I am honored and powerfully grateful to have been Tory's friend, partners in art and adventure. I will love her forever, and she loves us all, always and forever. She is with us all now.

Daniel Jordan, rising king. We found each other on a drive of darkness up the California coast, honoring lost Tory; in grief, we ventured farther from our homes, returning to Pescadero—stayed for three straight days, pulled back together by the gravity of sharp night stars and exposed truths, pulled into an embrace, a thousand seemingly random dots of our pasts connecting with the lines of a new picture:

Thank you for your friendship, your good instincts and perceptive mind clear as bright tropic water, your wild power to sway my soul *to trust*. I am deeply grateful for the magically empowering impact you've had on me; on Tory; on everyone you love. Your good energy is a wildly powerful force. Thank you for your unflappable belief in me and in the value of my creative work. You awakened my career, and my heart; and in your presence, I discovered I was enough. Thank you for your wisdom so far beyond the finite scope of only thirty-two years.

Kelly Sullivan Walden, interpreter of dreams, for your guidance and your faith. Thank you for our many rich Human Design sessions, which bring me closer to Daniel, and to myself; and for exposing your own heart with courage in those conversations. For sharing your private writing weekly and inspiring my own as I was writing this book. And thank you for reading an early draft of this memoir, offering your notes and boundless love.

Dana Walden, friend and sage. Thank you for teaching Daniel and me to honor the softness of a forming pearl. We love you.

Corrina Gramma, goddess girl. We found each other in a Greenwich Village café in the middle of the night; you came to my apartment and stayed for three straight days, pulled me in with the gravity of exposed truths, into an embrace, and lit my way to sobriety and the clarity that followed—the earthy place where I learned that I am tall enough to reach up high and turn on the light myself.

Thank you for your grace, your perceptive convictions clear as water, your quiet power to sway your friends in healthier directions. For showing me kindness, as a model and a practice. For showing me forgiveness and honest beauty. For the unwavering brilliance of your authenticity. Thank you for your profoundly positive influence on me; and thank you for your Blue Notes, especially the last. You teach me the morals of the stories I've been telling all my life. This book is peppered with your gems, shimmering with Gramma. Your light's trail is my guide. You are a truly great thinker, and woman.

I am grateful for my brother **Jacob**. For showing me what an extraordinary husband, father, partner, *human* looks like. For modeling diligence and commitment to a dream; to a family; to bold and wonderful creations, responsibilities much larger than yourself. For your forgiveness. My sister-in-law **Halle**, for your kindness and your grace. I love watching you be "Mommy Nest" for your two precious girls. **Robert**, my big brother, a fun and present father, sibling, husband, citizen, and friend. Both your children absolutely adore you, and they are tremendously fortunate to have you as their dad. Fearlessly committed to the causes you believe in, devoted to making our world better together, you are an inspiration to me. I am perpetually in awe of your limitless energy and passion. Also, thank you for "publishing" my first "book," stoking my sparks of dreams. I love you very much. My sister-in-law **Jenny**, for the important work you're doing with children who need your knowledge and guidance; for raising two extraordinary kids.

I am grateful for my nephew, **Tom**. For inspiring the better angels of my nature. For your humor, your friendship, and your joy. For trusting me. For making time and space to FaceTime with me weekly; to visit me in faraway places; to laugh and wander with me; and to love.

Emma Rudié, for reading draft after draft of this manuscript with compassionate attention and deep care; for discerning which of my memories were necessary to share, and which ones were irrelevant or dull. For encouraging my voice. Thank you for helping me find the puzzle pieces that fit well together, for making time for this story. I am endlessly grateful.

Justin Matis, who believed. Thank you for accompanying me to the place that made magic possible. You scavenged the streets of New York for materials to build the bed we shared.

The Matis family: Walter Matis; Lucy Matis—fellow writer. Jeffrey Matis; Bea Matis; Irving Matis. Newfound timeless family, for taking me in and never letting me go. Small but great. I love you all, for always.

The Weingart family, for our profound and illuminating dream oracle card sessions, and for your guidance and kind support.

I am grateful for **Dr. Nancy Feldman-Weingart**—you are brilliant and graceful in the midst of the hardest days. Thank you for helping my family with the great gift of your clarity and guidance. Thank you for being who you are.

I have limitless gratitude for **Nicole Solomon**, the most passionate, generous professor and friend a young writer could ever meet. The care and loving attention you devote to each and all of your students is mesmerizing, unparalleled. You are "one of the magic people," more fairy god-mom than writing teacher. Nic—this book was inspired by your wise words on a walk, simple and true. You freely share your literary contacts, your wisdom, your brilliant friendship like a sapphire in my hands. *Thank* you. Thank you for your many gifts.

Sarah Herrington, fellow writer, for reading the very first draft of this book, "a small ship tossed at sea," and helping to steer the turbulent narrative toward clearer and less erratic waters.

Thank you to **Andrew Blauner**, my attentive, kind, and tireless literary agent. I adore, admire, and respect you. Thank you, **Matthew Snyder**, my intrepid film agent at Creative Artists Agency.

Bryan Hurt, for answering the phone when I called for help and then reading my entire manuscript and offering careful notes. For inviting me back to Colorado College—that return has empowered me.

Cathy Elliot, for helping my heart heal. Thank you. I am forever changed by the **Landmark Forum** you led.

Lena Dunham, you brought me to the set of *Girls* and listened to my stories, and told yours. Thank you for your endless generosity. Your support has affirmed and fueled me more than I can thank you for. I feel so, so fortunate for that day, and for your kindness. I treasure it within me. It was the first time I felt noticed by an artist I admired.

This book is the creation of an amazing, unflagging pack at **Little A**—thank you all! I'm especially grateful to my brilliant editor, **Erin Calligan Mooney**, for wise letters rich with insights, the clarity you offer. For giving this story a shot. For believing in the value of my voice, encouraging my style, letting my literary lungs breathe freely. For your brilliantly clear editorial vision. For trusting me. For developing the scenes of my past to better represent themselves, shaping the tension and mystery of reality. For helping me to distill the characters of my life into their paper-and-ink counterparts, their distinct essences. I once read an interview in a literary magazine, a conversation with an acclaimed editor who explained that "a great editor makes a writer *more* of what they naturally are." You have done that for me. You have held a microphone to my heart's beating, at just the right height and distance—and told me, "Listen."

I am grateful to **Emma Reh**, extraordinary production editor, for your meticulous and flawless work to make my manuscript *this book*. And I'm thankful for all copyeditors, proofreaders, and fact-checkers who scrutinized every dash and semicolon, every species of flowering tree and proper noun.

Carmen Johnson, thank you for giving this memoir a place in the world, a home to grow in. Your faith in me has forever changed my story.

Sueann and Mickey Unger, matron and patron of the Wynnewood Writers Residency. I am tremendously lucky and grateful to have been a beneficiary of your dazzling bigheartedness and inspiring kindness.

Thank you for countless deep and stimulating conversations begun around your dinner table and carried through the house and through the years, the love you radiate. Thank you for your refreshing honesty and authenticity, rare and important. Thank you for encouraging Daniel and me to create, and for investing your time and energy and food and care and home-roasted coffee beans in hosting us—thus making this memoir possible. This book would absolutely not exist without you.

Your extraordinary generosity has transformed my life.

And above all, *thank you* for exemplifying the grace and warmth a devoted couple naturally and consistently emits after fifty years of steadfast love. For living your days with benevolent intention, showing me the expansiveness of the beauty of commitment to another soul. Your marriage is a union for the ages.

Thank you for the residency you selflessly created for Daniel and me—for your breeziness and forgiveness of our messiness, our immaturity. For honoring us with the privilege of your trust.

ABOUT THE AUTHOR

Photo © 2015 Christopher Lane

Aspen Matis is the author of the critically acclaimed memoir *Girl in the Woods*, published by HarperCollins in 2015. Called "a powerful read" by *O, The Oprah Magazine*, the book made the *Guardian*'s annual top fifty list. The *New York Times* called Matis "a hero."

Her short-form writing has been published in the *New York Times*, the *Atlantic, Tin House, Psychology Today, Salon*, and *Marie Claire*. She now lives in New York City, where she visits cute cafés, writes madly, and studies philosophy, following the threads of her fascination. To learn more, visit www.aspen-matis.com.